BESSIE
HEAD

BESSIE HEAD

SUBVERSIVE IDENTITIES IN EXILE

Huma Ibrahim

University Press of Virginia
Charlottesville and London

The University Press of Virginia
© 1996 by the Rector and Visitors of the University of Virginia

First published 1996

⊗ The paper used in this publication meets the minimum requirements
of the American National Standard for Information Sciences—
Permanence of Paper for Printed Library Materials, ANSI Z39.48-1984.

Library of Congress Cataloging-in-Publication Data

Ibrahim, Huma.
    Bessie Head : subversive identities in exile / Huma Ibrahim.
        p.   cm.
    Includes bibliographical references and index.
    ISBN 0-8139-1685-2 (cloth : alk. paper)
    1. Head, Bessie, 1937–   —Criticism and interpretation.
    2. Feminism and literature—Africa, Southern—History—20th century.
    3. Women and literature—Africa, Southern—History—20th century.
    4. Africa, Southern—In literature.   5. Decolonization in literature.
    6. Exiles in literature.   I. Title.
    PR9369.3.H4Z72   1996
    823—dc20   96-17170
                                                                   CIP

0-8139-1685-2 (cloth)

Printed in the United States of America

For Rashid, my father,
Zohra, my mother,
Rashu and Sasha, my children,
Joe Kubayanda,
whose council I miss terribly,
and
Thelma, exile, friend and sister

Because it is a systematic negation of the other person and a furious determination to deny the other person all attributes of humanity, colonialism forces the people it dominates to ask themselves the question constantly: "In reality, who am I?"

When you examine at close quarters the colonial context, it is evident that what parcels out the world is to begin with the fact of belonging to or not belonging to a given race, a given species.

—Franz Fanon, *The Wretched of the Earth*

CONTENTS

ACKNOWLEDGMENTS

I AM grateful to the Center for African and Africanamerican Studies at the University of Michigan, Ann Arbor, for awarding me the DuBois-Mandela-Rodney Post Doctoral Fellowship in 1990–91, without which this project would not have been completed in a timely manner. I would like to thank Lemuel Johnson for his friendship, advice, and encouragement and Michael Awkward for reading parts of the manuscript.

I want to thank several colleagues in my department: Richard Sha read parts of the manuscript, but most especially Jonathan Loesberg, who not only looked at the entire manuscript but was always there to give invaluable advice about publishing.

I would also like to acknowledge my friends and colleagues in the field who continued to believe in me and in this book; among them are Brinda Metha, Obioma Nnameka, Ketu Katrak, Arlene Elder, Cecil Abrahams, and Thelma Ravell-Pinto. These friends and colleagues were forthcoming with their support and encouragement. In particular I want to thank Simon Gikandi for all his comments and help.

I would like to thank the office staff, Caren Saxe, and Dan Crawford for keeping me sane through every computer disaster.

I would like to thank my teacher, friend, and inspiration, Emile Snyder, who is no longer with us but whose spirit and work continues to be cherished by the entire community of postcolonial scholars.

I am also very grateful to my readers, especially Linda Susan Beard, and my editors, Cathie Brettschneider and Adrienne Mayor, for last-minute advice in bringing this project to fruition.

Lastly, I would like to thank my twins for creating a welcome diversion from Bessie Head.

Bessie

You who had died in the desert growing vegetables
You who had paused for a brief life in that desert
You whose soul crippled by hate—knew joy very briefly
You, who must finally rest.

Was it so hard for people to understand
The fat Coloured woman
With the soul of a gazelle, who was to live
Very quietly in the desert—growing flowers.

The desert became her soul, the flowers became her life
One slowly despairing and dying
The other flourishing—sometimes! Yet
She lived as she died, rather quietly in the desert.

To all those who live in the desert of my dreams
I give you flowers unseen
I give you many growing things
All for Bessie's garden-of-dreams.

BESSIE
HEAD

INTRODUCTION
Feminist Discourse and a Crisis of the South African Identity

I think I was so sensitive to that question of dispossesion.

—Bessie Head, interview by Linda Susan Beard

Bessie Head's synchronic and syncretic genius mixes media; she is story-teller, historian, choreographer, agronomist, and chanteuse. Bessie Head is the avatar of disconcerting paradox.

—Linda Susan Beard, "Bessie Head's Syncretic Fictions"

Exile is a soulless Country.

—Salman Rushdie, *Satanic Verses*

IN THE decades before Nelson Mandela was inaugurated May 10, 1994, Black South African writing was always driven by the tension between an individual's exile and her political and personal resistance. This tension causes a crisis in the South African cultural identity because of the individual's political intention toward the apartheid system, especially before it was dismantled. This crisis contributes to the definition of the self which is in conflict with oppressive institutions as well as the self which is writing a literature of resistance. The struggle for locating the self can be most easily perceived in the literature emanating from specifically South African systems of oppression, where the writer or political activist's exile does not occur out of voluntary migration.[1] The most

1

renowned Black South African writers, Alex La Guma, Bessie Head, and Peter Abrahams, have charted aspects of this crisis in their narratives. They have also attempted to negotiate a definition for identities that are inherently subversive—subversive to colonial, imperial, apartheid, and patriarchal structures.[2] In order to understand the way resistance and subversion revolutionize subject identities within oppressive institutional patterns, one must analyze both the particular experiences of oppression and the dominant systems of oppression. My own claim is that the desire to belong, what I call the "exilic consciousness," initiates the resistance that subject identities confront. My notion of exilic consciousness includes an escape from systems of oppression that give rise to desires which encompass the sphere of belonging not to your own but to another people. These anxieties and desires are very important because they are the foreground for the enactment of Head's narratives. Her main characters exhibit an acute awareness of their own desires to belong both to where they came from and where they must live. This awareness forms the backdrop of my analysis and constitutes the exilic consciousness.

An exilic consciousness is usually manifested by individuals or groups of exiles who leave the country of their birth voluntarily or involuntarily. Being a woman and a South African, Head was engaged in two kinds of exile: one from patriarchal institutions and the other from the apartheid state. Head's exiled characters are anxious about the loss of their birth place and their desires to belong to the place of exile. The exiled psyche of her characters is one divided against itself, for the characters often wish to return to the phantom of the old home even as they try in an exaggerated way to leave, for it is only through leaving that they can belong to the new home. It is useful to study the unresolved conflicts arising out of a state of being in exile in Head's narratives because the exilic consciousness forms the nucleus of her writing. In addition, I use the term "exilic consciousness" to imply how a subjectivity responds to exile. The state of exile is often imposed on a subjectivity torn between a sense of not belonging as well as a desire to belong to one's gender, linguistic group, community, and nation. The consciousness arising out of this ambivalence is the basis of the exilic consciousness.

My purpose is to evoke the most misunderstood and oppressed voices from the spectrum of South African writing, and since Bessie

Head's interests reside in the particular exploration of exile, gender, and resistance emanating from usually silenced voices, she is the most appropriate writer for my analysis of subversive identities in exile. Bessie Head has become the Western feminists' icon—a Third World woman writer who is interested in women's issues. This book hopes to relocate that assumption. Bessie Head has dispelled the silence existing between colonial and feminist discourses by "talking back" through her careful and multifaceted portraits of women's sexual and political identity crises, and by examining their exclusion from dominant national discourses.[3] Her "talking back" suggests a different reading of Third World women's prescribed roles. What my study suggests is that unless we are able to look at how women's sexual, political, and gendered identity merge and seek to redefine each other in the neocolonial, postapartheid national milieu, the careful configurations created in Head's oeuvre will elude us. Power relationships, as they inform and are informed by exiled identities who seek to subvert the social and individual institutions of the nation, are the particular concern of her novels. One has to study Head in order to perceive how identities manifesting the ambivalence of an exilic consciousness subvert the center, the metropole, and the patriarchy as they seek greater understanding of their own subjectivity. The conclusions to these problematic issues vary in progression from novel to history. This variational yet consistent development creates a rationale for studying Head's works in sequence.

This book outlines the way that the identity of Head's protagonists emerge, not only from the materiality of the author's act of writing her "own" story-autobiography, but also from her quest for revolutionary change as a woman inhabiting an exile's displaced space as she clamors to "belong" to human systems of interaction, that is, individuals and societies as they create institutions that represent power. It is through the explosion of the individual's political and personal identity as it comes into being through writing, in part, an autobiography that Head is able to unfix the "fixity" of Third World women's identities. In other words, the autobiographical gesture creates dimensions of identity that have been frozen and fixed through stereotypes of the Third World woman's condition. By including postcolonial feminist analysis, such as Trinh T. Minh-ha's work on women's resistance and identity, as well as Edward Said's many notions of exile—which is often, though not inherently exclusive of women—I hope to present a serious critique of existing notions of postcoloniality which are often exclusive of women's "identity politics."[4]

Furthermore, my book takes issue with current critical analysis of Head as primarily a feminist writer. When postcolonial feminist scholars, and the term must be used advisedly, who are acutely aware of the woman's world view claim Bessie Head as a feminist writer, what do they mean by that? Does her critique add to that much neglected part of colonial discourse which has yet to include women's specificity and experience? The forging of an authentic postcolonial feminist ideology, by no means monolithic, is the task of the feminist scholar and critic who must, as a primary responsibility, inform postcolonial discourse from the perspective of Third World women as they experience their own identities. I believe that Head's examination of the subjectivity of women's experience not only subverts Western hegemonic notions of the Third World woman but becomes a critique of postcoloniality. This critique becomes particularly important in terms of South Africa's position, especially in the 1980s, as it increasingly implied a post-apartheid state. Bessie Head constitutes a good subject for such a study primarily because her enduring interest in the theme, structure, and consciousness of an exilic identity creates "stealthy negotiations" of her feminist concerns.[5] This book focuses on the point at which Head's fictive interests engage her feminist concerns and culminate in a discourse on women's exiled identity, be it within the national discourse or within the boundaries of women's autobiography. For Head, the question of autobiography is not just an issue of identity as the "cultural feminists" understood it but a query into "micropolitical practices."[6] In other words, Head's enormous autobiographical gestures suggest her interest as primarily personal, but I believe that her emphasis is consistently on the political, and only as it engages with the personal. I naturally agree with Biddy Martin's further elaboration of Teresa de Lauretis's view about women's subversive identities when she says that "practices of self-representation . . . illuminate the contradictory, multiple construction of subjectivity at the intersections . . . of gender, race, and sexuality," but I would also add that they constantly collide with dominant national discourses.[7]

The insights of women in South Africa are unique because the quest for identity arises from a simultaneous struggle against apartheid and against patriarchal structures within their own communities. For South African women, the struggle for a definition of self or identity, within and outside the context of imperialism, has immediate currency and leads to what one experiences in Head's writing as a crisis of the political being: woman as she is "otherized" and as she begins the process of defining herself in order to rejoin her unchosen/chosen society. For the purpose of reading Head, this crisis is a forerunner of dynamic redefinitions. These redefinitions radicalize traditional concepts of gender in relation to the postapartheid world. I am deliberately collapsing the distinction between Third World women's quest for identity through Head's writing and her attempt to define herself through the dialectics she creates in the same writing, because Head does both simultaneously. For my purposes, this quest for self-definition as part of a radical subversion falls under the dialectic of what Biddy Martin, among others, has called "identity politics." She argues that the problems of maintaining sexuality as the constituting ground of identity and claiming that autobiographical gestures are the exclusive ground of politics defy the fixity of identity. These problematics are distinct, in some ways, from the ones that the configurations of sexuality or identity and autobiography or politics present to the postcolonial feminist when she turns her critical glance to postcolonial women's texts. Even though Martin often talks about the lesbian as other, her definition can easily be applied to Third World women when they raise questions of their own identity. The politics of women's identity, especially since the expression or quest of that identity is by definition subversive, coincides with Bessie Head's feminist inquiry which tends to manifest her experience as a woman writer exiled from South Africa. I use Martin's idea of subversive "identity politics" as linked to women writing autobiographies, strongly evident in Head's third novel, *A Question of Power*.[8] The problem of an autobiography that emerges out of individual, yet extreme experiences that the Immorality Act, an act passed into law forbidding sexual relationships between Black and White South Africans, poses for a feminist discourse on identity is not because of its "fixity," as Martin would have us believe. Rather, the writing of the self becomes itself a political gesture of resistance, even before we critically examine texts, and it certainly provides liberation from the fixed presuppositions that cultural identities often imply. Teresa de Lauretis suggests that the "female self" can emerge only out of the "materiality of her writing" and "the historicity of her experience," which, for the purposes of my argument, is the act of writing the self through autobiography, even though Lauretis never mentions autobiography per se.[9] I claim that, for Head, the act of writing autobiography often merges with the politics of "resistance."

As we know, several notions of the concept of "subversive identities" have been extended by various cultural critiques. Given the structures of dominance and power, women's identity as it manifests itself in women's writing and questions pertaining to that subject space are, as feminisms suggest, always subversive. My interest in the term *subversive* resides in its association with race and gender as Head problematized them. In order to study Head we must look at exile, and what I call the exilic consciousness, as inherently interconnected with subversion. Taken together, these two concepts suggest the relationship of margin and center as well as colony and metropole, connections that postcolonial discourses expound. Concepts of distance and dominance become part of the larger questions of subversion, identity, and exile.

An identity is often called subversive when it defies or challenges its prior definition—a definition that usually emerges from the center or metropole. The reconfiguring of definitions of women's identity interests me most in Head's work. Since the colonial patriarchal definition is external to itself, its context, and nations, especially colonized nations, their peoples seek to redefine and recontextualize themselves in regard to the discourse of the metropole as well as the radical reconfigurations of cultural-national, individual-gender meanings emerging from within the new postcolonial nations. In the twentieth century, the need for definitions expressed by every "otherized" or colonized subject or group has taken precedence over all other political activities in the sphere of postcolonial feminist discourse. Women as political exiles constitute two spheres. In one area, women are exiled from their countries for political activities, as is the case in South Africa. In the other, women are political exiles from their own communities when they are delegated relative positions of powerlessness in established patriarchies. Bessie Head epitomizes and explores both forms of women's exile in nearly every one of her works. Women exiles have sought definitions of the self as well as the self or the "many selves" in relation to the other, that is, the external colonizer, and to internal patriarchal institutions and other symbols of the same. Subverting the internal

patriarchy occurred as an affirmation of the colonial and imperial onslaught, for it changed the structures of precolonial patriarchy forever,
and not necessarily as part of a revolutionary dialectic leading to progressive ways of viewing issues of gender, but rather as a way to rees-
tablish corrupt and old patterns of power.

The discussion of exile as an inherent part of subversion and identity
is the foreground upon which this book is inscribed and is manifest by
the complex writerly investments that Head projects onto her narratives. Exile permeated Head's life and those of her characters long before she left South Africa for Botswana, because apartheid, which determined her problematic parentage, also displaced her out of its vast
geography. She was to remain in exile in South Africa as well as inside
Botswana, a short respite notwithstanding; but in Botswana, she began
to articulate a whole series of Janus-faced responses to that same exile.
Through an exploration of these ambiguities that overflow in her novels, short stories, and histories, I aim to show how what I call the "exilic
consciousness" problematizes women's identities but always seeks to
"name"—define this self or selves—without in any way essentializing
them. Most Head critics are unable to perceive that it is this "naming"
of experience that positions both the political decolonized self and the
gendered self in a stance of resistance in the postcolonial and postapartheid milieu. In Head's narratives one finds that women's exile and
women "naming" their experience occur in sequence.

Through the exploration of women's experiences and lives Head is
able to rename and redefine women's subversive identities in the dominant national and patriarchal milieu, as well as chart their limitations.
Through this renaming Head is able to reclaim women's experience
and identity from both patriarchal and colonial apartheid objectifica-
tions. The many permutations of the exilic consciousness manifested
by subversive identities are relevant here. Even though Head was very
relieved to be outside South Africa, her domicile was never without
ambivalence. Head's first response to her exile in Botswana was the
nostalgia for "Old Africa," an Africa she thought she saw in simple
village life in Botswana. But at the same time she wanted to reject
tradition definitively, or as her South African protagonist calls it, "tribalism." Instead, she wanted to provide a vehicle for using some of the
traditions of cooperative farming and graft it onto her exile's desire for
economic progress. But the very dichotomy of "tradition" and "moder-

nity" indicates her desire to locate African women's identity in sociopolitical as well as in an emotionally revolutionary "flux."[10] For example, her characters Pauline and Maria are not primarily revolutionary feminists, and it is unimportant that they be so. But given the context that they are seeking to redefine women's roles and identities in their own world, Head's reference point always remains the larger postcolonial context.

In *A Question of Power,* the conditions exiles are subject to were channeled through the rigors of a disturbed emotional economy, where "a sense of belonging" was sought above all else in an Africa where the protagonist did not belong linguistically or socially. The apparent loathing Elizabeth felt against the "Bloody Bastard Batswana" was tempered by her extreme love and respect for women's work, her friend Kenosi, and the Cape gooseberry. This ambivalence compelled Elizabeth to be of and from Africa and Botswana, as well as totally external to it. The latter is what her universal personality encompassed, the problematics of which I shall discuss in the body of this book. Head's universalist identity is important only in that it defied what Biddy Martin calls "fixity" and rejected the dichotomy of "tradition" and "modernity," placing the artistic emphasis on the critical inclusion of female "identity politics" within the parameters of a cultural critique. Even though Head herself was not aware of current trends in postcolonial theory, she was certainly aware of problems that individuals and nations have within the postcolonial context.

Bessie Head's autobiographical narratives emerge out of both the personal and political "historicity of her [own] experience," and it is through the "materiality of her writing" that her "female self" realizes the ultimate seduction of belonging to a home. She comes out of the political legacy of apartheid, the literary yet illicit daughter of Shakespeare's exiles, Othello and Desdemona, unacceptable and unaccepting, a doubly exiled being, just as a child of their union would have been. Like her literary father Othello, Head seeks, in retelling her story-biography, however incomplete, an understanding of the configuration of the makeup of her own identity which falls in the framework of how apartheid affects her gender, her class, and her mixed race.[11] She would not and could not "belong."[12] Let me hastily add that the concept and discussion of racism that I include in this book hinges on how Head perceived and problematized racial prejudice—racial prejudice as it informed identity politics within national spaces. She is interested in prejudice as it is tied to the concept of sociohistoric and racial differences between peoples and especially how it affects African women's gendered identities. For Head, identity was always problematic. When one no longer understands racism as an external inscription on the identity or self but begins to recognize its familiarity and interiority to the self, the problems of identity and desire multiply. The process of interiority that occurs is what I see as the supreme exile, part of the makeup of the exilic consciousness.[13]

For women, far more than for men, identity and questions relating to identity, as Teresa de Lauretis has suggested, can only be negotiated through cultural and political strategies. For the purposes of reading Head, one has to extend Lauretis's idea of women's identity. Elaborating on that dimension, Trinh T. Minh-ha argues that for her, women's consciousness and identity, which in my reading incorporates the exilic consciousness, is a "way of re-departure," or "the pain . . . of having to live a difference." Using the term *exilic consciousness* allows me to invoke simultaneous reference to the South African exile-writer and the gendered subversive subject seeking self-definition. This is precisely how Head explicated her exiles. In Minh-ha's model the question of identity is integral to the state of exile and is therefore more appropriate to the discussion of Head. Minh-ha writes: "Identity is a way of re-departing. The return to a denied heritage allows one to start again with different re-departures, different pauses, different arrivals."[14] For Head, the quest for the definition of identity is a quest for subjecthood within and outside phallocratic systems of power.

I believe that feminisms informed by the colonial experience suggest a very fundamental departure from Western feminisms. Third World feminisms are defined by a need to resist but not reject the world we are given, phallocratic though it is.[15] Like concepts of postcoloniality, Third World feminisms have consistently aimed to bring new understanding to questions of identity and nation. Cornel West rightly suggests that, in the 1980s, the most ground-breaking and radical work "toward a new cultural politics of difference has been made by the powerful critiques and constructive exploration of Black diaspora women."[16] When studying postcolonial women's literature, concepts of "resistance" become integral to the issues of exile. And let me suggest here that resistance by women is always against the exiled space delegated to women in their own societal and national frameworks. For Head, the resistance occurs as a refusal to be contained within the discourse of an exiled identity. Her novels both explore resistance against the state and reclaim women's space while subverting notions of exile and manifesting aspects of the exilic consciousness. Each woman character in Head's narratives resists being dismissed or misused just because she "became" a woman or because there was no place for her in the phallogocentric economy. These women claim a space within the equivocal boundaries of neocolonialism. Resistance becomes part of the dialectics of women's identities in exile, which become subject places "negotiated as strategies." They not only claim a place for themselves in the postcolonial economy but they have to define themselves within that sphere. Even though it is that very resistance which informs the exilic consciousness, for Head a mere desire for subversion is not enough, for none of her female protagonists are able to efface exile entirely.

In her analysis, Minh-ha adds yet another twist to the notion of "identity politics." Her analysis of the problematics of identity closely resembles the dialectic set up by Head, especially in *A Question of Power*. The divisions within each group and individual identity constitute the crux of the problem for both Head and Minh-ha. My analysis of Head's texts shows that it is the dialectical relationship between an "authentic core" and the "foreign . . . non-I, other" within the politics of each identity or self-representational practices which constitutes exile, as well as the consciousness it inhabits.[17] In other words, exile is both internal and external to the subjective and subversive identity. Head's exiles are always trapped in an exploratory relationship with good and evil as manifested by power structures that are determined by the individual and collective self. The many selves that constitute societies, communities, and nations inform and reform the question of inherently subversive "identity politics." Both writers come to the same surprising conclusion at the culmination of their discourse on identity. Minh-ha, like Head, seems to feel that an understanding of identity can emerge only out of a "sly negotiation" between the "authentic core" and "foreign . . . non-I, other" residing in each identity space. She argues that any understanding of subjectivity comes from the dialogue between the appropriate as well as "the inappropriate other within every I."[18] Head's characters "name" their experience through this dialogue.

I will begin my argument with Head's notion of women's identity as it constitutes variations of "inappropriate" selves, because it is through their dialogue with themselves and other national and patriarchal institutions that they seek to define themselves anew, while remaining members of their societies and nations. Elizabeth, Head's protagonist in *A Question of Power*, can only achieve the "gesture of belonging," that is, a complete subject position, when she can successfully reconcile the two aspects of a gendered and exiled identity. It is only through the recognition of the "inappropriate other in every I" that she reaches an uneasy level of "belonging," in exile, to her exiled identity. In other words, she can be at home with her own exilic consciousness, as well as re-form a cohesion within women's identities as they uninhabit displaced spaces in order to inhabit social national ones.

Head's interest in the conditions and structure of exile informs other exile literature from Southern Africa. There are, however, several biographical, linguistic, and sexual-political problems that constitute her narrative. What are the problems of a writer who does not *choose* to be a "linguistic mulatto"?[19] The issue of a colonized being writing in the language of the colonizer is specific to certain kinds of alienation and exile. This linguistic angst is especially evident in *A Question of Power*. And further, language, as Julia Kristeva and Luce Irigaray have suggested, constitutes yet another domain of the phallocratic economy. The alienation of women from this linguistic economy is only part of the problem for women writers. The notion of subversive identities is complicated in a useful way if one adds the dimension of writing with a tongue used historically, first by the colonizer to enslave, and later learned and used by the colonized to empower herself against her colonization. It situates not only a horrendous strain on the relationship between a writer and the language that constitutes the materiality of her writing, but also perpetuates the experience of exile. As a result of this, definitions of identity emerging from such writing are often rife with contradictions. Language is, of course, also a means for expressing desire. How is a doubly colonized/exiled woman and writer going to artistically relocate her experiential writing material? How does the relationship between language and material inform the patterns of exile we find in Head's novels? And how does the question of women's identity inform the problematic relationship of her language, sexuality, and exile? The analysis of these difficulties as they inform and reform Bessie Head's oeuvre forms the nexus of my study.

The corpus of Bessie Head's uncollected and collected novels, short stories, histories, and other works constitutes an agonized inquiry into the South African identity within a complex framework of personal and political, feminist, and colonial dichotomies. She absorbed her woman writer's exile in ways that were different from other South African writers in exile. Head's language constitutes the condition of sexual and political exile, especially as it concerns women of different classes and groups in a milieu of political and personal upheaval.[20]

In talking about a certain kind of exile, Edward Said argues that exile is part of the human condition specific to the twentieth century, which he calls a severe "contemporary political punishment." He further adds that the state of exile is "the unhealable rift forced between a human being and a native place, between the self and its true home: its essential sadness can never be surmounted. And while it is true that literature and history contain heroic, romantic, glorious, even triumphant episodes in an exile's life, these are no more than efforts meant to overcome the crippling sorrow of estrangement. The achievements of exile are permanently undermined by the loss of something left behind forever."[21]

For Head, both leaving and not leaving South Africa constitutes such an "unhealable rift," which took many forms. Since her novels suggest, at once, a desire to surmount the "crippling sorrow of estrangement" and the sexual, personal reality of being always undermined by the "loss of something left behind forever," they present a complex dialogue of the experience of gendered and colonized beings as they subvert and re-form the politics of identity. Head's personal loss included the loss of her mother, a potential Desdemona, distant and passive, whose madness and untimely death haunt *A Question of Power*, and of Africa, the m/other who simultaneously denies her patrimony and punishes her for not "belonging" to the imperialist language group. This m/other, sometimes symbolized by the character Medusa, taunts her lack of any ties to the peoples of Southern Africa. Elizabeth, her protagonist, has not only lost her "home" and can never go back, but is constantly reminded by Medusa that the home and identity she thinks she has left behind were never hers to claim. It is no wonder that Head's novels are so fiercely about a "belonging," forever problematized by the exilic consciousness—a consciousness of being rejected by the exile's "host" culture. In *A Question of Power* the protagonist is acutely aware of her "crushing isolation and the world's indifference." Said contends that it is only in these circumstances of "loneliness and despair" that an exile can work ambivalently in order to "belong" even as she simultaneously "insists on her right to refuse to belong."[22] My own argument emphasizes that this enormous loss is the foreground for Head's exploration of female identity in the postcolonial context.

The "identity politics" of someone who is "prevented from returning home" *is* tragic. The ambivalence one feels toward questions of subjectivity as well as the imposition of the socionational framework on that self are concurrent with the anxiety of not belonging. Said calls the "the exile's predicament" a modern "tragedy."[23] One of the most poignant tragedies of all time, *Othello,* is also drawn out of the "unnatural" complexities of relationships manipulated through tensions that must exist between exile, race, and national discourses; all raise questions of "belonging." Earlier, I mentioned that Bessie Head was the illicit daughter of Othello and Desdemona—exiled racially, socially, and nationally. Out of the generality as well as the particularity of her own apartheid experience, she moves backward to take account of her past, and forward to meet the sociopolitical future of postapartheid South Africa.

The complexity of identities determined by race and gender, often in confrontation one with the other, is acted and enacted in Bessie Head's *When Rain Clouds Gather, Maru, A Question of Power, The Collection of Treasures, Serowe: Village of the Rain Wind, A Bewitched Crossroad,* and the posthumously collected works and letters, *A Woman Alone, Tales of Tenderness and Power, A Gesture of Belonging,* and *The Cardinals.*[24] Since each of Head's novels and short stories exemplifies one aspect of a long "journey" that informs the development and progression of the exilic consciousness, it is useful to examine them separately. The four posthumous collections form another whole, and it is important to look at them together as early indications of the profound political engagements and commitments that were more clearly expressed in her major works. The discussion of her histories belongs together, for here the subversive identities are replicas of a damaged collective historical consciousness and are being reclaimed through memory and desire.

Chapter 1 steers away from the main focus of the book in that it does not concentrate on Head's exploration of subversive identities per se but examines how her earlier writing contributed to the development of various forms of women's resistance. After looking at Head's dialogue on subversion, resistance, and identity, it is imperative to discuss her earlier writing, in which she sought the direction she was inevitably to take in her major work. In addition, this examination is especially important since she is now recognized as one of the finest African writers and is certainly among the most prominent women writers. Head's increasing reputation in the canon of African fiction has been immediately instrumental in her smaller pieces being collected posthumously in three volumes very shortly after her death. The first of these volumes, *Tales of Tenderness and Power*, was published in 1989, three years after her death, and the second, *A Woman Alone: Autobiographical Writings*, in 1990. The third, *The Cardinals*, was published in 1993. Very shortly after the first two volumes were published, Randolph Vigne, who had corresponded extensively with Head, edited her letters to him in a collection called *A Gesture of Belonging*. The volume of letters gives us an authorial text without fictive mediation. There is considerable overlapping in the first two posthumous publications; nonetheless, they are of great importance for the Head reader, teacher, and scholar. The first two volumes are, at the very least, testimony to Head's varied interests in philosophy and the politics of race and gender, as these issues addressed questions of identities in exile. These early writings indicate the directions that Head was to take and the conclusions she was to draw in her major work. In addition to the first two collections, there is some writing that came after her major works about the opinions and thoughts she had held about the South African woman writer and exile's role in the neocolonial world. The fact that every conceivable bit of earlier writing is being published is testimony to the increasing recognition of the complexity of Head's writing.

In the first chapter I talk about these posthumous collections in two parts because that division separates Head's dual understanding of exile. The writing that she did while still in South Africa anticipates her exiled status as a woman writer and concerns the identity spaces she was to inhabit in a voice that did not belong to the seasoned writer she later became. These earlier works have to be studied within the context of the tensions and ambivalence created between belonging and not belonging in both South Africa and Botswana. The work included in these volumes, written after she had moved to Botswana, some of which was finished after she had written her major works, is distinct from her South African writing. I chart the writing in Botswana as tending to account for the inscriptions on an African woman's body, sexuality, and creative work space. Head was later to develop a more specific interest in women's lives as she wrote and recorded her stories in *The Collector of Treasures*. Here, I clarify those distinctions, evaluating how the South African writing contributed to the euphoria Head felt, at first, upon entering a country with a large Black government and population instead of apartheid. Additionally, this chapter takes issue with Head for glorifying Botswana and what that means in political terms. I elaborate the seduction and denial of the exilic consciousness in the first pieces she wrote about Botswana.

Even though by Head's own admission she was able to write in exile as she was never able to in South Africa, the subjects with which she engaged and the intensity of her writing remained the same. Her South African writing anticipates, in numerous ways, the concerns that endured through out her life. For example, I intend to show her lifelong exploration of how oppressed people, especially women and those in exile, inform and re-form "identity politics" in such a way that their understanding brings new and startling insights into the nature of "Good and Evil." This early engagement shaped Head's later writing and led her to make conclusions that appear in the posthumous publications. These early statements provide clues to her long-term interests. She seemed, like her first protagonist, Makhaya, to be looking for "goodness" in individuals as well as in national identity spaces, especially those which they shared with the rest of the world.

In the first chapter, I show that even the awkward, sporadic, journalistic writing of her South African days seems to reach out for the kind of coherence that instructs an exile's desire and longing to "belong." Head desperately wanted the world to surpass the psychologically unfathomable racism of apartheid, "the culture of hate."[25] This desire led her to seek a comprehensive world view under the influence of Asian peoples and philosophies and traditional African religions. It thus harkens to a universalist world view in which the national and the individual have personal and historical consequences, making it necessary for all people to come to terms with the good and evil in themselves while they re-form their identities in the postcolonial world. Here I will chart how her notion of universalism emerges directly out of what I call the exilic consciousness.

In the first chapter I often speculate, when it is not entirely clear from the content and date of publication, whether a certain piece of writing was composed while in exile in Botswana or prior. This speculation is important in terms of the progression of Head's unsuccessful search for a writerly voice in South Africa toward one that became very distinct in its goals and achievements in Botswana. It can be claimed that the inability that Head talked about to "just write," which assailed her in her own home country, is a component of the exilic consciousness.

In the second chapter, I discuss the interrelated tensions between Head's tone of nostalgic reminiscences about "home" and the compulsory exile in *When Rain Clouds Gather.* Head's desire to recapture "Old Africa" was unexpected because she had always insisted on seeing "tribal" Africa as detrimental to the progress toward African "modernity." The temptation of the mythic past, of getting back to precolonial times where life was assumed to be, if not perfect, certainly socioeconomically well ordered and emotionally viable and whole, is perhaps understandable from a South African exile, problematic as it was for Head. This nostalgia radically subverts the experience of colonialism, for it emerges out of the desire to efface socioeconomic apartheid. The protagonist leaves behind his home but also his own internalization of apartheid. Though the intensity of this desire is understandable, it causes an inherently problematic situation for the exile's identity and Head's definition of the same. The protagonist, Makhaya, finds himself looking both forward and backward at the same time. I argue that this simultaneous view, of both future and past, positions the politics of subversive identities in a false dichotomy. Head is not looking toward the precolonial or colonial past as inherently separate from one another in order to arrive at some truths about cultural identities. In *When Rain Clouds Gather,* Head explores truths about systems of desire within identities as they entered a dialogic confrontation between the

past and present and as they are simultaneous with, rather than separate from, each other. Head's dialogue on the dichotomy between past
and present compels the question of women's identity to be renegoti-
ated so that women can claim a new subject place in the neocolonial
milieu.

The writerly process of the second novel is compromised by Head's
desire to write something "so beautiful and so magical that [she], as
the writer, would long to read and re-read it." She adds, "I achieved
this ambition in an astonishing way in my second novel, *Maru*."[26] My
third chapter examines a certain visionary quality that permeates the
overall design of Head's work after the illusion of nostalgia is dispelled.
The visionary aspect of Head's writing was to develop further in her
last novel and her histories. The nostalgia is replaced by a vision, a
dream which *Maru* (1971), Head's favorite novel, carefully constructs.
Even though this novel is ostensibly about the romance between an
underclass woman and two chiefs, it raises complicated issues about
the possibility of merging dominant national and marginal gender discourses. In chapter 3, I argue that gender and other minority discourses
are not and cannot be negotiated as implicit to the construction of
dominant national spaces by privatized gestures of desire, as Head
seems to indicate. Here, I discuss Head's enduring desire to use narrative devices, like the character Margaret Cadmore who does not fit into
the narrow labels of "race or tribe or nation," in order to fulfill the
author's "universalist" obligation, commitment, and desire.[27] This obligation and desire constitutes part of the exilic consciousness. I argue
that the dream itself is an illusion given the realities of classist and
racist Botswana. The construction of Head's dream is like a fairy tale
that merely outlines the "possibility" of "belonging" for a pariah who
does not belong and must always remain an outsider.

Head formulates her novel out of a "simple" understanding of racism, and she explores how discourses of oppression can be incorporated into the dominant discourse of the nation and its laws. In the
third chapter, I show how Head fails in her attempt to merge dominant
and marginal discourses but instead produces a strong authorial system
of desires emerging from the exilic consciousness, superimposed on
the characters as they become different representations of exile.

In chapter 4, I examine Head's turn inward, toward her own resources and psyche, in order to raise issues that she had only teased

into tentative existence. This chapter examines the complex autobiographical novel of 1973, *A Question of Power,* in which Elizabeth, the protagonist, is exiled by her country of birth, for the accident of being a woman and for the choice of becoming a writer. These various senses of exile contribute to the complex picture of women's subversive identities. I argue that in *A Question of Power,* Head poses the questions of personal and political autobiography, simultaneously and interchangeably locating the South African, woman, and exile's subjectivity in startling identity spaces, which of necessity remain in flux. The patterns of "resistance" through writing and through "journeys of the soul" contribute to the understanding of Third World women's cultural and national identities.

In Head's work the politics of resistance and subversion are parallel abilities manifested by identities in crisis. In other words, even though writing the autobiographical self as an act of defining the subjective self is simultaneous to the resisting self, the two activities are different. It is through the experience of her autobiographical gesture that Elizabeth, the protagonist of *A Question of Power,* can emerge out of the materiality of Head's writing as a "female-self" with multidimensional understandings about the way she views both her exiled being and also the being that experiences a "sense of belonging" at the end. This novel sets up a dialogue between the actual self and the written, autobiographical self. This confrontation of the many selves culminates in subversions and exiles pertinent to my study. For Head, at least theoretically, one can be in exile even as one belongs to a particular geography, even though her novels often contradict that. Woman's self and experience, especially that of a Third World woman, can be theorized if one begins, as Zoe Wicomb stipulates, at the "level of nomenclature."[28] This aspect of naming as one defines one's experience is an idea crucial to the understanding of Head's exploration of subversive identities.

In this novel, more than in anything else Head ever wrote, all of her sociosexual guards are down, and she writes about a woman's life in all its stark, racial-gendered interrelationships. Elizabeth, the protagonist, has a remarkable biography. But this life is rendered perfectly mundane and commonplace through apartheid reality. It is because of Head's understanding of this external and internal reality, which Elizabeth carries into exile to Botswana, that Head's protagonist suffers her mental breakdowns. Within the contexts of these breakdowns, complete with personifications of Good and Evil and the simultaneity of good/evil, Head begins to resolve individual and institutional power relationships and formulates questions of women's identity within systems of domination. It is through the understanding of individual and group identities that she poses and positions questions of women's sexuality, which is one aspect of women's identity—a question that she pries out of exile, silence, and false mythologies located by patriarchal discourse. Head creates and draws on women's mythologies instead, in order to discuss issues of women's writing as it coincides with women's nudity, sexuality, and even women's work, that is, the role of Elizabeth and Kenosi as vegetable farmers, and she examines how these affect the identities that emerge from a multiplicity of conditions of exile.

Here, as I mentioned earlier, Head does not shy away from questions of identity, exile, and madness in their relationship to good and evil manifestations of power. It is through this intense "soul searching" that she develops the theme of "universalism," an aspect of her writing that has come under considerable attack. This view may seem naive at first, but it claims an imperative subject space for all individuals in all societies. Head accomplishes this by fictionally taking us to the individual and societal edge, the "point at which you become evil."[29] She slowly builds her argument away from that abyss, where nothing more can be lost, where Elizabeth would either find a series of meanings or abandon life altogether. In *A Question of Power,* her protagonist comes very close to murder and suicide. Head relates this to the question of power and engages personal and universal symbols of evil to work out, messiah-like, her own salvation as well as the salvation of all of womankind. For Head, this salvation emerges out of Elizabeth's defining her own identity within the community of residence. Even more important is the concept of work as it relates to the individual and that community; thus work becomes fundamental to questions of belonging.

In chapter 5 I discuss Head's anthology of short stories, *The Collector of Treasures* (1977), particularly in its construction as a collage of women's oppression in the villages of Botswana where Head lived. In this chapter, I claim that these portraits of women, taken in the context of their lives, constitute the basic feminist commitment and engagement that Head always denied having. These stories indicate that even though Head was terrified of labels of any sort and assiduously avoided them, she expressed overwhelming interest in the minute details of women's lives and experiences as they shaped their identities. However, these stories do more than express outrage at the treatment that women encounter when their definitions of themselves collide with male-dominated institutions such as marriage and the social, legal systems governing any nation. Head shows that in most societies, spheres of power delegated to women which are often manipulated by the women themselves still disenfranchise them to a large degree. This "power" that women often have is extremely limited, precarious, and easily lost to other younger women, especially as societal taboos surrounding women's sexuality are controlled by aspects of patriarchal discourse. Head's exploration of the limitation of women's power marks a fundamental departure from the simplistic feminist notion that even the smallest power in women's hands somehow advances the cause of feminism.

These stories not only criticize patriarchal institutions and discourse, but through the "materiality of the writing" they formulate an understanding of women's experience of their own identity and thus contribute in significant new ways to postcolonial feminist discourse. Further, I argue that these portraits are meant, in part, to provide the common ground for dialogue between so-called Third World women of different classes and the patriarchal culture in which they function as social and national entities. This dialogue begun by women is primarily feminist. Even though this dialogue was inherent, it has been extremely hard to implement, especially for societies struggling out of colonialism, because the postcolonies arrested the critically conscious dialogue between men and women and silenced women's demands. In large part, men and women in Southern Africa have led separate lives since colonialism, the women rearing children and growing crops in the villages and the men tending to the "white man's mines," often in isolation and exile from family, home, and nation. This gendered separation successfully crippled, as Head documented in *The Collector of Treasures*, any previous understanding that tradition and history had instituted between men and women. Head critiques colonial economic trends in the family structure that are experienced in Southern Africa today. Her method is not to heap the entire blame on imperialism but rather on the ways that predominantly patriarchal societies responded to that situation. For Head, the burden of dialogue has to be placed on the decolonized men and women—this again is a fundamental departure from the postcolonial critical tradition. Bessie Head could see a window opening in the interrelationships of women and men, as well as of women and national and social institutions, to redefine, inform, and re-form women's subject place in the neocolonial world.

Said tells us that "it is not surprising that so many exiles seem to be novelists, chess players, political activists, and intellectuals." Even though he evokes the picture of an elite class of exiles and not the hundreds of thousands of "guest workers" in Germany and France, the distinction between a nonexile and an identity in exile is relevant. In correspondence with Said's maxim, "Much of the exile's life is taken up with compensating for disorienting loss by creating a new world to rule," each of Head's protagonists' "projects" in the adoptive community seems to be an attempt to "belong."[30] And each attempt to belong represents a new failure. The tension between a desire to belong and the failure to belong is fundamentally created and recreated in Head's narratives. Each activity undertaken in exile manifests a desire for a place to belong. For Head, exile dulled as much as it liberated, and it brought into sharp relief certain kinds of experience that she could commit to paper only in Botswana. With her earlier shorter writing, Head began to articulate the experience of exile in its totality. Thus, her first novel in exile comes as the beginning of her understanding of the dialectical relationship she was to have with Botswana as Bessie Head, woman, South African, and writer.

History is one of the most important aspects of the neocolonial intellectual and sociopolitical challenge facing a colonized peoples as they begin to take account of a severely tampered-with history. It is no wonder that Bessie Head contributed two histories about Botswana and several shorter pieces that complement those histories. This is where Head's interest shifts from individual identity toward collective identity. In chapter 1, I chart the theoretical and creative links between the shorter pieces and the two longer histories. In chapter 6 I discuss the whole notion of historiography and "rememory." Head was evasive about South Africa and its complex and problematic history. Instead, she chose to deal as a research scholar with a history with which she was entirely unfamiliar. Relying heavily on Head's histories, *Serowe: Village of the Rain Wind* and *A Bewitched Crossroad,* as texts, I explore how she implements the idea of rewriting history. I argue that this exploration of history is part of a radical understanding of cultural identities; for this rewriting becomes a process of informing, reforming, and redefining colonial and postcolonial histories.

In the final analysis, I am not claiming that Head is either a raving feminist or indeed even a champion of women's causes. What I am trying to bring to a reading of Head is an inclusion of her problematic examinations of nations, individuals, societies, history, exile, gender, and women's subversive identities as they become part of a larger sociopolitical framework of issues relating to Third World feminisms and postcoloniality.

1

GEOGRAPHY OF SUBVERSION:
Struggle for a Writerly Identity

IT IS crucial to discuss Bessie Head's earlier writings, in which she sought direction as a writer, especially since she is now recognized as having an "extraordinary contemporary voice." Linda Susan Beard has called upon the necessity to listen to a voice which is being "discovered and rediscovered in the process of a remarkable Bessie Head renaissance."[1] As noted in the introduction, *Tales of Tenderness and Power* was published three years after her death, and *A Woman Alone: Autobiographical Writings* appeared in 1990. *The Cardinals*, written while she was still in South Africa, was published in 1993.

Head has talked about the effects of apartheid in terms of her inability to write; her longer pieces, written as soon as she came to Botswana, are testimony to the simultaneous liberation and constraint she experienced as a writer, both liberated and hyphenated by exile. In retrospect, it is difficult to say whether she was, as a young writer, still looking for a voice in South Africa, or whether apartheid, by its horrendous systems of oppression, renders impossible the kind of creativity in which she was interested. The publication of *The Cardinals*, her only longer piece written in South Africa, certainly contradicts Head's own idea that she was unable to write in South Africa. Head documents the difficulties of writing in several pieces. In *The Cardinals*, both the difficulty of writing in South Africa and the desired breakthrough coincide.

Head's letters to Randolph Vigne provide an unmediated biographical text. I believe one must remember that for Head the gesture of developing the writing self coincided with exploring the autobiographical self. In order to study Head one must remember that these selves were never identical even though they often overlapped. In this chapter, I trace the early development of these two selves in their relationship to exile and belonging.

I will discuss the posthumous collections in two parts. With the exception of *The Cardinals,* the writing that she did while still in South Africa anticipates and exemplifies her exiled status as a woman writer in a racist, patriarchal society. The concerns she had in her South African writing, and the identity spaces she inhabited in a hesitant voice, did not belong to the seasoned writer she became. At first, upon entering Botswana, Head was euphoric—she wanted to consolidate what she frequently called the "eternal" beauty of Botswana.

In this chapter I take issue with Head for glorifying Botswana. As I show in chapter 2, this enthusiasm for "Old Africa" was much more clearly developed in her first novel, *When Rain Clouds Gather,* which emphasized traditions and customs without problematizing them. However, this tendency could be detected, quite easily, in the shorter pieces she wrote when she first arrived in Botswana. The shorter pieces seem to anticipate her first novel. At first, her stance toward her host country is entirely uncritical, even as she gathers firsthand tales of problematic family life from the women in her community. What seduces her completely, especially as an exile, is the peaceful environment of Botswana village life, which must have seemed so utterly distinct from her life in apartheid-torn South Africa. This seduction can be perceived very easily in the first pieces she wrote about Botswana, paying minute attention to the natural environment there.

I shall begin by taking issue with the material that Head published in various anti-apartheid journals and magazines before she left South Africa with an exit visa. In some of the first pieces that she committed to publication, the struggle for a relevant voice in the chaos of apartheid is very clear. Head's inability to voice anything in a "culture of hate," as well as her struggle to create something beautiful in spite of internal and external realities, is seen most forcefully in "Let Me Tell a Story Now," first published in 1962.[2]

Even the title indicates the frustration and enormous will involved in the telling of this story. It exemplifies apartheid brutality and the resulting revulsion for "a place that crushes dreams." She was constantly debilitated by the apartheid paranoia. Head writes about being watched and undermined by people she came into casual contact with:

"Because they can bust your ego to bits and you won't know what's happening to you, especially if your enemies are around and watching the terrific beating you are taking from one who knows all the answers."[3]

The identity of the protagonist is especially undisguised: it is clear that Bessie Head is speaking for herself. She wants to escape from the scrutiny of the glib political lawyer, who does not seem related to the story at all, but she is trying hard to explain something "delicate" to him. She also lacks confidence in anything she might want to contribute as a story of her life and time to other people. Head stalls before she "begins" to write, and even after she finishes "telling" her story she is still not sure that she has accomplished the task she set out to do. Here, and in a lot of other shorter pieces before she left South Africa, the voice is quite unabashedly nonfictive. The extreme ambivalence toward the process of writing, toward its possible value and toward public condemnation, is acute. She finishes this particular piece with "Whatever my manifold disorders are, I hope to get them sorted out pretty soon, because *I've just got to tell a story.*"[4] The urgency of this self-imposed task is closely tied to her identity as a "survivor" and chronicler of the apartheid situation. Head's engagement with the survivor's identity indicates an awareness of her writerly identity and her personal "manifold disorders," which are all jumbled in a big and slowly unfolding mass. The second part of her paranoia is fear of what the constant concentration on politics will do to her writing. She flounders as she tries to articulate her difficulty in writing: "Perhaps it's because I have my ear too keenly attuned to the political lumberjacks who are busy making capital on human lives."[5] This desire to run away from grand political actions and schemes is one of the most enduring refrains in her novels and short stories. Her protagonists all want to run away from the madness of apartheid into exile, which at first seems to entice and then haunts them afterward.

What Head is struggling to "tell" in her story is interesting simply because of her twenty-year exile, which commenced only four years after the publication of "Let Me Tell a Story Now." The story is about two people who plan to travel because they have an opportunity to do so but at the last minute they get off the train, realizing that it is pointless to leave friends and the familiarity of their way of life and language just to be in an alien place. Perhaps this story is indicative of why Bessie

Head chose not to leave Botswana and the environment of Southern Africa when the opportunity presented itself. The story itself tends to evoke the same kind of pathos that one is to find in her "Letter from South Africa: For a friend, 'D.B.'"[6] Like the story, the letter seems to be about herself more than the friend who has left. She writes: "For those of us who are still here, life becomes lonelier and intensely isolated."[7] The dilemma of "identity politics" that a South African woman writer faces is whether she should reside in a state of exile in and outside her country. This internal and external reality of not belonging clings to each aspect of life regardless of which subject position the characters in each piece seem to be inscribed within. These pieces indicate Head's enormous struggle before and after she entered into her dubious "voluntary exile."

Head's creative frustration was very closely allied to her political and emotional loneliness while she was in Southern Africa. The "Letter" talks about the one and only consequence of anti-apartheid political involvement. Political involvement always led to eventual exile, and it was only a year later that she herself got an exit visa to leave South Africa forever. Thus, the alienation and exile manifested by her "nervous breakdowns" in *A Question of Power* were experienced by her before she came to Botswana. The "nervous breakdowns" had something to do with "not belonging," of being in a culturally and emotionally unfamiliar and therefore barren space. The imbalance and agonizing erosion that apartheid creates in the emotional structures of Head's friendships recurs throughout her early and later work. The intensity of outrage in the "Letter" against the "unceasing torment of hate, hate, hate," is precisely what debilitated Head, an intensity that she was allowed to escape only through exile.

In spite of the debilitating influence and unceasing pressure of the political environment in South Africa, she remained politically astute and active. Even the reviews she wrote of local events, including one about a Black local artist who was receiving a great deal of artistic and monetary attention from White South African liberals, were critical of escapist art. She sums up Gladys Mgudlandlu's success in astute sociopolitical terms, contrasting realist and escapist art:

> Who wants to be reminded of the terrors of township living? It is ugly, horrible and sordid. So, let the ambiguous Mr. Ngatane rot; the fate of all those who shatter the calm of society's built-in illusions.

Miss Mgudlandlu, on the other hand, performs a kindly service. She is an escapist.[8]

Even as the political situation seriously hampered her ability to write, Head still had a strong and articulate political voice—a voice that developed to encompass the not-so-immediate universe of her South African days. But it is the same integrity and harsh honesty that she brings to the expanded notion of politics in her concept of "universal brotherhood," which developed gradually in the three novels written shortly after she went into exile. Identities and questions relating to individual subjectivities in South Africa are always determined by, and determine, politics. Thus, Head is critical of, as well as grateful for, escapist art given the political reality of black lives under apartheid.

On the other hand, the sketches she has written about the Cape "Coloured" are interesting for her dissociation from this group of people to whom she herself was supposed to belong. These short pieces indicate her understanding of, and her impatience with, the "infuriating character" of the Cape Coloured because he is "the uncommitted man." She adds, "He has given his loyalty to *no one*. How can he when he cannot even agree with himself about what he is thinking?"[9] There is an implication here that mulattoes are unable to belong to anyone, including themselves, simply because they are racially mixed. Even though there have been bonafide Coloured communities in South Africa for a long time, Head is able to see what it must be like for a child who belongs to neither one of his parents entirely but is something else. Apartheid exacerbates the dislocation of primary loyalties and gives rise to the exilic consciousness, even within the borders of one's own country, community, and peoples. Here, Head deliberately throws a monkey wrench into the notion of "identity politics," which was never personally or politically unproblematic for her. The notion of the "inappropriate other in every [personal and political] I"[10] is hinted at in this early work but not developed until *A Question of Power* and *Maru*. Ambivalence toward involvement in destructive apartheid politics dogged Head's footsteps and those of her characters throughout her writing career. This ambivalence is perhaps one of the chief reasons why Head is always loath to characterize her major characters as rigidly belonging to one sphere of political influence as opposed to another. The mulatto fits her subversive narrative purposes more completely even though she tends not to use mulattoes in her novels, except in her last and most acclaimed novel, *A Question of Power*. But again, the issue of the protagonist Elizabeth being a Coloured is almost irrelevant to the "plot" of the novel, though not to the negotiations of gender and identity that Head manipulates in the narrative itself.

I believe that this inherent subversion in her narratives is perhaps the most overtly revolutionary feminist aspect of her writing. In the South African political milieu where not taking sides is immediately classified as reactionary, Head insists on systematically decoding class loyalties by having a paramount chief marry a Masarwa woman in *Maru*. She further decodes race loyalties by depicting "goodness" in White characters as well as "evil" in Black characters. This deliberate flip-flop can be perceived most clearly in *When Rain Clouds Gather*. These attempts to change the epistemological structures of race, class, and nation began with her hesitant writing career, and toward the end they became a full-blown theory of what she later called "mankind in general" not "exclusive brotherhoods."[11] When she talks about the Coloured man not giving his loyalty to anyone, she implies that the lack of "commitment" on the part of those who know how and by whom they are oppressed comes out of a need again expressed by Head herself and several of her characters to be left alone to lead a trouble-free, nonpolitical life. Head is frustrated by this attitude, though not entirely condemnatory of it. She wonders what might be responsible for this mentality because she knows that it comes out of deliberately set-up apartheid divisions, and thus the manifestation of this weakness becomes all too human. Head notes, "We all love our comfortable grooves and somehow feel safe in patterns of living that have been imposed upon us; even though those patterns are unjust. A time of change is a time of upheaval that disrupts the status quo. It is also a time when violent passions rampage and terrifying acts of repression are perpetrated by those who wish to resist this change. The sane man will resist being swept into this cauldron of hatred."[12] Here she does not make an excuse for why the Cape Coloured need to remain "un-committed," but she implies how they have become a political buffer for the Whites in South Africa to keep the 80 percent Black population in a racial and economic bind set up by apartheid, in spite of the fact that the "underdog" knows who the real oppressor is.

This earlier writing is very limited in its scope and in its ambition. Head never gets beyond the sketching of life as she saw it in South

Africa, and she almost never develops it into a full fictional account as she did soon after she left. From this phase in her writing career one notices that she draws small, often incomplete pictures as she tries to "tell a story," which is nearly always camouflaged by straight commentary. As she began writing her longer pieces, gradually becoming a more accomplished writer, the narrative began to speak for itself, though the commentary never disappeared entirely.

Yet again in her piece titled "The Isolation of 'Boeta L,'" she begins with a commentary on how a young male lover is treated by the young girl's family and how this is directly linked to so many children being born out of wedlock.[13] In the last five paragraphs of this short sketch she finally gets to the subject of her story, Boeta L, who she describes as a "fierce political individualist." This aspect of Boeta L would not be so problematic if he did not live in Atteridgeville, which, Head tells us, strikes the outsider as rather a "cowardly" community.

The "point" of the story is quite simple. Boeta L is fed up with the apartheid situation and screams at one of the Boers as he waves a Bible in his hand: "'Take back your Bible, White Man. This is an eye blind. You tell us to go to church while you are in the battle-field!'"[14] Even Atteridgeville is saved from its cowardly malaise in the last paragraph. The "watch boys" at the guard post destroy this means of apartheid control, but with the same sense of humor that they displayed when they objected to Boeta L's singular reaction to the Boer. At a certain level the sketch makes light of individual heroism because that can only result in "jail," and besides, they argue, the Boer did not "invent the Bible." The two points that Head makes are that it is often better not to act singly in the apartheid situation and that communal humor about the conditions in South Africa is a survivalist tactic. Her talent remains in the actual storytelling. The meaning and the picture must be gleaned from the text carefully. The human balance of sanity in an insane system through humor marked by occasional spurts of anger at an unchosen historical and political identity is testimony of the author's struggle to analyze an impossible situation. But contained within the analysis is the whole idea of resistance to this situation, which oppresses 80 percent of the population.

"Snowball," set in Cape Town, is perhaps the only "story" in this early period of Head's writing that remains a story without too much authorial intervention, from beginning to end.[15] It is one of the only pieces that remain consistently on the subject of the story, Snowball, and the acute pathos evoked by a person who is not only accident-prone but also helpless and simply cannot fight for himself. In this story, the "authorial intervention" is woven into the narrative. This voice was to get more subtle with each work. Snowball seems to be intimidated by everyone from his landlady to his brother-in-law. They all seem to exploit his very passive nature just as the apartheid government exploits the Coloured people caught in the double bind imposed by racism. Head expresses affinity with Snowball and outrage that people who cannot defend themselves are robbed out of any peace of mind or any personal space. And it is no surprise when Snowball's dinghy capsizes; like Head's friend "D.B.," he too disappears into the peripheral margin of her transitory memory as yet another sacrifice to apartheid historical reality.

Several pieces of Head's writing are very specifically about South Africa but the date of publication is often not enough to determine whether it was done before or after her exile in 1964. Perhaps the only way to simplify this issue is to pay careful attention to the subject matter and style, which becomes distinctive in exile, and let that determine whether a particular piece was written before or after she left South Africa. Some of these pieces are reviews written by Head and commissioned by *The New African* on current African writing, such as *The Wedding of Zein* by Tayeb Salih; *Not Even God Is Ripe Enough: Yoruba Stories* by Bakare Agadamosi and Ulli Beier; *Potent Ash* by Leonard Kibera and Samuel Kahiga; and *African Religions and Philosophy* by John S. Mbiti.[16] In this group one could include the review she wrote on Miriam Makeba's music.

These reviews are less notable for Head's opinions on the work under discussion than for her opinions about topics unrelated to the text she is analyzing. The review of Mbiti's book is most pronounced in this regard. As the reviewer, Head tends to use the book only in order to talk about her own concept of what God should mean to the disenfranchised people of Southern Africa. The review's overemphasis on religion as Mbiti describes it, as an "attitude of mind of any people who have never been wanted by the rest of mankind," seems to emerge directly from Head's apartheid experience.[17] Toward the end of this review she talks about African religion as part of the everyday life of the African, as opposed to the Asian, who must leave life behind in order to pursue a religious life.

The article on Makeba's music is similar to the review of Mbiti's book, for Head wants to construct her opinions while writing, an opportunity that she still had not been able to exploit fictionally. She draws an unlikely similarity between Boris Pasternak and Makeba because they "eventually said the same, eternal, everlasting things to my heart."[18] She praises Makeba's music for speaking truthfully about the human and political situation in South Africa.

Curious for its subject matter is another article Head wrote for *The New African* in 1966, titled "West-East-South."[19] "West-East-South" links the suffering inherent in the Afroamerican experience to the Black South African situation under apartheid. This review discusses three books as well. Head chooses to spend two-thirds of her review on Malcolm X, and most politically moving in this regard is Bessie Head's discovery of Malcolm X. She sees him as a political activist who finally transcends the immediate situation of the Blacks in America to discover, through books on Africa, "black empires before the black slave was brought to the United States."[20] This mutual epistemological discovery, for it was not until the end of his life that Malcolm X discovered African writers, is what underlies the strength of Head's review. Once again, like some of the other articles written during this period, the value of this article is based primarily on the direction of Head's development as a writer and thinker.

There is one other noteworthy piece from this period in Head's life. "Sorrow Food," which was first published in *Transition*, is a critique of politicians.[21] The first date of publication, 1967, does not help determine where she wrote this piece. This could very well have been written either before 1964, while she was still in South Africa, or right after she went into exile in Botswana. "Sorrow Food" is striking in the very same way as the one poem ever published by Head. Her poem, "Things I Don't Like," was published in *The New African* in 1962.[22] The poem, obviously written and published before she left for Botswana, is, unlike the article, extremely strident and "angry." "Sorrow Food" is strident in the same way even though it is more cynical, especially in the way it is constructed. There is minimal direct interference by the authorial voice and it is spoken from the point of view of a very corrupt and ineffectual politician on the periphery of the political arena.

"Things I Don't Like" comes directly out of her apartheid experience in South Africa. Her only poem, as she told Patrick Cullinan in 1982, filled her with "horror." (Patrick Cullinan often appears in her letters to Randolph Vigne and helped her with her publishing career.) This poem had been written right after the massacre in Sharpeville in 1960. In Botswana, two decades later, the poem grew to upset Head, for it "advocates indiscriminate violence and bloodshed." The protagonist's voice, impotent with rage, implies a collective Black South African voice and seems to demand recognition of the systematic suffering of Black people from a world that just stands by and refuses to do anything about the plight of a whole nation. The defiance, pride, and repetitive variations of the refrain, "I am Black, / Okay?" stand out, not so much as contrast, but rather as an explanatory gesture about the back-breaking life that most Black South Africans live. This poem is witness to the real puzzlement and bitter anger of a man who can only explain the reasons for his life's trauma through incident—the color of his skin.

The protagonist seems to be an older man, perhaps at the end of a life's struggle just to survive on "eggs and polony," without family and without achievement. His life has been completely wasted by the racist apartheid system, and everything that he was as a human being is thrown back at his feet. He has no patience and only offers a very bitter truth to young people, who should not be "Grinning as though life is good." However, the anger does not get channeled into political action until the very last stanza. Head writes:

> Oh no.
> Today is my day.
> Going to get back tit-for-tat,
> All you stole.
> Going to fight you till you or I
> Lie smashed and bleeding dead
> And don't care who dies,
> You or I,
> But going to fight—
> OKAY?

This poem is indicative of Head's complex response to racist politics as they displaced the identity of South Africans. However, even in this 1962 poem, she anticipates the postapartheid era, which reveals her investment in the liberation struggle. In the verse just quoted, it is clear that Black people in South Africa have borne misery and suffering to the point where they cannot take any more, "don't care who dies, / You or I." It seems that "don't care who dies" anticipates the history which until recently was just a dream. After Mandela's release and presidency, the whole negotiating balance of the political and historical future of a free South Africa becomes imminent as it does in Head's poem with the finality of the last "Okay?" This nonconciliatory era is vastly different from Peter Abrahams's conciliatory politics of *Mine Boy* (1946). Even though the last "Okay?" ends in a question mark, it is not indicative of uncertainty but instead sounds bullying, demanding, threatening. The implication is that there is no place for those who do not wish to be part of the free South Africa.

In this period of Head's sporadic, troubled writing, the most difficult piece, in terms of its purpose, is the one I mentioned earlier, "Sorrow Food." The ideas expressed in this sketch, because it does not quite resemble a short story, are very enduring ones for Head. From the first pieces of her writing she expressed great discomfort with politicians who tended not to care for the "people" they were meant to serve, but instead seemed rigidly and hypocritically self-serving, shamelessly getting on any political bandwagon. "Sorrow Food" looks at such a person in all his complexity but tends to remain one-dimensional. Even though he is disgusting, he does evoke pathos largely because he is not as slick or fashionable as the other politicians and as a result loses his position of power.

Character and identity especially in South Africa are determined by politics. In "Sorrow Food," the corrupt, immoral politician can only come from an opportunism that survival has made imperative. Head is interested in the morality of a common man who is the typical politician defeated by the ethics of "tribalism." His morality seems to be summed up in a very simple question, which he asks himself, "To be or not to be—a day-light robber, or an under-cover robber?" He seems contemptuous of people who are underhanded about stealing from the poor in order "to get rich quickly," only because they do not steal in the light of day. He thinks that everybody, like him, wants to cheat poor people and become rich. So when they "find out" that he is misappropriating political funds, he disdains their supposed honesty because he thinks they are doing underhandedly exactly what he does openly. His assumption is that that is what every politician does.

This extreme antipathy toward politicians, for it is never clarified whether the protagonist of "Sorrow Food" is wrong about the motivations of his accusers in the sketch, remained an enduring attitude of Head's. In her first novel, she tends to make an uneasy and short-lived peace with what she calls "tribalism," and she goes further by having her South African exiled protagonist, Makhaya, look at the benefits of "Old Africa." But by the time she wrote *Maru* and later *A Question of Power,* the balance between old and new Africa was abandoned, and what took its place was bitter and relentless criticism at any oppressive structure or any institution symbolic of power, old or new. She believed that the misuse of political power affected the politics of identity and the "evil" pervasive in individuals and societies. For her, a relief from this evil could emerge only if one recognized one's humanity along with the humanity of others, Africans and non-Africans. In 1985, a year before her death, Head was to say, "I have my national, my African side but I am also very much an international kind of person."[23] And in spite of her obvious acceptance of her "African side," the "international" side took precedence even though she chose not to leave Africa, except for short periods, when the opportunity presented itself.

In addition, "Sorrow Food" anticipates some of the most startling language that Head was to use later on in her writing.[24] When the protagonist is giving examples of his "honesty," he says he is one of the few people who pays for everything he gets, including prostitutes. He says that unlike other guys, he pays. "When I get a woman I say: "Here's your five bucks. Africa is one big, loose penis female. Thanks for the ride." The extremely exploitative and vulgar language is jarring, but the concept of "penis female," even though far from a positive image, is typical of Head's complex understanding of new, more "androgynous" construction of relationships between men and women. The language of this piece is explosive like her poem, but "penis female" seems to imply a collapse in structures, whether family or gender, that opportunistic politicians, of which Africa has seen an overabundance, indeed the entire "third world," exploit in order to continue to maintain colonial class structures. "Penis female" remains the icon, not of ineffectuality, but rather of the complexity of the postcolonial, postapartheid era. It also indicates Head's awareness of the impending complexities intrinsic to such an era.

Turning to Head's smaller pieces written fairly soon after she came to Botswana, one finds two clear strains in her writing. The emphasis is on two journeys, one in which she explores the self by going inward, toward her own psyche, and the other going outward, toward Botswana and the ambivalent peace she found between two new homes. The writing of this period suggests an inward journey toward the self and the outward journey toward the community and represents a desire to bring the peaceful, simple life and community into the psychological mechanisms of the individual self, which in Head's case was undergoing an intensive healing period after leaving apartheid South Africa. Head writes: "In South Africa the white man took even the air away from us—it was his air and his birds and his land. In Botswana, I have a little bird outside my window every day. No one laid any particular claim to him, so I am able to confide, to the whole world, that he sings like this, and he sings like that, without some white man or woman snickering behind my ear: "Why, you people don't appreciate things like *that!*"[25] The process of being able to own one's experiences were the most early and liberating experiences that Head had in exile, short-lived though they were.

Less than a year after she got to Serowe, Head wrote a tribute, "For Serowe, a Village in Africa," published by *The New African* in 1965.[26] The most poignant aspect of this article is the balance between her euphoric response to Serowe and her "bewilderment" and loss of her home. There is another precarious balance that Head is acutely aware of in this article. She seems to be examining the internal perspective of how Seroweians have viewed and lived their lives for hundreds of years as opposed to how they are perceived by the external eye of groups bringing them "development and aid." There is, in this acknowledgment, a great gratitude for and euphoria about the simplicity and quiet beauty of Serowe, what she calls a "sense of wovenness," intertwined with the insider/outsider perspective. Her narratives are built around a search for this very "sense of wovenness," or the universal good of mankind, as she was to call it in her third novel. However, Head is very troubled by the viewer/viewed dialectic that colonialism sets up. She writes: "They say this and that about aid. They seem to know nothing of the desperate longing to bring out our own creativeness."[27] Head was trying to salvage one part of the "desperate longing" in her two histories, *Serowe: Village of the Rain Wind* and the sequel, *A Bewitched Crossroad.* It is clear from her commitment to the idea of seeing life as it is lived in Botswana, in spite of colonial impact, as inherently separate from the way it is viewed by external spheres of influence. An outsider might call each village in Botswana "timeless," but for Head, the determinants of a time and place were the people who lived and struggled within that frame.

Even though the article is a tribute to Serowe, her thoughts always include, as in much of everything Head ever wrote, her home. Head notes, "Southern Africa isn't like the rest of Africa and is never going to be. Here we are going to have to make an extreme effort to find a deep faith to help us live together . . . people are not going to be destroyed. Not now. There is all this fierce hatred and it is real. There are the huge armies prepared for war against unarmed people and we are all overwhelmed with fear and agony, not knowing where it will end."[28] Head draws a comparison between the fierce struggle for "our own creativeness" in Botswana as well as in South Africa. She points to the fundamental issue of Black and White people needing "deep faith" in South Africa in order to live with each other, the kind that is not necessary in Botswana.

At the end of this article she adds remorsefully, "Some of us cannot battle with this conflict. I cannot. But wherever I go I shall leave a chunk of myself here because I think of myself as a woman of Southern Africa. . . . There was this immense conflict, pressure, uncertainty and insecurity that I have lived with for so long—I have solved nothing. I am like everyone else—perplexed, bewildered and desperate."[29] She seems almost apologetic about having left South Africa. Her remorse is part of the exilic consciousness—a part she was to combat the rest of her life. Her statement also suggests, as Edward Said says, "desperate loss" and "longing" for South Africa. However, there is also a great helplessness about coping with life inside South Africa. Exile did not solve all the "uncertainty and insecurity" for Head, and she continued to experience it after she came to Botswana. This ambivalence about her home and the space that was not-home was to dog her writing throughout her life. She was exiled—caught between cultures and emotional economies—and agonized by a "Janus-faced" allegiance and a "Janus-faced" psyche. In exile, Head experienced an uneasy reconciliation with the place of her birth as well as her un/chosen home, Botswana, all the while remaining "like everyone else—perplexed, bewildered and desperate."

An article that was not published till 1972 in *Listener* as "An African

Story" is collected as "Dreamer and Storyteller" in *Tales of Tenderness and Power*.[30] This article belongs to the period during which Head still agonizes about life in South Africa even though the distance, for her, was always one of degree. In this article, her exile remains like "borrowed clothes," and despite her ambivalence about leaving, Head continued to hope that "Southern Africa might one day become the home of the storyteller and dreamer, who did not hurt others but only introduced new dreams."[31] It is clear that even after the eight years spent in exile in Botswana she longs for home and considers herself a South African writer who must "introduce new dreams." She links the role of the artist and writer with nationalistic interests, though not necessarily political engagement, as it relates to the immediate apartheid reality of Black South Africans. She writes, "It has surprised me, the extent to which creative writing is often regarded, unconsciously, as a nationalistic activity, and perhaps this expression of national feeling is rather the subdued communication a writer holds with his own society. I have so often been referred to as 'the Botswana writer,' while in reality the Botswana personality isn't as violent as mine. I wasn't born with the gentle inquiring eyes of a cow but amongst black people who always said, when anything went wrong: 'Why don't we all die?' And the subdued undertone was: 'since the white man hates us so much.'"[32]

Even though most of Head's text was set in Botswana, she recognized herself as a South African writer. From the foregoing passage one gleans the tremendous survival mechanism that Head must have mobilized in order to stay afloat from the time she was born. I believe that it was the tension between the desire to emulate the peaceful Batswana personality and her own violence and anger against injustices that contributed to her creative endeavor. However, in the passage just quoted, her reaction to the violence under apartheid makes her a distinctly South African writer. The problem of identity raised by "Why don't we all die?—since the white man hates us so much" situates itself in the exiled imagination giving rise to a permanent tension, which leaves her vacillating from gratitude about life in Botswana to guilt at having left South Africa. In the next paragraph she talks, for the first time, about the overt discrimination, like benches for Whites only, that she encounters and the violence that it engenders in both victim and victimizer. In "Dreamer and Storyteller" she talks about the material available to the Southern African writer: "There are not people but complexions and hair textures—whites, coloureds, Indians and Africans. Who can write about that?"[33] It was precisely this writerly inability that she was to escape through exile. But through exile, specifically exile in Botswana, she was to encounter the perfect tension for her narrative skills which she would not have in Europe or America. In other words, it was very important to Head's identity as a writer to remain in Southern Africa.

"God and the Underdog: Thoughts on the Rise of Africa," published by *The New African* in 1968 is almost a verbatim description of all the ideas Head used in her second novel, *Maru*, in 1971.[34] Stylistically, this essay seems to imitate her earlier writing. She does not limit herself to the subject matter: instead she records her scattered thoughts on the sudras of the world as if she were recording in her diary, going from image to image and idea to idea. One of several important ideas in her second novel is the claim that the sudras and outcasts of the world can claim a higher spirituality than others because of their suffering. This demand obviously comes directly out of her apartheid experience, where Black people cannot even lay claim to appreciating nature. Head's delight at the bird outside her window, which she recorded upon first arriving in Serowe, is part of that spiritual claim, part of claiming an identity that escaped apartheid.

When she talks about the "underdog's" claim to spirituality she means it to be in a certain sociopolitical context. Her heroine in *Maru*, Margaret Cadmore, is a Masarwa, and her avocation as an artist prohibits her from engaging in political overthrow of oppression; but rather, she lives her artist's life regardless of those demands. For Head, this aspect of spiritual engagement privileges the spiritual position of the sudras. She writes: "I had also just been relieved of the sight of the Afrikaner Boer and was correspondingly anxious to fill the great chambers of my heart with something beautiful like a God who was just quiet and full of common sense."[35] It is obvious that even though she invokes "God" she means something quite different from the god of grand schemes. For Head, spiritual engagement and God represented the daily life and small tasks of common people. For her, it was in these tasks that human and God found a unifying principle. The god in her second novel, *Maru*, was quite different. There, a god enters her characters and they in turn represent goodness of all kinds. Head wants to give the Masarwa schoolteacher, Margaret, a spiritual life that no one can take away from her.

Historically, part of the survivalist identity politics of Black South Africans has been to develop something that could not be taken away. Religion plays that role in Southern Africa—and indeed the same patterns could be traced for Afroamerican spiritual interests and history. The phenomenon of a religious and spiritual identity, where, regardless of external suffering, one can still be human, was a recurring theme for Head.

Given the problematic, survivalist relationship to Christian religions that Afroamericans and Africans have experienced, Head counsels the same sort of faith. "I feel in my heart that our Pharaoh has already been born. It may be that I shall not live to see Pharaoh's day but I want all those who now live in anguish to be comforted. For one day, due to the length of his roots and depth of his wisdom, all nations shall dwell under his shadow."[36] The coming of the Pharaoh is much like the coming of the savior who passes judgment and liberates his oppressed children, holding sway over all of humankind and not just some specific groups. This ideology is problematic in its advocacy of pacifism even though it is fundamentally survivalist in both the Afroamerican and the African tradition: if you have only one pharaoh coming to save a whole multitude of oppressed people from misery then you do not need to do it yourself.

Head's "Nigra" Goddess indicates the strong commitment to women's issues that Head showed during her writing life and brings together the spirituality which is not exclusive of fighting back systems of oppression. She is very clear about this preference for a female god, even though the Pharaoh, who is going to save humanity, is male. This idea of a feminine god is linked further to her tribute to Afroamerican womanhood:

> But Africa is going to rise to a great height of civilization and this is going to be done, in the last resort with African brains and my "Nigra" Goddess.
>
> I am one African who needs and wants my God Black . . . preferably of the feminine gender. There is something wrong with God, expressed as masculine. You don't see the fire and thunder in him the way you do in his feminine counterpart.
>
> And if I say—My God, she's a "Nigra" it is because I slightly confuse in my mind That which is double-edged, That which is made of fire, That which is eternally alive, with the personality of a certain Afro-American woman who was my friend and comrade for a period of almost two years in Botswana.[37]

Later she talks about how Afroamerican people can instinctively understand the "underdog" because of what they themselves have suffered. She links the "rise of Africa" with women as goddesses and revolutionaries. This feminist writerly persuasion was inherent in everything she wrote even as she denied the necessity of being "feminist." She remarks, "I do not have to be feminist. The world of the intellect is impersonal, sexless."[38]

In this article on the "underdog" Head continues her tribute to Afroamericans: "But one thing I do know, that all this suffering has made Afro-American people catch a little of this fire from heaven and bring it down to earth to us. I wish, with all my heart that they bring it to Africa."[39] This is one of the few times that Head was to see the commonality of the struggles of Black South Africans and Afroamericans. This tribute does not take into account the differences between the ingredients of the two struggles against racist economic oppression, but perhaps that is not Head's intention at all. Here, as in *Maru,* as well as in her analysis of women's oppression in Botswana, she consistently tends to privilege the position of the "underdog." However, it is not until *A Question of Power* that she rejects the political ideology that privileges "special groups."

The tribute to Black womanhood continues in her piece titled "The Woman from America," published in *The Classic,* 1968.[40] It is highly likely that the woman mentioned in this article is the same one that she talks about in "God and the Underdog." The air of wonderment about everything that Head encountered in Botswana pervades the narrative techniques and style of this period in her writing. A sense of wholeness, harmony, and belonging, in spite of the rigidity of the society that she was to live in and which she never ceases to notice, constitutes the strength of these pieces, written very shortly after her sojourn in Botswana. This sense of wholeness, hyphenated only in some parts of her writing, was to continue through the major part of her first novel, *When Rain Clouds Gather.*

In "The Woman from America," there is a struggle between the traditional community and anybody who represents foreign influences. This struggle was glossed over in her first novel but in this sketch there is harmony even in the intolerance of the village people for this strange woman who is a bit like an "avalanche." She draws a sharpe distinction between just people and people from Botswana. "Basically, we are mean, selfish. We eat each other all the time and God help poor Botswana at the bottom."[41] Even though she is aware of the narrowness of the society, she effectively divides Botswana from it. She simply uses the two camps of people, "those who feel a fascinated love and those who fear a new thing," to continue her tribute to this woman who ultimately becomes a symbol of the possibility and potential of Botswana.[42] In this piece, Head's tribute to the Afroamerican woman is tied to the fascination and respect that she continued to have for Botswana even when she became more critical than she had been in the earlier pieces.

Head, only a year earlier, in 1967, had written a longer tribute to Botswana in *The Classic*. "Village People, Botswana" is the continuation of Head's musings on poverty and tradition.[43] In spite of the peace and beauty of Botswana, the poverty was irreconcilable for her. "Do we really retain the right to develop slowly, admitting change only in so far as it keeps pace with our limitations, or does change descend upon us as a calamity?"[44] These thoughts are indicative of her fascination with the Afroamerican woman who came to a small village in Botswana and unreservedly advocated change. Head's question shows a Makhaya-like determination to "end poverty in Africa." Makhaya, in *When Rain Clouds Gather*, was impatient with his own poverty and wanted everybody to be a "millionaire."

What is most notable in this longer piece, which is divided into smaller sketches, is that Head the author is looking at herself from the point of view of a Batswana who has to struggle with poverty and semidesert conditions. In fact, even when she is talking about South African refugees she looks at them as a Batswana would, which anticipates Head's longer and more complicated works on a need to "belong" to a certain place if not a particular time. She writes in the section titled "The Green Tree,"[45] "Many strangers traverse our land these days. They are fugitives from the south fleeing political oppression. They look on our lives with horror and quickly make means to pass on to the paradises of the north. Those who are pressed by circumstances and forced to tarry a while, grumble and complain endlessly. It is just good for them that we are inbred with habits of courtesy, hospitality and kindness."[46]

Even her impatience with foreigners who do not understand "the passion we feel for this parched earth" emerges from the simultaneous desire to protect the poverty of Botswana from criticism and a desire to belong—one feeding into the other. So even as she describes Botswana as a stranger would, "Our women with their tall thin hard bodies can drive a man to the depth of passion," she claims a oneness in her tone. The description could closely fit Pauline, one of her first in a series of strong, passionate female protagonists.

Interestingly, this is one of the very few times that Head uses a male narrator. At the end of this particular sketch there is a curious twist of the male protagonist being consumed by the complex and phantomlike relationship he has developed with a woman who has taken up "the mask of adaptability" but is really a "deceitful stranger." This part of the sketch is indicative of Head's ambivalence toward outsiders and being one herself. She deconstructs her own idea of an exile's superior motivations. The "deceitful stranger" wearing within and without the "mask of adaptability" becomes "the inappropriate other in every I." The pretense of "belonging" to a culture that is not one's own is an act of deceit against oneself and the inhabitants of the place of exile. Yet the "sin" of this pretense does not seem so great except to the exile herself, as she balances her desire to belong with a longing for the lost home to which she cannot return. These essentially parallel parts of a "homeless" identity make the exile schizophrenic, for they are innately unreconcilable. The simultaneous ambivalence and euphoria about her exile in Botswana was to come to an erosive psychological conflict in Head's last novel, *A Question of Power.* In "The Green Tree," it is not just that strangers and natives threaten each other in sociopsychological ways, but that they become each other's phantoms, reflecting and reflected by each other. The idea of exile and native as necessarily causing great discomfort and grief to each other is more fully developed in her third novel.

The sketch "Summer Sun" is straight narration and not as effective as "The Old Woman" which is more of a short story, more poignant simply because there is development through dialogue rather than a narration of the hard life of Botswana women.[47] In "The Old Woman," Head's immense respect for the graciousness of a society under siege of poverty is most apparent. In her settling into the semidesert conditions of the south she cuts herself off from the opportunistic immigrant and allies herself with the poverty of the people she lived among. Thus the deep respect that is apparent in *When Rain Clouds Gather* is anticipatory of her first long glimpse of Botswana.

"Tao," first published by *Freedomways* in 1967, continues the exile's fantasy of being one of the people she is among, even as it nurtures the idea of being distinct from those very people.[48] The story's narrator is a Batswana schoolteacher who is explaining to the rest of the African continent why the Batswana react the way they do and how unfair it is to call them defenders of "British Imperialism." The narrator explains that it is not that they defend colonialism but perhaps the rest of Africa does not understand that "we were never subjects under colonialism. We were protected people." For Head, this intense desire to understand the lack of a Batswana political consciousness after she experienced the seductive peace was a subject for great sociohistorical debate.

In the last seven years of her life, she was to puzzle out this complex historical reaction to political challenge through a historical analysis of the various tribes that came to be called the Batswana. These two histories, *Serowe: Village of the Rain Wind* and *A Bewitched Crossroad*, offer an explanation to people who accuse South Africans of "playing into the hands of the settler governments!" Head writes: "We defend ourselves. We make a long speech about how our country has always been peaceful and a refuge for those in trouble. We tell them the ancient story about the Kalanga tribe who fled from the persecution of the Matabele tribe and for three centuries have lived in peace here, though being a different nation with different customs."[49] She was to look at the Batswana fear of change in the same uncritical way as she was to look at their desire to be left out of divisive politics, which she always claimed was the fundamental reason that she found herself a home in Botswana.

"Tao" is a more important piece of shorter fiction than others Head wrote at this time simply because it anticipates and outlines not only the two histories she wrote but also her most important novel, *A Question of Power*. One of the ideas that she implies in "Tao" was to be more fully developed in *A Question of Power*. Here, the idea of sexuality and sexual attraction is suppressed as quickly as it is raised. Head writes, "I would rather efface myself than face torment of a naked and unashamed desire for an unattainable man with the face of a brooding thunder cloud." The character was to explain, "I have no courage in this upside-down world. I flee." Head was to "flee" her sexuality and any overt political involvement, even as she left a literary trail of clues about questions of resistance and identity. Later, Head was to create in Moleka, one of the main characters in her second novel *Maru*, a personality much like Tao's. Moleka, too, drives at "tearing speed amid the twisting, dusty circular paths of the village," scattering outraged goats and other domestic animals. Moleka, like his predecessor Tao, is a dashing figure whom Margaret Cadmore never stops loving in spite of her marriage to Maru. Head later wrote that this repetition occurred as she tried to develop one kind of male character.[50] Working and reworking the image is testimony to the accomplishment she was to achieve in her later work.

Head's antipathy toward opportunistic politics inspired by individual politicians springs from a real fear that she voiced in "Tao." She describes a political gathering where Tao is giving a speech. It is very clear that she is seduced by the aura he is able to create through his personal and political charisma, just as other poor people are. "Few have such a powerful creative intelligence," she writes. "A man, vividly, passionately alive, awakens all life around him. Strange that he should be one of us and yet a contrast, a new thing, the awakener of deep, hidden suppressed feeling. Such a man, with evil intentions, could cause wreckage and disaster all around him."[51] For Head, individual power was always connected with evil, and this issue was explored more fully in *A Question of Power*. In this novel, the interplay between good and evil within every identity space gave Head a chance to come up with the synthesis of what humanity relied on. Head's idea of "universality" situated her as an idealist, but it is the most problematic concept, especially for an exile, to hold. Tao had the same male sexuality and charisma as Dan and Sello did in her last novel. Tao anticipates them in terms of the complex interplay of the power of good and evil that always implicates female sexuality.

Head was to turn away from politics more and more as she began to settle in Botswana. Her article "Chibuku Beer and Independence," the original title for which was "Borrowed Clothes" before it was later published in *The New African*, constitutes yet another testimony to the necessity for peace and regularity, what she called well-trodden "grooves" in her private life. Even though this article celebrates the independence of Zimbabwe, it ends with Head, after the raucous celebrations, admiring "the ever-familiar thorn bush lit up by the brilliant fierce beauty of a desert sunset."[52] The natural beauty and curious history of Botswana were to become the most enduring political interests that Head claimed during her exile from apartheid South Africa.

One of the pieces she wrote for *The New African* in 1966 came closest to resembling the style she was to cultivate as a mature writer. "Looking for a Rain-God" shows Head's absorption of life as it is lived in Botswana. This story was later anthologized in *The Collector of Treasures*. In this story, she seems to understand the poverty caused by the whimsicality of the weather and the desperation of people dependent on rainfall as their only salvation. Since this story was published, Head mentioned that her source was a newspaper report on a trial of two men who sacrificed children to draw rain. She remained unjudgmental about the extreme response to poverty and desperation that people faced in her host country. She continued to have sympathy for the two men who were hanged by the state as reparation for the sacrifice of the two little girls. The "ashen, terror-stricken faces" of the family and the "wailing" of the women in the bush are poignant images. These tropes of misery that cause the cruel death of the children remain present in "Looking for a Rain-God," rendering superfluous any halting readerly judgment.

Though Bessie Head always considered herself a South African writer, she continued to manifest an enduring interest in Botswana history very soon after she got there. In her 1977 article "A Period of Darkness," published in *Kutlwano,* she indicated the beginnings of her biographical interest in historical personalities.[53] Here she talked about Chief Motswasele II's rule as a period of darkness, a darkness she was all too familiar with, especially given her distrust of political leaders and governments and apartheid.

The whole village decides to get rid of their chief in one collective gesture because he has violated their fundamental trust in him. What interests Head is the "triumphant statement . . . that people had always held a position of ascendancy in matters of government." She was to later utilize this idea of fundamental democracy in her first novel, *When Rain Clouds Gather,* in which Chief Matenge hates "common people" and is deposed by them even though no one actually gets rid of him. In addition, Head explored African civilization and history and the way that disputes were settled and bad leaders were overthrown (this idea of reworking history is more clearly developed in my sixth chapter).

"The Prisoner Who Wore Glasses" was published fairly early in Head's literary career in *London Magazine* in 1973.[54] From the late 1960s on, Head was to display very definite talents for narrative writing. "The Prisoner," which really belongs to the South African period because of subject matter, seems to resemble in style the more accomplished pieces she was to write in exile. This short story, like "A Period of Darkness," is really concerned with the strength of collective political action—and in this case, the validity and efficaciousness of that action even if one has been "neutralized" in jail.

In the 1980s Head published three stories that complimented her second history, *A Bewitched Crossroad*. All three were published between 1980 and 1981. "A Power Struggle" was published by *Kutlwano*, "The Lovers" by *Wietie*, and "The Coming of the Christ-Child" in *Marang*.[55] There are three main components of Head's interest in history: first, the careful preservation of tragic folk legends transmitted orally from generation to generation; second, the contextualizing and reinscribing of ancient wisdom in traditional Botswana; and third, partly related to the second, the reclaiming of history from the colonialist point of view.

In "A Power Struggle," Head creates a delicate narrative balance between real power and violent power. Her agenda is very clear. It is impossible to have real power through force—that is why the younger brother fails in his attempt to rule an unwilling population. The older brother, on the other hand, through the inspiration of love and trust, can rule his people even after he is deposed. The people choose displacement and exile with a leader they love instead of staying at home allowing a tyrant to rule them. "A Power Struggle" engages Head's long-term interest in the precarious balance between society and powerful individuals.

"The Coming of the Christ-Child" echoes the loneliness of a people who have "abandoned the religion of their fathers." This story is about a man who replaces religion with political action because, as a young man, he has seen land taken away from Black people when they could not pay the poll tax, while his father, the pastor, was left completely undone by the brutality of apartheid. The story of the young man is not very different from a lot of young Black South Africans involved with political struggle. The fact that he could have lived an easy life because of his education and job, but chooses not to, is incidental to the retelling of the sociohistorical events that took place in apartheid South Africa. He recognizes the need for young men like himself to fight oppression instead of simply helping themselves. At the end of the story Head compares the protagonist to the Christ-child, somebody who sacrifices his entire life for the liberation of his people. In so doing she separates the actual events of the birth and coming of Christ from the institutional religion that uses those same events to oppress people.

"The Lovers" is documentation of another sort of tradition. One aspect of the tradition that Head always deplored is the lack of what she understood as a tolerance for individuality. Even though the tale is really about the tortured love of two young people, she chooses to link the intolerance of society to migratory trends of the Batswana. The tale itself is very touching and forces readers to question the superfluous demands made by a strictly ordered society of deviant individuals.

The only three stories collected in *Tales of Tenderness and Power* that were never published before are "Property," "General," and "Son of the Soil."[56] The second two manifest Head's interest in the history of South Africa and individuals who have political power. Even though she never wrote a book-length history about the country of her birth, she did tend to read and record her ideas about the specific historical happenings there. "Son of the Soil" records the brutal aspects of Boer rule in South Africa and the sinister aspects of Bantu education. The justification that the Boers gave the rest of the world for Bantu education was this: "'Our Natives are unlike Natives anywhere else in the world,' they said, contentedly. 'They are capable of progress. Once they work for us they will become civilized.'"[57] Head records that the only people who did not accept this cruel Boer justification were the young schoolchildren in the townships. They rebelled against it, thus beginning the legacy of children of nine being placed in solitary confinement by the apartheid government of South Africa.

"General" remains an undeveloped story and is indicative of Head's belief that anyone who was a benevolent person turned away from political or other kinds of power that gave them visibility, in order to "till the earth."[58] Along with this belief is the suspicion that anyone who chooses political power does it for his or her own self-interests; it is also clear that Head does not want to believe this of the general, for she spends a great deal of time developing his traits as someone who "disliked being saluted more than is necessary."

In "Property," Head wanted to write about a new mode of relationship between Black men and women. In this story, when men and women want to change their roles, tragedy occurs. The theme of amicable relationships between men and women became more than a pleasant possibility in her collection of short stories, *The Collector of Treasures*.

Head's novella, written before she left South Africa never to return, *The Cardinals,* indicates that she was always very interested in exploring nontraditional ways for men and women to negotiate each other's presence. This piece really stands out in terms of its depth and scope. It is presumably the only longer piece emanating from Bessie Head's South African sojourn, a multilayered documentation of the early career of an artist. The subject matter might explain why this story remained unpublished for so long. In this novella, the pervasive desire to belong to a community is less important than belonging to oneself as a woman writer. Miriam or Mouse, the curious result of apartheid, inhabits this story as a young journalist struggling to function with the discoveries and contradictions of her catatonic sexual-emotional self and as an artist coming into being. Characteristically, she finds an older, more jaded colleague who immediately takes an interest in her development even though at first he wishes the relationship to be sexual and she does not. M. J. Daymond remarks in the Introduction to *The Cardinals* that "the love plot . . . rests on a cliché: Handsome, worldly man meets and loves shrinking violet. This was the basis of many escapist romances Bessie Head handled each week at *Golden City Post*."[59] I believe that Daymond is simply skimming the extremely deceptive surface of this novella, leaving several dimensions unexplored. If anything, *The Cardinals* seems to be an earlier rendition of her most complex work, *A Question of Power.* The novella begins with an introduction to the precariousness of intimate relations between White and Black people under apartheid. Head gives minute details about the White woman's betrayal of the beautiful Black fisherman, Johnny. Their unusual relationship is followed by the birth of a child. Both parents disappear from the newborn's childhood. The manifestation of the father as lover in Miriam or Mouse's life is in part indicative of Head's defiance against and in part her critique of the Immorality Act.

The incestuous refrain in the novella is startling in its subtlety, in that the main character, Mouse, never shows any acknowledgment of the actuality of incest. The only criticism of incest occurs when her adoptive father tries to rape her while she is still a child, but his actions are halted by the adoptive mother. Miriam would not be found in a brutal foster home if her White mother and Black father had been allowed to keep her. Miriam's response is typical of sexually abused children everywhere—she leaves the scene of the impending abuse and perhaps finds another somewhat similar emotional economy as an adult. Johnny mentions that he loved his sister in ways other than strictly brotherly ones. But as Daymond suggests, "Head does make us believe that her protagonists have the right to love each other."[60] Johnny believes that his sister needed his love and protection, and he could only provide the former; the text implies that the perpetrators of the Immorality Act, apartheid, and poverty are greater criminals than the two people trying to save their own and each other's lives in that milieu, even if one is a parent and the other a child. Ruby and Johnny's love form the impossible parallel to Mouse and Johnny's attraction later in the novella. The implied local wisdom is that neither one is incestuous.

It is unusual for Head to create obvious incestuous overtones in Mouse's relationship with Johnny without a grand acknowledgment of a taboo. In *A Question of Power,* the protagonist appeared to be terrified of any sexual deviance, but in *The Cardinals* there is an inevitability and acceptance about this social taboo.

The plot itself is not as well developed as is the character of Mouse. She has been "harnessed" into a recognition of herself first as an artist and second as a woman. At first she is loath to even open her mouth, but toward the end she has lived through important experiences primarily as a writer and secondarily as an emotional being. Johnny is her mentor *par excellence.* Daymond's point about Head's usage of incest as an icon for the risk-taking writer is one way of sublimating her explosion of taboos. It is conceivable that an apartheid society that respects racism more than the incest taboo would not care to enforce records and names of underclass parents and their children, and certainly if the child were mixed, both the apartheid system and the White family would be interested in erasing, rather than preserving, such records. In this novella, the simultaneous desire for erasure as it coexists with the fear of incest becomes an issue integrally related to apartheid.

There are three interrelated ideas in *The Cardinals* that are important to the narrative and to the world view Head was to develop more fully later. Head's ideas about individual identities as they relate to their art, politics, and Africa are explored mainly through Johnny. Mouse, the novice, primarily listens and absorbs his ideas, for they seem to correspond with her own. Johnny tells Mouse, "If any crazy bastard stops you in the street one day and asks you to join his political party, don't. He's actually asking you to let him do your thinking for you. You'll find yourself tied up with a lot of dogma and cock-eyed ideas."[61] Elizabeth, in *A Question of Power,* was to repeat these ideas by expanding the role of any responsible individual in a society. The man who tries hard to find Mouse a wheel-chair has that same sense of moral and social responsibility that Head recommends to humanity at large. Joining a political party is not politics, Head would argue. For her, politics is the profound engagement with fellow humans—an engagement that is not race-bound or nation-specific. This is what she was to later call "universal brotherhood" in *A Question of Power.*

The task of the writer is to "understand . . . man and try to figure out all the complexities at work inside him." Later, Johnny continues to tell Mouse, "The task of the writer is to serve humanity and not party politicians and their temporary fixations."[62] In Botswana, Head was to notice the "eternal" quality of her new home. Head was to return over and over again to this cross-pollination of values that she placed on her writerly expectations and her desire to belong to a future Africa.

"Africa is the one thing I can't afford to be uncommitted about and yet I, and every writer, should be—especially at this time of change, of patriotism and nationalism."[63] Head's belief about writers being critically engaged with a postcolonial postapartheid Africa is especially insightful, for she warns against a premature euphoria. But in the foregoing passages from *The Cardinals,* Johnny is talking about a different kind of political commitment—an "eternal" one to "goodness and truth," not to "temporary fixations" and ephemeral ideologies. It was this profound commitment to "humanity" that constituted the fundamental basis of her focus in all her novels, short stories, and histories. Most of the pieces I have analyzed in this chapter contribute directly or indirectly to Head's larger world view, as her world view becomes more defined in her novels, stories, and histories. These seedlings that have been collected in the posthumous anthologies were to bear fruit when she got down to writing her longer, more mature work; but at the same time, there is a tenable connection between Head's earlier interest in exiled identities and spheres of power, and especially as these spheres control and determine oppression.

2

EUPHORIA AND SUBVERSION
IN EXILE

IN *When Rain Clouds Gather* there is a tension between Head's tone of nostalgic reminiscences about "home" and the compulsory exile that her main characters face. Head's interest in "Old Africa" conflicts with her view of "tribal" Africa as impeding "modernity," a progress that she envisioned for the continent of her birth. In Botswana, she reasserted, "What was valuable for me, with my South African Black background, was to find a society where the African experience is continuous and unbroken."[1]

The temptation to re-create the mythic past was great: if only it were possible to get back to precolonial times where life was assumed to be orderly and emotionally viable. Such desire aims to radically subvert the experience of colonialism and emerges out of the longing to efface socioeconomic apartheid altogether, but it is regressive in regard to several issues, especially that of gender. The desire for the past causes an inherently problematic situation for the exile's feminist identity. An exile is especially equipped to see the past and present more clearly simply because she occupies the displaced zones that people "at home" cannot perceive. Head's exiles can look both forward and backward with ease because they are not part of the social context. Head invests her exiles with the power of simultaneity and vision so that they may evaluate life lived by Africans today.

The protagonist of *When Rain Clouds Gather,* Makhaya, looks both forward and backward. Head's simultaneous view of both future and past offers a false dichotomy, however. It is not that one has to look to the precolonial or colonial past in its relationship to the postcolonial present as inherently separate from one another in order to arrive at some truths about cultural identities.[2] In *When Rain Clouds Gather*, truths about systems of desire within individual subjectivities become prominent in a dialogic confrontation between past and present, as they are simultaneous with rather than separate from each other. These systems of desire that emerge specifically for each subjectivity out of an exile's consciousness tend to display truths about peoples and, given Head's interest, particularly about women's aspirations in the last two decades of the twentieth century.

As Head affirms again and again in her writing, to an exile *"nothing is secure."*[3] In this novel, exiles abound. Each looks for a different security, thus forming, informing, and re-forming a pattern of identities while in exile. In writing about the exile's consciousness, Edward Said remarks, "Exile is a jealous state. What you achieve is precisely what you have no wish to share, and it is in the drawing of lines around you and your compatriots that the least attractive aspects of being in exile emerge: an exaggerated sense of group solidarity and a passionate hostility to outsiders, even those who may in fact be in the same predicament as you."[4] Granted that Said's concern is primarily with one set of exiles—Zionist Jews trying to inflict genocide on another exiled nation of Arab Palestinians—the animosity between the South African refugee exile and the Botswanan nation in its role of representative, as delineated in Head's three novels, is somewhat similar. Her South African exiles are often unwelcome in Botswana and are not granted residency for decades. In her first novel she negotiates the animosity between the Batswana government and South African refugees amicably, through the use of utopian nostalgia, or through what Simon Gikandi has called a false debate between modernity and tradition.[5] Head's treatise on power relationships as they inform and are informed by exiled identities seeking to subvert the nation are the particular concern of her novels, and the conclusions to these problematic issues vary in progression from novel to history.

Stuart Hall postulates two modes of cultural identity that problematize Head's identity dialectic:

> One defines cultural identities in terms of one, shared culture, a sort of collective "one true self," hiding inside the many other, more superficial or artificially imposed "selves" which people with a shared culture and ancestry hold in common. Within the terms of this definition, our cultural identities reflect the common historical experiences and shared cul-

tural codes which provide us, as "one people," with stable, unchanging and continuous frames of reference and meaning, beneath the shifting divisions and vicissitudes of our actual history.

[Cultural identity] is not something which already exists, transcending place, time, history and culture. . . . Far from being eternally fixed in some essentialized past [such identities] are subject to the continual play of history, culture and power. Far from being grounded in a mere "recovery" of the past which is waiting to be found, [they] will secure our sense of ourselves into eternity; identities are the names we give to the different ways we are positioned by, and position ourselves within, the narratives of the past.[6]

Even though the "actual history" of Hall's cultural identities would be seriously thrown out of joint by what Judith Butler has called "gender trouble," especially as it relates to gender definitions of subjectivity through the addition of feminist definitions of female identity, his distinctions and definitions have relevance for women. A simplistic notion of an identity, never a cultureless one, seems to be the bane of Head's exiles. However, the driving force behind the exiles in Head's first two novels is to strip away "superficial or artificially imposed 'selves'" in order to reach the "true self." This "true self," that is, a general African self, can function in a society with minimal historical intervention and does so in Head's first novel, which comprises a policy of amnesia about the past that is replaced by a whole-hearted acceptance of the exiled present in the new home. The construction of the "pure African self" is problematic because the complex racial structures of a postapartheid South Africa were changing rapidly. Bessie Head was not only increasingly aware of this change but a living embodiment of it.

Makhaya does and does not try to obliterate "the continual play of history, culture and power" represented by his apartheid South African past in favor of his peaceful present. Even though the authorial system of desire wishes to position Makhaya where he can "secure his sense of himself into eternity," Head is unable to extend this to any of her other protagonists. Thus, *When Rain Cloud Gather* is characteristic of an early stage in the development of an exile's system of desires and the consciousness out of which they emerge.

Desire, even desire for the past, is always, as Christopher Miller has implied in his discussion of Yambo Ouologuem's *Le Devoir de Violence*, a component of exile.[7] I believe that Said's avowed fierceness, which he believes the exile has, and Miller's desire both coincide in Head's exile, Makhaya. There is an inherent desire in the structural makeup of Head's characters for the precolonial past as well as a desire projected onto the text in the case of Head as author. Quite specifically, in *When Rain Clouds Gather*, this desire is manifested as a longing to situate her exile within the parameters of "Old Africa," which is how Botswana at first seemed to her. However, this desire is not uncritical of the past, but seeks a direct link between African past and present, with an intense longing to efface colonialism. Especially for an exile, historical movement certainly stops for a while; history is halted, life seems jarred, and emotions are withdrawn from the present. Contexts do not change, but events and lives that are tied to them float in uncontextualized displaced zones, emphasizing levels of exile unsuspected even by the individual under such a regimen.

Head privileges exiles and political and personal motivations as they take up domicile in countries that they want to be able to call "home," a term rife with contradictions. The tension between this longing for home and the reality of exile unfolds very slowly in Head's first novel, but not as relentlessly as it did in *A Question of Power*. When Bessie Head herself got an exit visa and left for the neighboring state of Botswana, she, along with other refugees, was first housed in refugee camps where she saw several people occupying the exile's displaced space just as she did. However, the exile that engaged her was an exile within an exile, and perhaps this is where her analysis of women's experience as exile emerges. She writes, "A young refugee from Zimbabwe quietly detached himself from the group and held long dialogues with me. He wanted an alternative to war and power. He had no faith in the future leadership of Zimbabwe. There was no one articulating the hopes of the people and he did not want to die for a worthless cause. I latched eagerly on to his dialogue and my first novel provides an alternative for young men. I created a symbolic type of refugee. I implied that he was a man of talent. I made him briefly face implications of black power and then turned him abruptly away from the madding crowd to spend a lifetime in a small rural village, battling with food production problems."[8]

Here Head not only indicates the dilemmas of the exile but also manifests a tendency to create a utopic and euphoric space, namely, "a small rural village." The euphoric space suggests a haven, an escape from immediate political struggle against apartheid. This "looking back" into the distant African past of rural village life, or what Hall has called "fixed cultural identity," implies that the unattainable past is the only aspiration of a colonized people. However, what Head wishes to achieve through her longing for the past is a search for a higher quality of life, even for humans in political transition. The desire for a better, more peaceful life is legitimate in human terms, but extremely problematic especially given the long bloody history of Southern African politics.

As I mentioned earlier, *When Rain Clouds Gather* sets up a dialectic between the euphoric space that the exile wants to occupy and the political activism that he or she does not wish to abandon, the displacement notwithstanding. Makhaya has to leave the intense political activism of South Africa for a less politically charged situation in the village of Golema Mmidi. Carol Boyce Davies has argued that there are "three structural modes or levels of narrative self-representation" in African women's autobiographies—in other words, in their quest for definitions of the subjective self. For her those three modes are the self as synonymous with political struggle; the self in dialogue with family and/or social-cultural history (and I would add national history); the self in resistance to patriarchal-racial systems.[9] In Head's first novel, these three categories function both in conjunction and in confrontation with each other. The six exiles in the novel manifest sometimes one and often all of Davies's modes of self-representation. Makhaya's and Gilbert's expatriate identities are usually not distinct from the ones that are in dialogue with "political struggle" in the home country, nor are they sociocultural, racist-patriarchal systems of dominance. However, all three modes function simultaneously in order to position the exile as a subjective being who can "belong." For Head, belonging is the key to any political action or resistance, for it is only through belonging that one can explicitly stake a political and social claim in any society.

Head uses exile as a vehicle, not only as the enactment of displacement for her six characters, but also as a way for exiles to "belong" outside their immediate home. These six characters represent and enact the exilic dialogue, and this dialogue itself takes place at several levels. Dialogue exists between Makhaya and Gilbert, between Makhaya and the rest of Golema Mmidi, and among the six exiles. These dialogues evoke Head's desire and nostalgia for an amended visual image of "Old Africa."

It is important to remind oneself that for Head, even though some of her main characters are men the voice and the problems you hear through them are women's. It is in this way that she breaks down gender roles in traditional settings and is thereby able to consolidate a vision of "brotherhood." Even though the plot of this novel is deceptively simple, it is far more than a treatise of "innocence and experience" as Arthur Ravenscroft would have it.[10] As usual, Head's simple ambience is a fictive backdrop for more complex issues. Perhaps this simplicity is responsible for the novel's popularity among Peace Corps volunteers who are given this book as an introduction to their stay in Botswana. This carefully constructed atmosphere is rooted in the exile's nostalgia for "Old Africa." Golema Mmidi is presented as a wondrously idyllic, almost utopian place. Gilbert sees the village in its essence. For him, Golema Mmidi is "paradise." There is a fundamental air of contentment in the smallest element of the village. Even the goats in Golema Mmidi seem to want to talk to the people, if only they were not in such a hurry to get home, Head adds as an afterthought. The author expresses the South African exile's delighted wonder about the peace integral to village life, almost as if she did not quite believe it. The stark contrast between South Africa and Golema Mmidi is the point of departure for Makhaya. His story recalls the situation of the South African exile, writer Nat Nakasa, who could not believe that in New York the police were not going to chase him down as they did in South Africa, and he plunged to his death from a multistory building. However, Head exaggerates further, by making Golema Mmidi into a "special" village, a village like no other in the world or even in Botswana.

For Head, "Old Africa" consists not so much of traditional Africa but rather a habit of desire. She utilizes several devices to make this exile's paradise special. For instance, there is a god in this village. This god does not allow Makhaya to kill Matenge but carefully orchestrates the demise of the chief's brother in order to spare Head's exile protagonist. Makhaya's exilic consciousness requires Makhaya to be rescued from his anger and fury against unfair oppression by a sense of belonging orchestrated by the same God. Head reports: "Therefore the Good God cast one last look at Makhaya, whom he intended revenging almightily for his silent threat to knock him [Matenge] down. He would so much entangle this stupid young man with marriage and babies and children that he would always have to think, not twice but several hundred times, before he came to knocking anyone down."[11] There seems to be a magical quality about this particular village in Southern Africa that is like a promise of possibility and creativity, especially important to the exile. It is not only that a god exists outside the characters, but all the characters are components of this godliness while at the same time remaining entirely human, complete with small imperfections. Head goes to great pains to describe this embodiment of goodness in her perfect village as it emerges in complete symmetry right from precolonial times. This duality of godliness as well as human error represents an exile's system of desire, and it is through this desire that a fundamental faith in human goodness emerges. Head writes that

> the God with no shoes continued to live where he always had—in the small brown birds of the bush, in the dusty footpaths, and in the expressions of thin old men in tattered coats. . . .
>
> The way this God . . . carried on might easily delude you into thinking he was a charming halfwit like Paramount Chief Sekoto or hesitant about truth like Mma-Millipede or tortured and tormented like Makhaya. He changed about from day to day contradicting and confusing himself by all he had to learn, never certain of anything the way the fortune-tellers were.[12]

Complicit with this duality are kingdoms of creatures like goats. There is a very visual quality about this traditional idyllic design and there is order to the world that Head describes in this novel. This order, which the author controls completely, anticipates the postapartheid era in several ways. This love for orderliness comes directly out of a reaction against the chaos of apartheid that Makhaya has only very recently left behind. Couched in this desire for personal and sociopolitical order is a nostalgia for "the way things were." Head wants to explore how the two variants, the "way things were" and the "way things should be," can become the possibilities for direct or indirect change in national and "tribal" structures in Africa.

This nostalgia expresses idealistic desires that Head's exiles often need to have, with an intense desire for good deeds, characteristic of Dinorego, Mma-Millipede, Gilbert, Maria, Paulina, and Makhaya. However, the first five exiles tend to be much more at peace with themselves than Makhaya, whose South African experience is far too immediate. Thus he is still unsure of what he wants to do with the peace he has found in Golema Mmidi.

Head shows that the dialectic arising from the personal conditions that enforced the departure is most problematic for the South African exile, Makhaya, who is escaping political activism and looking for an idyllic situation in Golema Mmidi. It is no coincidence that this village "consisted of individuals who had fled there to escape the tragedies of life."[13] There is, in addition to the desire to escape to a "perfect little village," a feeling of guilt for leaving the struggle in the homeland. The need to work exceedingly hard in the borrowed homeland surfaces out of the idealism of the exiled characters in this novel. Salman Rushdie, another modern-day exile, has said about his own agonized departure: "I have never come to terms with leaving," almost as if the lingering effects of "voluntary" or "involuntary" exile are extremely difficult psychologically, emerging slowly over the course of a life. A curious dialectic that the exile often ignores is the eventual return and the location tied to that return. The euphoria emerges out of the need and desire to return to precisely what one left behind. And of course one can never return to the same time and place that one left, for "home" has changed irrevocably.

It is pertinent here to make a distinction between the condition of exile and the person who left, especially since Head implies it in her writing. I would argue that the agony of the exile is personal and is usually turned inward in questioning him or herself about the act of leaving; whereas the person who had to leave for personal or political survival is unhappy for the discontinuity between the known, yet dislocated space, particularly for South African refugees, and the little-known space in which they are forced to lead sociopolitical lives.

Makhaya, on the verge of entering the little village in which he decides to spend his life, says, "Well-educated men often come to the crossroads of life. . . . One road might lead to fame and importance, and another might lead to peace of mind. It's the road of peace of mind that I am seeking."[14] We know that he has just come out of jail for carrying political pamphlets that recommended using explosive devices in order to get rid of the apartheid system. He decides that he wants to leave the road that is uncomfortable, though marginally spectacular in its containment of "fame and importance," and opts for peace of mind and hard labor in a village where his work would be valuable only to the few inhabitants.

This desire for simplicity and order characterizes the exile in *When Rain Clouds Gather*. However, along with this love for order is a pervasive mistrust for "tribalism" and people in power. Thus, the longing and nostalgia for "Old Africa" is always hyphenated by a glance in the opposite historical direction. The condition of postcoloniality impels this Janus-faced consciousness, characteristic of the exilic principle, which is always immanent in Head's fiction. There is a great personal and individual vulnerability in this novel which is manifested through Makhaya's mistrust of people. Makhaya also wishes to maintain his personal space impenetrable and inviolable to the almost unknown new community or new "home."

It is curious that Head does not wish to deal with any racist tension at all in this novel, even though apartheid, which seeks to exile Black South Africans, is based on racist ideologies. She is interested in breaking down these binaries rather than encouraging them. For her, this breakdown leads to the possibility of "universal brotherhood," to an anticipation of postapartheid societies, a concept she untiringly ascribed to. One of the fears that all well-known South African writers have had is that they have seen the danger of collapsing every issue into one of race—of Black and White. Ezekiel Mphahlele warned all South African writers in his autobiography that "the main weakness in South African writers is that they are hyper-conscious of the race problem in their country. They are so obsessed with the subject of race and colour that when they set about writing creatively they imagine that the plot they are going to devise, the characters they are going to create and the setting they are going to exploit, must subserve an important message or important discovery they think they have to make in race relations."[15] Bessie Head was also very aware of this reductionism. She told Lee Nichols in an interview after she had written *When Rain Clouds Gather*, "I didn't use a black-white theme like black versus white man. I used my own theme to work out what I'd say was a kind of universal thesis on racialism."[16]

The way she deals with the White characters Gilbert and George Appleby is interesting because she does not problematize their positions of comparative power in the South African milieu but creates another dichotomy dependent not on troubled race relations that colonialism intensifies, but rather on the good or evil intentions of individuals. When Makhaya says, "I want to feel what it is like to live in a free country and then maybe some of the evils in my life will correct themselves," it is like the beginning of an exile's promise to himself to remain out of the relational mechanism apartheid imposes on White and Black peoples.[17] He does not wish to deal with the whole question of how racism has been used divisively by colonials in order to render a people sociopolitically powerless. Rather, his exile is a symbol of a desire to escape this problem altogether in order to find a peace unriddled with racist issues.

Thus, the only White people who are allowed character status in Head's novel are Gilbert, who represents well-motivated goodness, and Appleby, who wants progress and independence for the people of Botswana. The evil in this novel is also represented by the forces of exile, yet Head is careful not to let them emanate from White colonialist oppression. Matenge, who is Black, is totally divorced from himself and the people he claims to govern in spite of his roots—or perhaps because of them. He represents old but corrupt and evil power. Thus, he has to be removed from the immediate interactions of the village. He is dislodged from his sphere of influence in a completely unbelievable way at the end of the novel. "Matenge had to barricade himself up, not because the villagers were about to rise up and tear him to shreds, but because he was an evil pervert and knew it."[18] This extremely simplistic removal of the "forces of evil" is unbelievable, but Head utilizes it because she wishes to get back to her own agenda without wasting too much time on evil. By its very nature evil would self-destruct in her ideal village, Golema Mmidi. Patterns of resistance engage her interest in Golema Mmidi and not the evil that needs to be resisted. However, there is a refrain, as perceived in Matenge and Makhaya, that evil or goodness can only come from within. This idea was to be further elaborated in her third and most important novel, *A Question of Power*, and reveals a desire to block out the past. Even as she gets rid of Matenge, the representation of traditional mechanisms of evil power, she encourages his counterpart Chief Sekoto because he is benevolent.

It is significant that in this novel all of Head's White people are good, and the only evil person is Black and gets power through traditional political systems. I believe that this too is indicative of the mechanism of longing I spoke of earlier, inherent in an exile's system of desire. Head always wanted to be able to treat her characters as humans rather than people belonging to any racially determined ideologies. This desire to have each person transcend racial loyalty became part of the exilic consciousness expounded by Head.

Unlike Head herself, Makhaya has not even been given an exit visa—he has had to leave illegally across the apartheid border. This crossing into another space and time is part of the relevance of the Zimbabwean refugee, after whom the main character is modeled. Head wanted somebody who was disillusioned with apartheid politics and so she could not have evil manifested by White characters because that would topple the careful balance she was trying to create. She was trying to get away from the Black/White dichotomy of apartheid South Africa. Makhaya could not, thus, be a radical revolutionary trying to oust the government of his host country (just as he had tried to do in South Africa) because the government was Black and Head did not wish to criticize it openly. He had to be someone who can see both good and evil in White people as well as in Black people. An exilic consciousness refuses to allow race to determine every human interaction. Thus, Makhaya had to be a former revolutionary looking forward to a life different from the one he lived in South Africa. However, there are pockets of evil in every society and she rationally chose to attack that evil—not chiefdom itself but rather Matenge, who represented "Old Africa" at its worst. She dissociated Whiteness and evil, which simply could not be done in apartheid South Africa but could be managed in Botswana to a successful degree, since in the country of her exile there was no White/Black dichotomy serving the purposes of the White elite. Head consistently backed away from an overt critique of apartheid racism even in her novel on "racism," *Maru*.

It is always problematic when a writer very deliberately wishes to get away from the complexities of race and economics, especially in their relationship to imperialism. Head's desire to avoid race can only be understood in the context of one exile's longing for "Old Africa," for the well-ordered life of precolonial days. When we examine Makhaya's motivation for leaving behind everything connected with apartheid, we find that he wishes to leave corrosive race relations behind as well and in the worst possible way. Over and over again, the emphasis is on Makhaya's future in Golema Mmidi, and there is no indication that he might want to go back to South Africa, or that his past, complete with his individual/communal history and family, is a concern for him. Indeed, Head's implication is that his illegal departure seems to cut off his emotional ties to his homeland. Perhaps this aspect of his portrait is not entirely "true to life," since Head was to come back to the theme of never having left apartheid, even while she was exiled in Botswana, as becomes evident in *A Question of Power.* The only possible explanation is the one embedded in the exilic consciousness. In her first novel, the strongest desire is the exile's longing to make herself new—to be born again in a different nation—to have crossed the boundary linking her to the problematic concept of the apartheid homeland. These aspects of the exile's system of desire are clearly not as easy to implement psychologically as they are in terms of literal and legal geography.

But this aspect of the exile's limbo is a moot point in *When Rain Clouds Gather.* As a tribute to a possibility of harmony between races, the novel refuses to dichotomize Black and White—almost as if colonialism and racist oppression never occurred. This refusal displays Head's reluctance to stay within the present realities of race. Maria and Gilbert's relationship falls under the same rubric. They are less troubled by the difference in their races and more concerned about gender.

Gilbert represents another exilic dilemma; he is so thoroughly involved in the production problems in Golema Mmidi that one would have to constantly remind oneself that he is White. However, Head wants her audience to dispense with pathological ties to the race issue. She does not want us to remind ourselves that Gilbert is White. For Head, it is the exile's reality that is preeminent, not race. Like Makhaya, Gilbert has such a dire need to escape his own homeland that he needs to belong entirely to the people who need his labor and expertise, and he desires to join the community in concrete sociopsychological ways. He marries Maria soon after the book opens, stepping right into the integral family structure of the village; even though the relationship is problematic in terms of education, neither the complexities of racial unions nor cultural differences are ever mentioned. The only thing that Dinorego wants to ask Maria is whether she likes and wants to marry Gilbert; Mma-Millipede is concerned only whether Maria loves Gilbert, given her "quiet ways." The question of this racially mixed union so spatially close to the realities of the Immorality Act is entirely mute before, during, and after the entire marriage ceremony. Even the two young people who are getting married in violation of race and class are entirely silent about the effects of race on their marriage. Head simply evades this issue, as she does many others, systematically prioritizing the exile's consciousness over and above any other.

There is another issue that is never touched upon in Head's novel. Makhaya, even though he is an exile like Gilbert, can never repatriate while his country is controlled by apartheid and has left home with just that expectation. However, Gilbert has not left never to return. There is an interesting scene between him and Maria at the wedding, where he asserts his right as a husband to control the environment of his wife. He tells her: "You're are not Dinorego's daughter any more. . . . You're my wife now and you have to do as I say. If I go back to England, you go there too."[19] This assertion and Maria's response has more to do with a recognition of male power rather than his desire for acceptance within the community of his exile. Head is more prone to problematize gender relations than racial binaries. The power struggle is between Maria and Gilbert, man and woman, husband and wife, not between a White man and a Black woman; however, the struggle between the newlyweds is really an articulation of Maria's fear and not Gilbert's. Head's texts always privilege the woman's discourse and anxieties.

One cannot imagine Gilbert going back to England for more than a quick visit and, oddly enough, this show of power comes right after he recognizes that "he had not felt free in England . . . the polite women kept on remarking about how you were such a big-boned lad with an ungainly walk and didn't somehow quite fit."[20] Perhaps he needs to rely on the only thing that links him up with the other men in Golema Mmidi, his maleness. The connections he makes are gender connections. By asserting his commonality with other men in the village of his exile he becomes a man without the complex imperialist overtones of being a White man.

Although Gilbert and Makhaya share maleness, Makhaya cannot go back to South Africa. Again, this unevenness between the two men's exile is something that is neither problematized, nor constitutes a subject area of concern for Head, and it is never allowed to enter that sphere of the novel. The other White character is also male and has a considerable degree of power in and around the Golema Mmidi district. George Appleby is a police officer and has direct control over Makhaya's tenure in exile. He can refuse to grant him residency, that act would be in perfect accordance with the wishes of the Black government. However, Appleby, a benevolent character, does the exact opposite in a grand gesture of conspiracy with the exile's consciousness.

Again and again there is a reaffirmation of how people are good or bad regardless of their color. For someone escaping apartheid South Africa, the separation of White and evil is crucial to survival. One must live a life informed by a belief in humanity to legitimize the constant struggle faced by an exile. I would contend that Head deliberately does not see the presence of these two White male characters in *When Rain Clouds Gather* as problematic, simply because she needs to restore Makhaya's faith in the essential goodness of humanity, especially given the context from which he has escaped. Thus, the only evil in this novel is represented by the domestic power structure, by the nonexiled Black chief, Matenge.

Head shows Makhaya that even the dreaded "tribalism" can be of use if old customs are respected in a new context. She takes the protagonist by the hand and lets him learn all the things that are wonderful about people and about cultures. Makhaya seems very much the product of a Western education that has historically condemned all "tribalism," whatever form it may take. Dinorego is the one who shows him that customs, like people, can be good or bad—it simply depends on how you use them. This seems to appease the young man who sees "tribalism" as oppressive for both men and women, and at first it does not inform his views through a good hard look at the aftermath of those same customs in postcolonial times.

As I mentioned earlier, euphoria is concomitant with the valorization of the exile's motivations. Both Gilbert and Appleby seem to be motivated by the best possible intentions toward their hosts. Appleby "sticks his neck out" for Makhaya, which is surprising, especially since he works for a government that discourages refugees. However, since he is an "exile," and thus a well-intentioned person, he can spot the good in an incoming exile. The position and suffering of the exile is generally privileged in Head's writing. However, in her first novel in particular, the exile's privileged status remains unproblematized. It is almost as if the exiles have suffered enough after being expelled from their home and begin finding a "home" in a place which is not their own. That homelessness itself renders their motivations above suspicion. This faith in the exilic consciousness is part of the euphoria—not so much for "Old Africa"—but rather for the simple "goodness" that the picture of a well-ordered precolonial, Africa must have inspired.

However, this euphoria becomes a denial of fundamental issues and questions. For instance, the people of Golema Mmidi or Botswana may not desire the existence of refugees in their country, even for purely economic reasons, no matter how pure and unselfish the exile's motivations would be. Botswana is not a rich country and Makhaya probably would never have gone there if he had not needed to escape apartheid. It is true that Head does not deal with the ambivalence that the exile feels toward the people who house her or him until her third and last novel, *A Question of Power*. However, when she includes the people of Golema Mmidi in complete praise of Gilbert and Makhaya in opposition to one of their own, the carefully designed narrative reveals the author's motivations toward exiles.

Head manages to dispel the claims that traditional societies do not care how and why they are poor. The myth is that poor people are uneducated and cannot escape a traditional malaise which oppresses them. Everyone in Golema Mmidi is very interested in bettering their lot. This is not problematic in and of itself but it is dubious to say that they have no problems in overthrowing traditional authority or that they distrust with great enthusiasm anyone who feels negative toward foreigners in their culture.

Head seems to be so intent on valorizing the position of the exile that she depicts the exiles as essentially the unchallenged and respected leaders of this village without examining the problems that can entail from doing so. In *When Rain Clouds Gather,* there are no leaders in the idealized village of Golema Mmidi that are not foreigners. Matenge, the native traditional leader, is obviously loathed by everybody and therefore cannot be a leader.

Why is it that everybody unanimously consults Gilbert about their problems regarding cattle farming and then immediately grasps the "scientific," untraditional sense of his suggestions? Even the endorsement of Dinorego is not enough. When the village council meets after they have returned from the devastation at the cattle posts, they go immediately to Gilbert, who feels at perfect liberty to criticize traditional cattle farming and tries to introduce them to cooperative agriculture and animal husbandry. He tells them: "What would you say if I said that the deaths of all these cattle, in Golema Mmidi, are a miracle . . . I was hoping it would happen?"[21]

In fact, as he had done earlier, Gilbert was reintroducing them to their own African traditions of cooperative farming with a few variations. In this way Head resolves the tension between euphoria for the past and the present realities of a primarily agricultural community. Gilbert does remain a potential colonial who takes it upon himself to teach African customs to the Africans. His role is reminiscent of a recent news item about French chefs trying to teach Australian Aborigines traditional culinary habits from ancient aboriginal culture. The only difference about Gilbert's suggestion is that earlier the land was owned cooperatively, whereas the produce was not; now he suggests that both the produce and farming be cooperative ventures. This incident about the cattle farming is really just an echo of his earlier struggle with grazing. When he encloses land in order to optimize cattle grazing, the village council is very unhappy with him, in spite of Chief Sekoto's permission. It takes them a while to see that he is not violating African tradition in spirit but is intent on maintaining an intelligent old African custom of collective farming.

At one level, what Gilbert says makes perfect sense—given the climate of the region—but it seems that the villagers tend to yield inordinate decisionmaking power to him. The narrative wants to accomplish two things. First, it argues that exiles, even White ones, are geared toward doing good; and second, that the colonial dichotomy of Black and White must be dissipated. They succumb to his persuasiveness and listen to him even though he has not been in Golema Mmidi very long at all. It seems to me that what is at issue is not that Gilbert, as either an exile or as a character, is untrustworthy, but that the argument "all good things come from the outside" sounds suspiciously like colonial ideology. However, Head refuses to problematize the issue of "all good things coming from outside" in her first novel, even though she is acutely aware of this aspect in all her succeeding novels. Instead, here she deliberately dissolves oppositional relationships, resolving tensions between binaries.

Within the context of her narrative, Head can get away with valorizing the "good" that comes to Golema Mmidi from the outside by opposing it to the evil leadership that exists inside the village. She makes Matenge almost inhuman in his desire for power and profit. He represents the kind of evil that is only there to be rid of, a narrative device that is clearly a symbol and nothing more. She writes, "The greatest moment of his life had been when he had inflicted suffering on his fellow men. People were not people to him but things he kicked about, pawns to be used by him, to break, banish and destroy for his entertainment."[22] It is with tremendous relief that one sees a Matenge hang himself. And even though we are told that he is crying when he watches the people gather outside his house, the detail is really meant to evoke only minimal sympathy; he exists as an idea that evil people cannot be satisfied by doing evil but instead regret it in numerous ways and continue to remain unhappy. He cries, one suspects, because all good people know that he is evil and perhaps he knows it too.

Through Head's exaggeration, Matenge becomes the only representative of traditional evil and power. The evil both fits and does not fit in this tension between nostalgia and exile. To elaborate, the evil is and is not part of "Old Africa" as represented by Matenge. He becomes the direct result of the colonial aftermath even though one finds close facsimiles of him in traditional Africa. By contrast, Sekoto, his brother, is presented as a closer tie to "Old Africa," and Head compares him to the "god in Golema Mmidi," his womanizing and love for food notwithstanding. However, his evil is small and always overshadowed completely by the exile's consciousness, for that is composed only of goodness. Thus, here the exile is played off against the nostalgia at the cost of the latter. Head accomplishes this smoothly, for Matenge's evil lies in contradistinction to the evil of Southern African apartheid because it can be contained and localized geographically in a small place; thus, the evil is never overwhelming and can be overcome quite easily. The smallness of this evil determines its manageability. It is peculiar that Makhaya, who represents the exile's consciousness, never once doubts the destruction of evil in Golema Mmidi whereas he has had grave misgivings about the evils in South Africa. And thus do all characters in Head's novels look for small places where they can effect societal change, where their personal existence is of some value and where they can escape the impotence that a political activist must feel against the vast machinery of apartheid. The existence of extremes tends to complicate and simplify the development of the narrative. Matenge is so evil to his own people that it becomes vital to have him removed from the scene; some of the tension between the past and present is dissipated by his removal. Since Matenge atones for Isaac's death, it serves as a catharsis. But his death is still too convenient. No one is going to feel sorry for Matenge, so he can only be substantiated through his own removal, whereas his presence was somewhat super-fluous to the plot—though not to the overall fictive design.

What is being done, however, is extremely problematic in terms of sociohistorical colonial and postcolonial realities. To return to the idea that good can be brought only from the outside undermines the idea that viable change can and must come only from the inside. It is not just with the arrogance of an exile that Head can claim that the out-sider brings reforms to a society; here the assumption is that this change is desirable to the natives. Change, filtered down from the Westernized locale, comes back to haunt developing countries because the patterns of change have been determined by capitalist-industrialist interests, which seem, at best, only marginally relevant to the postcolo-nial situation, and at worst they destroy indigenous economies, cul-tures, and peoples.[23]

It is doubtful, however, that Head was consciously creating a milieu where any progressive change came from the outside, for her focus is always on internal individual reaction rather than on scientific prog-ress. Her primary interest remains in resolving tensions, not enhancing them. She wanted to locate her exile in a sociopsychological home base, which meant that Makhaya had to accept Golema Mmidi and had to be accepted in turn by its inhabitants. Unlike the avoidance of racial issues, which becomes deliberate on Head's part, the unprob-lematized outsider does not seem deliberate. It is possible that she sim-ply did not wish to deal with shades of motivation but wanted to pack-age her characters as extremely good, uncomplicated people against the background of one evil person against whom they all struggled. This is part of what Head developed and what I have called the exile's consciousness. Head elaborates this consciousness by evoking the "sim-ple, good truth," which indicates a lack of racial or economic tensions between people in *When Rain Clouds Gather.*

As I have mentioned earlier, there is an overabundance of exiles in Golema Mmidi. Even the bastions of tradition and good will, Mma-Millipede and Dinorego, do not "belong" strictly to Golema Mmidi but are northerners exiled to the south. The context of the novel raises an odd question of privileging the voice of the exile. Why does the exile want or need to be privileged? I remember how my own mother, who at thirteen was forced to flee Kashmir, her home, to live in the Punjab at the time of the Pakistani-Indian partition, would claim that same privileging. When I suggested that Punjabis may not have wanted her to live among them, she was exceedingly upset, reiterating how much her family had to suffer and how many privileges they had to leave behind in order to get to what became West Pakistan.

Knowing that her outrage, that of a "Mhuajar,"[24] was a bit overdramatized because she was only a girl when she left and rather excited by her first train ride, I never stopped to examine the other part of her discourse. She was an exile, like Head, like Makhaya. Exiles, like Head, must resolve the tension between their past and their present. They claim a recognition for their suffering by valorizing the status of exile and privileging the purer motivation of someone who leaves the comforts of home in order to travel to an alien land. "All good things come from outside." This privileged space emerges out of the rhetorical question, Why would anyone leave home except with motives that are, ipso facto, completely above suspicion? Thus, exile becomes the sole condition that creates enormous tension between the home that is left and the "home" of adoption. The exile's consciousness becomes the catalyst where different streams of belonging meet. In this novel, Head collapses the distinction between home of exile and home from which her characters are exiled. This collapsing constitutes the desire for what I have earlier called the euphoria about "Old Africa." The rationale is interesting: if you are a Southern African, surely you can "belong" in Botswana as easily as you could in Cape Town. Head was later to refute the actualizing of this "desire" principle because Elizabeth in *A Question of Power* has a consciousness of not being able to belong in Botswana linguistically or culturally. Thus, the "desire" of an exile to "belong" remains just that, and the exile remains an exile. Tensions between belonging and nonbelonging remain firmly delineated.

The motivations of the exiles in *When Rain Clouds Gather* are above reproach. Implicit in the novel is the fact that these exiles cannot help but do good. This novel creates what Michael Thorpe has called the "parable of goodness."[25] They can only do good for each other and the communities they have adopted. Exiles become the pioneers of progressive thinking in their host communities. Head implies that the Makhayas of the world would have done untold good in their own countries, which is precisely why they were exiled in the first place.

In fact, there seems to be a Walt Disney level of conspiracy of good people and goodness all over the village and its surrounding areas. The good is not just located in human actions but also in human and animal interaction. Head writes, "Once, for a year, almost at the exact same hour each afternoon, a big white goat would step into his office . . . both goats and people love George Appleby-Smith. And he appreciated this deeply."[26] Animals tend to express as much courtesy toward people as most of the people express for each other. The goats tend to want to "stop and talk" with the other inhabitants of the village, that is, humans. The perfect accord between animals and humans in this "utopia" is, I believe, part of the necessary euphoria typical of Head's exiles.[27] This euphoria is part of the tension created by an exile's consciousness in Head's fiction. The accord between nature and humans is necessary as a narratological device for negotiating an ontological space where an exile can function and heal after the apartheid experience.

Makhaya, at the instigation of Gilbert and the leadership of Pauline, begins to teach the women of Golema Mmidi tobacco farming. In most Head narratives there is tribute to human labor. For Head, this is meant to address fundamental questions of ontology that are tied to the tests and demands the adopted community places on the exile's consciousness. The response of the exile is always one of commitment to the process of "belonging" and everything that the state entails. Head's stipulation is that with a cash crop under their belt the villagers would really have recourse to a higher quality of life in every aspect of their existence. More wealth would mean that they would not need to send their young sons to the cattle posts, but would send them to school instead. Life, for the natives of the village, would become more integrated with a little more money.

This is obviously all quite true in terms of agricultural economics but what is improbable is the rapidity with which the women take to the tobacco-growing idea. Head, I think, would claim that Southern African women are traditionally agricultural (and thus, very sound in terms of decisionmaking, for they understand the market economy through actual market experience), which explains their enthusiasm for the tobacco-growing project. Additionally, their decision may also depend on the fact that an attractive young man like Makhaya was spending time and energy in order to help them. The decision of the women intensifies the romantic tension between "belonging," as Pauline does, and the exilic consciousness of Makhaya.

Yet, just one look at village life confirms that both men and women use their time very economically because the burdens of survival and the amount of work that goes into everyday tasks are great and often relentless. For the village women of Golema Mmidi to add considerably to their work they would have to have a clearer idea of what they were spending their days doing. There is almost no concrete information about tobacco farming given to them. Head indicates how persuasive the leadership of Pauline is, but surely even that would not be enough for the busy village woman. The simple adventure that they seem to all *want* to embark on would be extremely time-inefficient if the fiscal returns were not as great as they expected. A village woman would have to examine the pros and cons of any time-consuming endeavor. However, the reality of an actual village woman making an actual decision about additional work is not an issue for Head. Her writerly interests are concerned with the accord particular to Golema Mmidi—she uses this same accord as a symbol of possibility for a future Africa.

As I mentioned, the tobacco-growing project fits into Head's design of the prevailing theme of the exile's unquestioned desire to do good, concomitant with the desire and right to benefit his or her host country. The fact that this theme is never problematized in *When Rain Clouds Gather* is strange indeed, especially given the nature of the Botswana government's response to exiles. We are told several times that Appleby has to "stick his neck out" in order to get Makhaya residency status. However, this problem is swept away as a bureaucratic detail necessary only because Matenge is unreasonably malicious to everyone, without discrimination.

Immigration and residency laws aside, the notion of the villagers accepting all the exiles as their own is somewhat unbelievable. But as the narrative develops, it becomes very clear that the authorial interest does not reside in the tension between actuality and fictional account but rather between the euphoria or collapse between "Old Africa" and the exile's consciousness. The creation of this perfect village is the synthesis of these two strains of thought. If we look at the passage quoted from Head's response to the young refugee from Zimbabwe, we notice that there are several aspects of politics that begin to inform her understanding of an exile's consciousness. She realized fairly early that simply getting rid of the colonial powers was not enough to ensure the economic legitimacy of a "black government." She wanted, like Makhaya, to seek an alternative to "war and power." It was only through "battling" with the immediate needs of a given community—in this case the adopted community—that the wide-ranging control of apartheid power can be overturned.

In order to let Makhaya concentrate on the issues at hand, Head needs to grant him perfect acceptance and desirability by Golema Mmidi. Even though when he first arrives he has all the suspicions of some one who has survived apartheid, his suspicion evaporates as he learns to belong. He says, "It's not so much what I'm running away from. . . . It's what I'm trying to run into. I want a wife and children." And again later, he adds, "I thought it best to find a wife before I found anything else."[28]

After his harrowing and illegal escape, we are told that "his reasons for leaving were simple: he could not marry and have children in a country where black men were called 'boy' and 'dog' and 'kaffir.'"[29] There is something disconcerting and admirable about the simplicity of Makhaya's dream. Yet, the simplicity itself seems more like a justification for leaving a place of marginal belonging rather than a reason for entering a place of nonbelonging. He wishes to leave the ravages of apartheid behind and enjoy simple human privileges, like marriage and children, without the agonies that South Africa imposes on its Black population. Much later in the novel he tells Paulina that he wishes to take care of her and her children as part of his simple design.

This need for community that begins with wife and children might well be a natural pattern among most people, but it is not such a reliable desire especially in Southern Africa. Since every aspect of life is exclusionary for Black South Africans, the simplest possible human expectation becomes a luxury, and the desire for these human pleasures runs high in exiles like Makhaya. It is with this desire that he arrives in Golema Mmidi. He needs to be involved in very simple human activities like marriage, crop production, and raising children.

Through the process of belonging, Makhaya hopes "some of the evils in my life will correct themselves."[30] The past will be miraculously reconciled to the present.

Head refuses to see the problem with Maria's disengagement with cash crops. Since her marriage to Gilbert she becomes wife *par excellence;* she can only cook for the men, but not benefit economically from the cash crop, something to which the other women have instant recourse. Maria, unlike Makhaya and Paulina, tends to get excluded from resolutions of her own past and present. Marriage also removes her from the dialectic of belonging and not belonging.

Makhaya fits into Head's design for her protagonist. Makhaya finds exactly what he has been looking for, a country where his labor is valued and where love is not commercialized as we are told it was in the city of his past. Even though I have said earlier that Golema Mmidi is an idyllic little village, it is perfect only in terms of its idea, not its reality. It is true that the potential for this village to be "paradise" is as important for Head as it is for Gilbert. At the same time, the reality of the village, which is often quite stark, does tend to encroach on the dreams that the exile's consciousness wants to evoke.

The cattle dying by the hundreds has an extremely sobering influence on the general euphoria of the exiles bent upon affluence for their adopted community. Even Gilbert, when he sees the suffering in the bush on the way to Isaac's cattle post, is utterly remorseful about his earlier glee over the positive aspects of this disaster. The disaster allows them to perceive the real life and death struggles that a community, totally dependent on rainfall, would experience. Thus to the earlier tension is added another twist. There are thousands of cattle dying in "paradise." Their death becomes the exile's vehicle for implementing reforms in his new home. It also brings the pain and tension home to the exile who is still toying with the idea of belonging.

Even though Makhaya is grateful to leave the apartheid relationships between White and Black people behind and find a supporter in Appleby and a comrade in Gilbert, like any exile he has to start from scratch. He sets out to build a community of trust around him. Trust entails having to internalize the suffering of the community he wishes to belong to. And if one feels critical toward the perfect milieu of Makhaya, this can be dispelled by what he is taking on. Head emphasizes that he was used to leading life in an urban setting, and the rural poverty, though challenging, is still alien and harsh. But it is precisely through this poverty that he is able to establish the equilibrium in his own life. He throws himself in the work Gilbert assigns to him as if he were saving his own life, which as an exile he is doing. It is work that creates the only redemptive atmosphere for the exile, which is inherently tied to his belonging.

However, Makhaya is different in his spatial exile from the other exiles merely by being from South Africa. His bitterness and lack of trust of any authority, be it institutions or humans, is different from Gilbert or Paulina or even Dinorego. For him the escape to Golema Mmidi itself is cathartic—a life-saving device. For Gilbert it was a matter of finding a place in which he felt comfortable, and in his case it was a village in Southern Africa with "food production problems." He could use his expertise in agriculture under conditions of little or no rainfall to locate a familiar professional space for himself. Makhaya, on the other hand, has to carve a place where he does not feel displaced as he did in the country of his birth. Home for him, by definition, is not his home and is not to be returned to. For an exile, especially from South Africa, home could not be a geographical place with family and community because that has all been tainted for him through apartheid. Home has to be a place where his particular designs for a community can be implemented; exile becomes defined by such a desire, which Head's letters attest was her own as well. Thus, work as an abstract concept enables the exile's consciousness to heal itself and belong; the guilt about having left is redeemed through work and the tension between the exile's past and present resolved.

Thus, it is no surprise when Makhaya accidentally and magically finds Dinorego and is lured into going with the old man to the "paradise" of Golema Mmidi. Once there, he finds all the life tensions that he wishes to work out. The tensions that he does not wish to work out, such as Black and White antagonisms and "tribalism," are either not there or they are very peripheral to what he begins to define as real issues of day-to-day survival. Makhaya engages only with the most fundamental level of survival. Are we to assume this has occurred because of his disillusionment with politics and his subsequent stay in jail? Makhaya is reminiscent of Head's refugee from Zimbabwe who wants to leave politics out of his life because he is disillusioned with "the future leadership" of Zimbabwe, which is also predominantly Black.

There is a narratological problem with the assumption that even Black power in postcolonial times seeks to serve only itself. Disillusionment with politics cannot possibly have occurred in Makhaya's case because there has been no takeover by Black politicians in South Africa even though Head's fiction anticipates that inevitability. The "terrible" indignities he has suffered under apartheid must be fought against as they are. The political realities that are a luxury for Makhaya are not so for the refugee he is modeled after. Unlike the refugee from Zimbabwe, Makhaya has not been a witness to majority rule in his country. Is Head, without meaning to, indicating that it is fruitless to fight for emancipation from colonial rule because Black politicians would sell the people's interest just as their colonial counterparts did? This idea is informed by the same angst as Kwame Nkrumah's "How long will Africa be cursed by its leaders?" In Head's case, however, she is more engaged with anticipating a time where political struggle would no longer be required, that is, the authenticity of the postapartheid era coming into being.

Head specifically expresses an exile's desire to escape problems related to apartheid. As mentioned earlier, she draws deliberate and clear distinctions between Whites and evil, Blacks and good, often fictively debunking this racial/colonial dichotomy, having lived under apartheid politics and life. A troubling question for Head scholars is the extent of her political engagement with her country of birth. Would political engagement, like the kind we see in the narratives of Alex La Guma, be a value for someone with Bessie Head's interest in exploring the dialectics of belonging as they pertain to exiled, gendered identities? For Makhaya, and even perhaps for Head, *exile from* South Africa is an *escape to* a space outside, a realm directly controlled by one sort of politics or another. The Zimbabwean refugee certainly turns away from the immediate politics of coercion to the delightful simplicity of "food production." And Makhaya has deliberately turned away from killing people and blowing things up to participating in what Simon Simonse has called "Bessie Head's green revolution" in Golema Mmidi.[31] The god in Golema Mmidi does not allow Makhaya to kill Matenge, and the only blowing up he does is for the tobacco project. This space to which the exile's consciousness wishes to escape is located in the tension between euphoria and the struggle to belong; thus the escape is just a beginning.

Head has been severely critiqued by her fellow writer Lewis Nkosi for not having Alex La Guma's "rigorous political commitment." Indeed, he goes on to claim that Head "seems politically ignorant," possessing "*only* this moral fluency of an intelligent, intensely lonely individual, worrying about the problems of belonging, of close interpersonal relationships, of love, value, and humanity" (emphasis mine). Nkosi further elaborates: "Bessie Head is not a political novelist in any sense we can recognize; indeed, there is ample evidence that she is generally hostile to politics. Far from being an axiomatic proposition, as some critics tend to believe, this lack of precise political commitment weakens rather than aids Bessie Head's grasp of character. Makhaya . . . becomes blurred at precisely the moment that we fail to comprehend the nature of his political commitment."[32] The matter of politics is not as simplistic for Head as it seems to be for Nkosi. For Nkosi, as it was for other writers of Head's generation, "politics" implied an active participation in the dismantling of apartheid, but for Head political activity was an engagement with food production problems. Head deliberately does not set her novels in South Africa because she wanted to get away from narrow definitions of what a viable political activity was.

When Makhaya is talking politics with Gilbert and the latter claims that Africa needs a dictator, Makhaya's response is straightforward. "Not any politics in the world meant anything to him as a stateless person, and every political discussion was a mockery, he felt, of his own helplessness."[33] For Head, political battles were not fought for every oppressed person, and Makhaya's silent outrage is a result of the limitations of political activity. Exile becomes symptomatic of a mute rage. It is out of a need to find an alternative to certain kinds of political activity that the exile turns toward *work* in his new home. Gilbert becomes suddenly apologetic to Makhaya about his earlier statement after he notices his friend's silence. Makhaya's silence about politics seems to be pervasive and tends to be replaced by hard work, through which he realizes his existence. And it is precisely when he admits to Gilbert, "Nothing is quite clear to me," that his friend immediately sweeps him into the realm of the practical by asking whether he knows how to drive vehicles.[34] And it is through driving that he is able to provide help for his new community.

Makhaya's simple desire for a wife and children seems to be an assertion of that turning away from politics, a resolution to the apartheid past. Head writes:

> But the God with no shoes, with his queer, inverted reasoning, had brought Makhaya, a real and potential murderer, face to face with the body of Matenge just hanging there. . . . "Don't you see?" he said softly. "Murder is a small-minded business."
>
> . . . He made you take a long and perilous journey along a road where everyone threw things at you. Then he said you were small minded if you wanted to throw things back.[35]

Thus, an exile expects of himself messiah-like traits. An exile must not do unto others as they did unto him. The passage expresses an apology as well as an outrage. People who have to be part of politics in South Africa often cannot have a family, and that very situation leads to killing and destruction for the political activist and the system. Makhaya's outrage is directed against the effect an activist's life has on society, especially since the activist gives up so much in order to have a political life under apartheid. It is as if the turning away from politics is defined in contradistinction to having a family. A little later Head has the same god interfere in the larger scheme of Makhaya's life and make it possible for him to do less "small-minded" things. The assumption is that the natural task of human beings is to struggle to raise families within the interests of the community they find themselves in to the particular exclusion of politics. Thus, real work is always exclusive of politics in Head's narrative, but it is important to recognize that she had a profound commitment to social change. This desire and task of the exile Makhaya is defined by the words "I am going to bloody well adopt this country as my own, by force."[36]

The aforementioned assumption tends to set up hierarchies that on the surface seem to undermine the lives of Black South Africans who have families as well as political struggles to fight. Is Head claiming that all political struggle is "small minded"? She does allow her protagonist to be disgusted with South African politics, but one is never sure why. Surely Makhaya's discontent with the apartheid situation must predate his jail term. Black South African children are made aware, very early, of the limitations imposed on them. And surely Makhaya has seen enough of life in Southern Africa to know that both family life and politics must coexist in a state of total apartheid embattlement.

The assumptions made about Head's lack of involvement with politics are problematic. Are we to condemn a writer, even if she is from Southern Africa, for not writing overtly political literature? After quoting from Makhaya's line "All poor people . . . have to become millionaires with me," Nkosi is further aggravated by what he sees as Head's lack of political engagement. He writes: "It's an absurd dialogue, rooted in the author's confusion whenever she enters the realm of political ideas."[37] It is this very narrow and patriarchal definition of politics that Head resists, to the annoyance of her compatriots. Head's absence from earlier South African anthologies is an indication of the critical judgment against her. As I implied earlier, when she talks about murder as "small minded" she is expressing an outrage which is, to say the very least, profound. What she calls "murder" falls in the "should nots" of her fictional society and that is what makes murder "small minded," along with the "necessity" to destroy others. Head describes her disengagement with South African politics thus: "I was such a hot rod black nationalist. I very soon got over that phase because many people pointed out to me that I was not black enough." It is recorded that when Head, as a baby, was sent to be adopted by Afrikaans families, she was returned because she was "not white enough."[38] Given her autobiographical reality, it is not surprising that certain kinds of political engagement make her wary. What concerns Head most is the overall bankruptcy of movements, political or personal, because they tend to exclude rather than include humanity. For her the only political aim one could have is to uncategorically strive for the betterment of humanity as a whole. She carved out the balance between her duty as a political person and her role as a writer. She wrote: "There's a coolness and detachment in my work. . . . The cool stance means: you are up on a horizon, you have the biggest view possible. The story teller has to have that. It's not so much a question of being black as of having got control of life's learning. . . . I shape the future with this cool stance, the view that's above everything," but not everyone.[39]

Makhaya is making a not so subtle demand for his life. He wishes to live in peace and the only way he can do that is by leaving his country. It is not incidental that he leaves his country when he is no longer politically viable. His desire for a simple life of nonpolitical struggle and community is a legitimate desire. It can be argued, and Head does, that a peaceful life should be the inalienable right of every human. It is this right that Makhaya asserts after his experiences in South Africa. It is the desire for a life utterly uncontrolled by apartheid that lures him to the simple "food production" problems of Golema Mmidi.

Thus, Head's desire to create an atmosphere that is unproblematized with regard to the exile's ambivalence to "belonging" springs from the profound outrage she feels at the inhuman situation in which humans are denied basic rights, and which she had to escape from in order to claim those rights. The tension between the euphoric idealism and the exilic principle dealt with earlier comes directly out of the consciousness of exile, a consciousness that compels the search for a locationary force in a dislocated sociopsychological, personal, and political milieu. Even though it seems that the relationship between Pauline and Makhaya is a perfect, predestined match in practically every way, their dialogue represents the tension between enthusiasm for "Old Africa" and the exilic consciousness.

The plot seems to pander to Makhaya's eventual belonging in Golema Mmidi. Pauline almost immediately falls in love with Makhaya and pursues him in a rather simple, sweet way. Yet in so many ways she represents old tribal customs, the very customs he is trying to escape. Both Makhaya and Pauline exchange places with regard to who represents sexist traditions. For the second set of lovers, Head reverses the story of Maria and Gilbert, where Gilbert is the pursuer. Makhaya, like Maria, is very reluctant to get involved too quickly with someone in spite of his earlier claim about desiring a wife. However, the rather elaborate wedding of Maria and Gilbert is a preview of things to come. One of the things that dampens Makhaya and Pauline's union is the death of Isaac and the poverty in Golema Mmidi.

The problems between Pauline and Makhaya are inverted, as is their earlier courtship. Pauline is extremely haphazard about the way she runs her household. Even though she is a single mother, it is Makhaya who is meticulous. She cannot stand the idea of a man making tea for himself and he is annoyed at being treated in a "tribal" way. He is "liberated" and it seems that is one of the major reasons why he left his home. He had brought about a lot of changes in his own family after the death of his father. Head writes: "He had sisters at home. . . . But he was the eldest in the family, and according to custom he had to be addressed as 'Buti,' . . . and treated with exaggerated respect. As soon as his father died he made many changes in the home, foremost of which was that his sisters should address him by his first name and associate with him as equals and friends. When his mother had protested he had merely said, 'Why should men be brought up with a false sense of superiority over women? People can respect me if they wish, but only if I earn it.'"[40] He brings this lack of overt sexism to his relationship with Pauline. The quoted passage does not suggest that Makhaya manifests "feminist consciousness" simply because he does not go beyond questioning gender roles. He is upset when he is not allowed to make tea in Pauline's house because that is "women's work." Yet his consciousness is amazingly acute, based on his natural desire for equality rather than on any systematic analysis that would provoke the same decision. This tension between them remains unresolved through the novel.

Pauline is fairly "unwomanly" in some ways. When she admits, "You mustn't think I'm a cheap woman, but I love you," he responds thoughtfully: "There are no cheap women. Even those you buy love you, while we men rarely do. Perhaps I'll find out what love is like as we go along together."[41] This is a surprising and progressive revelation for Makhaya to have. I believe that Head is arguing that Makhaya's gender consciousness is part of the exilic mood as well. He might be suggesting that he is unable to love because that is a demand seldom made by women in traditional societies, or alternatively that men seldom love women they make love to. Or he may be suggesting that because of the pressures placed on the family by apartheid, men are no longer able to love women and children in the traditional ways that were the format for filial love in precolonial times. Even in his response to men loving women, his desire to belong notwithstanding, the tautness in the exile's consciousness is prevalent. Colonial disruptions of traditions have left him feeling ambivalent toward loving someone.

But it is Makhaya who brings to their relationship a higher consciousness of gender equality. He is the one who meticulously makes tea in order to show her that even a man is quite capable of taking care of himself. He is the one, not Pauline, who is repelled by the haphazard way that the household is being run. In spite of all these innovations introduced by Makhaya, it is Pauline who is the aggressive lover. When she sees him looking at the sunset, she is immediately attracted to him and sends her young daughter off to "greet" him. His response to this simple greeting is inappropriate but understandably one of suspicion and Pauline immediately regards it as a personal rejection. After all, Makhaya is a stranger and has no way of knowing whether he would simply be used badly by people in Golema Mmidi. In presenting this relationship as opposite to Gilbert and Maria, Head debunks and re- solves the gendered pursuer/pursued dialectic. For Head, there is no stigma attached to Pauline pursuing Makhaya.

Pauline continues to pursue him, however, and quite outside cus- tom, unabashedly stares at him while they are attending Maria and Gilbert's marriage feast. She is so unsubtle about her interest and at- traction that she provokes Mma-Millipede's extreme worry and cau- tion about observing the newcomer before letting him enter her pri- vate life. However, Paulina is quite undeterred by this cautionary voice. She is boisterous and challenging toward anyone who comes to live with them, but is unable to tolerate boiled goat meat; she even scolds Maria for putting up with foreign men's alien whims.

However much Makhaya is aware of cultural differences between the sexes, when he is being challenged about being able to eat goat meat and sour milk porridge by this woman who seemed to tower over him as he crouched, he is "relieved to see that he was a whole foot taller than she was."[42] This contradiction to his earlier "feminist con- sciousness" is interesting because when he takes Pauline in Gilbert's truck to look for her son Isaac on the cattle post, he is imperious with her. He denies her the right to see the remains of her son. Even though it is clear that his reasons stem only from a desire to protect her, he assumes that that is his role. In response to Pauline's protests about having to see the body because it is "our custom," Makhaya becomes ruthlessly critical about customs. Thus, custom and gender identities are often confused in this relationship, while they remain fairly con- ventional in Maria and Gilbert's marriage. Pauline is so stunned by her son's death that she simply does what she is told after that, or perhaps she does not need to take charge any longer since her lover has made it abundantly clear that he will "stay and help" her.

Later, after declaring that Pauline is his wife, he takes full responsi- bility for Isaac's burial without any consideration for what the child's mother may want. Burial customs are usually complicated in every culture and for him to alienate her from her son's death seems a little less kind than it is meant to be. His refusal to let Pauline see the remains of her child is a phallocratic one; he threatens to withdraw affection if she does not do what he wants her to do and she complies, though with a little hesitation. In this case, however, his demand for her obedience is complicated because he is sparing her not just the sight of death but a glance at her child's remaining bones, which are nearly picked clean by the time they find him. Thus tradition is always presented, in Head's fiction, as the ambivalent terrain of the exilic consciousness.

Further, it is Makhaya who finds the small bundle of carvings, the only remaining memory of the little child who died alone on the cattle post. He has denied Pauline not only the last farewell, and thus alienated her from her son's death, but by his actions she is left to be the secondary recipient of the artistry of her son. Pauline's son, who sat in a lonely place for months making wood carvings for his mother without any communication with anyone is denied a last farewell with her because the patriarchal world claims him. But Head does not present Pauline's segregation from her son by Makhaya as cruel or unthoughtful, in fact quite the reverse. Makhaya is painted as a man who takes control. Perhaps this is what he meant earlier when he said that he had to "earn respect." He does not hear any protests from anyone about the way he has behaved, and perhaps the implication is that he has "earned respect" in the eyes of Golema Mmidi. The respect is obviously tied to the work he has taken on in the village. But in his taking control, he represents the values of the traditional man.

When Makhaya is working with the village women on the tobacco-growing project, even Dinorego, who is the arbiter of good African traditional values, notices Makhaya's exemplary attitude toward the women who come into very close contact with him. Head writes: "Dinorego was very impressed by Makhaya's relationship with the women. It seemed to him that Makhaya was well versed in ancient African customs where the man maintained his dignity and self-control in front of women, except that in former times this man had maintained it over a harem of concubines, while Makhaya had none."[43] The last part of the description seems to be tacked on, and even though Makhaya constantly expresses suspicion of "tribalism," wishing always to dissociate himself from being thought of as "tribal," he seems to manifest positive characteristics of the "tribal." Another convenient resolution! This aspect of Makhaya's personality represents a general enthusiasm in this novel for the traditional values imbued in men before colonialism, especially with regard to the relationship they had to women. But such approval is always played off against the exilic consciousness. After all, Makhaya brings an abundance of good ideas to this precolonial village. Thus the exile's consciousness always supersedes the nostalgia.

It is notable that, in numerous ways, *When Rain Clouds Gather* traces the retrieval of an exile's faith. It is important that Makhaya recaptures his faith in humans and communities because that activity legitimizes his departure from the country of his birth. When he first arrives in Golema Mmidi, he talks to several people about how disillusioned he is. When he meets Mma-Millipede for the first time, Head writes that "he wanted to undo the complexity of hatred and humiliation that had dominated his life for so long. Perhaps, he thought, her life might provide him with a few clues."[44] This restorative influence continues for Makhaya, and it seems that it can continue only in exile.

This idea that Head seems to argue throughout her first novel, that what all exiles really need in order to "belong" is to have their faith restored in humanity, seems like another justification for having left. What Rushdie said about never coming to terms with having left is clearly not true for Makhaya, even though Head's consistent and elaborate design for Makhaya's restoration to faith makes one wary. The overemphasis on the conditions of this restoration are dubious simply because the place of exile cannot be as idyllic as Golema Mmidi is for Makhaya and other exiles like him. Then, Head's argument seems to be that if only every exile found a Golema Mmidi, then the poisons would go out of his or her life. Finding a "utopia" presupposes that there is one to be found and that human beings should only be asked to live in conditions that do not destroy their humanity.

The psychological and political pain of departure can only be accommodated by what can potentially exist in Southern African societies. Head talks about one possible method for human restoration in spite of the ravages of life. When Makhaya is listening to long discussions about the "marvels of the earth" he is very engaged by this aspect of village life. "There was much more than South Africa that he was running away from, and it included everything that he felt was keeping the continent of Africa at a standstill."[45] This altruism, though genuine, comes more sharply into focus and informs the objective reality that exiles have been rendered ineffective in their own sphere of influence for a number of reasons.

Apartheid renders Makhaya ineffective, which is why he runs from there to save his life from the malaise of hatred in which he saw himself drowning. "For he hated the white man in a strange way. It was not anything subtle or sly or mean, but a powerful accumulation of years and years and centuries and centuries of silence. It was as though, in all this silence, black men had not lived nor allowed themselves an expression of feeling." Trinh T. Minh-ha suggests that this unheard silence is not laid to rest through any one language, but rather through human interchange.[46] This monumental historical hatred makes Makhaya ineffective in the sorts of things he wished to do for Africa and as he was a representation of that Africa. Even his feelings seemed to have been frozen; Mma Millipede and Pauline help this thawing-out process. Gilbert was responsible for restoring his faith in the goodness in both Black and White races. He helps the new exile find profound meaning in his life through working hard for and with a community of farmers in Golema Mmidi.

Makhaya's dissociated apartheid exile's psyche is restored through his dialogue with Gilbert, who is operating on a world view which Head developed much more clearly in *A Question of Power*. It is the exiled consciousness of these two men that restores the narrative balance of this novel and resolves the tensions. Even though this dialogue takes place between men, it is nonetheless crucial to the resolution of any exile's identity. Head writes, "It was only through Gilbert that he discovered in himself a compassion for the whole great drama of human history. Only Gilbert admitted the mutual interdependence of all men."[47] In a characteristic way, Head indicates that not only do exiles find each other, but they find others like themselves as well. It is through Gilbert that Makhaya can repair his exile's psyche. This notion of "mutual interdependence" is explored much more fully in her last novel, but one can easily perceive the kernels of the same idea here.

The idea of the oneness of animate and inanimate phenomena is no longer as alien as it was to Western thinkers even as late as the beginning of the nineteenth century. Both Hinduism and Buddhism recognized the interdependence of life at least two thousand years ago, and moreover we know that Head was familiar with certain Hindu religious concepts. Thus, it comes as no surprise that she tries to restore her exiled protagonist's mental well-being by making him see the interrelatedness of all phenomena. To facilitate this, she establishes a distinction between White and evil, resolving the ambivalence inherent to the exilic consciousness. For Makhaya this is a crucial distinction, especially after his experiences in South Africa.

Once Makhaya discovers in "himself a compassion for the whole great drama of human history," he has moved into a sphere where universalist concerns become important, but not in terms of the similarity of all issues. I believe that it is a misunderstanding of Head's point of view to claim that she is whitewashing "difference" altogether by introducing "universalist" notions understood primarily as part of a hegemonic European discourse. Head proposes that one should step outside of one's immediate situation, as Makhaya does, in order to examine the historical cycles of human misery. The lessons of such an examination can be learned, perhaps, only by someone like Makhaya who can step outside his immediate situation, in a very specific geographical way.

Head is by no means silencing the "other's" discourse through the idea of "mutual interdependence," but resolving the exilic consciousness and tying it to the reality of "belonging." The movement toward ecologically sound farming, which seems to be part of political discourse, shows how small the world is in regard to the same "interdependence." No longer can a company pollute one lake and not be held responsible for affecting the rainfall or climate of a geographically different part of the world. As we know, one of the most sinister aspects of British colonialism in South Asia at the turn of this century has been the depletion of mahogany and teak forests in northern India for European furniture. As a direct result, floods take thousands of lives in Bengal and leave thousands, every year, malnourished, homeless, jobless, or dead.

The quarrel one can have with Head is that Makhaya sees these greater, more profound truths rather suddenly after his arrival, but, again, for Head, isn't that exactly what the exile's consciousness can perceive directly and without mediation? The recovery from that exilic ambivalence puts Makhaya on an equal footing with the innovators of Golema Mmidi and the rest of Africa. His desire to fulfill "god-like" functions in a very needy Africa is encouraged, with gentle amusement, even by Paulina.

It is the potential for harmony that the events in *When Rain Clouds Gather* underline, defining the exile's desire and nostalgia for "Old Africa," or "certain timelessness," as Head called it earlier. Problematic as the nostalgia is, it resolves the South African exile's quest for finding a "home." Once Head locates her protagonist in a sociopsychological space, she leaves him with the god who resides inside people as well as in Golema Mmidi, where he raises children with Paulina and works with Gilbert. Makhaya is left in a community that takes him in, "in a gesture of belonging," a recurring concept in Head's discourse. And this gesture of belonging emerges directly out of a tension between exile and enthusiasm for the "Old Africa." It is only through an understanding of how past and present affect subjective realities of exile that a sense of belonging can be attained. This accomplishment comprises the fundamental journey of Head's narratives.

3

RACE, GENDER, AND EXILE IN
NATIONAL DISCOURSE

The "locality" of national culture is neither unified nor unitary in relation to itself, nor must it be seen simply as "other" in relation to what is outside or beyond it. The boundary is Janus-faced and the problem of outside/inside must always itself be a process of hybridity, incorporating new "people" in relation to the body politic, generating other sites of meaning and, inevitably, in the political process, producing unmanned sites of political antagonism and unpredictable forces for political representation.

—Homi Bhabha, *Nation and Narration*

THE REASONS that Bessie Head's second novel, *Maru*, provoked more literary thought than her first are all too obvious at first. Head, herself, provides some of the clues that led her to embark on a "novel on the hideousness of racial prejudice," but she adds that she "wanted the book to be so beautiful and so magical that I, as the writer, would long to read and re-read it."[1] Head tells us: "In Botswana they have a conquered tribe, the Basarwa or Bushmen. It is argued that they . . . had been conquered by the more powerful Botswana tribes and from then onwards assumed the traditional role of slaves. Botswana people were also abhorrent to Baswara people because they hardly looked African, but Chinese."[2] There are two important coinciding components of racism here. The Basarwa could be discriminated against because they "hardly" looked African, and because of this difference they could be enslaved by the Batswana.

Head is sending a double message in this novel. At one level she wishes to explore sinister aspects of the ideology of racism, and on the other she wants her novel to remain a disconcerting children's story. Audre Lorde's direct and simple understanding of racism is well worth evoking. She tells us that racism is "the belief in the inherent superiority of one race over all others and thereby the right to dominance."[3] Given the fact of a shrinking world and the formation of a "global village" this "right to dominance" has little to do with literal "birth right"—birth right in terms of economic advantage and specific belonging to a geographical location. Head takes this argument further, for she is interested in the power of the dominant to exercise racism (and in this context racism seeks to exclude in order to gain control over) and thereby exile the oppressed from their own cultures, regardless of "birth right." In fact, the whole notion of birth right becomes a class-oriented issue as well. With this in mind, the Basarwa of Botswana fit the category of internal exile more explicitly than, for instance, Afroamericans because of historically and geographically determined physical displacement of a number of different peoples.

As with most of her novels, the choice of topic is again extremely personal and political for Head. In a letter to Randolph Vigne she says: "It's over Howard [her son]. . . . It was I who told him he was a Motswana. . . . No sooner did he go to school, this year, than the children at school told him he is a coloured. Apparently being a Motswana is a very exclusive thing. . . . Eventually he got assaulted by children twice his age, apparently on the grounds that he is a usurper into the race of Motswana, or some filthy specimen."[4] Perhaps it was as a tribute to her son that she wrote this novel for "the children's department of S and S."[5] However, as Head herself admitted, *Maru* became too much even for the writer. She told Vigne, "I wish I had not written *Maru* after all. It is personal and brings back many bad memories. . . . *Maru upsets* me" (emphasis mine).[6] And indeed *Maru* does upset, but primarily because of the assumptions Head herself makes about the dilemmas of race. Her book sets out to resolve race issues but in doing so she poses equally troubling solutions. From her first novel where resolution was carefully orchestrated, we rapidly move to *Maru* where "illegitimate meanings percolate."[7]

Even Head's reason for writing the novel, painful as it was, is curious in that it emerged out of the tension between her desire for her son to belong and his exclusion from the dominant national discourse. The exile's consciousness constitutes a tension between a desire and long-ing to belong to a nation-state but the fear and reality of unfulfillment of that same desire. The strength of the novel remains in being able to ask questions of gender oppression as they are related to issues of belonging to dominant social systems and nations. Head continues,

> I knew the language of racial hatred but it was an evil exclusively prac-ticed by white people. I therefore listened in amazement as Botswana people talked of the Baswara whom they oppressed.
> "They don't think," they said. "They don't know anything."
> For the first time I questioned blind prejudice:
> "How do they know that? How can they be sure that the Baswara are not thinking?"[8]

From Head's initial statements one can delineate a simple outcry against injustices the author perceived in an "all black" country and its stark similarities to the horrendous apartheid she had just left. As a result of her exilic consciousness, that is, her simultaneous desire to belong to a place but always haunted by not being able to really do so, she wanted to reconcile her choice in moving to Botswana. In her new home she experienced an equal longing for solutions to the problems of racism and prejudice. She wished to create a space that justified leaving South Africa because she did not want to move again. She writes, "The research I did among Botswana people for *Maru* gave me the greatest insights and advantages to work right at the root of racial hatred. I found out above all that that type of exploitation and evil is dependent on a lack of communication between the oppressor and the people he oppresses. It would horrify an oppressor to know that his victim has the same longings, feelings, and as sensitivities he has. . . . Nothing prevented me from slipping into the skin of a Masarwa per-son. And so my novel was built up in blinding flashes of insight into an evil that hung like the sickness of death over all black people in South Africa."[9] Since the phenomenon of racism exists over the globe, a novel about caste prejudice does have more universal appeal than a novel about the hardships of life in a small Botswana village. This could explain general critical interest in this novel. The quoted passage, how-ever, is crucial in terms of understanding Head's inclusions as well as her omissions of what she says about racism in this novel. She makes no mention, for example, of how racism is often an economically moti-vated societal symptom. Her words "exploitation" and "oppression" suggest economic disadvantage but Head wants to focus on different distinctions. It seems that Head foregrounds issues of race in an effort to transcend local apartheid versions of racism, but this transcendence is at the price of not engaging this subject with all the seriousness it deserves.

The author's initial motivation and the background of this novel is important, but what emerges from it is an ambiguous and very disturbing picture of feminine identity as it subverts and is subverted by the nation, the nation as it represents traditional prejudice, laws, and hierarchies. Even though Head creates a haunting "fairy tale," and not something "magical," she is in the last analysis unable to position female identity as it epitomizes oppression within the dominant discourse of the nation, indeed, even as it resists and subverts the nation. I believe Head's purpose is the opposite, namely, to create a space and a demand for feminine liberation, as it constitutes a minority discourse within the dominant national one. The character of Maru is the representation of the nation, which in turn acknowledges the status of oppressed peoples, as well as other patterns of institutional oppression, such as slavery. The stipulation of this novel is that the dominant nation desires to merge with the marginal discourse of oppression, and vice versa, in order to formulate a complete, or even Head's idealized state. However, the marriage between the dominant and marginal nations is very uneasy both at the level of gender and at the level of the liberation of the Khoisan, or Bushmen. But Head is able to position the questions relating to subversive identities in the forefront of her "love story." The importance of this novel resides in Head's refusal to foreground issues of oppression as they collide with the realities of liberation. She raises embarrassing questions for the new nations about marginal and gender issues within the macrocosm of newly emerging decolonized national constructs.

Maru is remarkable in its expression of the author's shock at the existence of racism in an entirely Black country. Head must, at the very least, have been marginally aware of the kinds of racism that can percolate within a Black community, especially since she came from Cape Town, with its large population of "Coloureds." Even though the scramble for power is almost entirely determined by the Whites, the apartheid structure tends to be absorbed in the interrelationships between people in the same community, and although Head seems to show a clear awareness of this phenomenon in her other writing, she refuses to acknowledge it in this novel "on racism." Her son's experience notwithstanding, she says that her primary goal was to write a "magical" book. Does her statement quoted earlier suggest that she is yet once again holding an understandable but unpopular position? Does she wish to imply that race is secondary to creating a novel that only engages with race issues superficially? And does her subordination of the subject of race, in this novel, jeopardize the magical quality which she is at great pains to develop in her novel?

In *Maru*, difference in physical appearance is of vital importance. As Head correctly assumes, if someone in your own country or nation has the capacity, for whatever reason, to say that you hardly look like other people from "home," but instead look Chinese, that statement itself constitutes tremendous leverage against you. Is that a racist attack? This sort of statement immediately displaces—exiles—one from one's "legitimate birth right."

When I was asked in my own country, Pakistan, whether I was Indonesian, I was helplessly angry at the unwitting double displacement I was subjected to, simply because this person had decided that all Pakistani women looked a certain way. Of course, this sort of immediate displacement is differently exacerbated when you are not part of the majority's socioeconomic or cultural system.

The Khoisan or Basarwa, constitute the marginal in Southern Africa and do not "belong" to anyone or anything, for they were institutionally declared slaves by the more dominant Batswana. The main characters Maru and Margaret imitate and constitute the individual and gender component of the national dialogue, which is between the dominant national center of Botswana people's class and race issues and the marginal reality of the Basarwa people.

Arthur Ravenscroft's critique of *Maru*, "a more transparent imaging of the renouncement of political responsibility and power could hardly be devised," is somewhat hasty. And even though he retracts in the next sentence, "But with Bessie Head things are never so simple," he does not locate the complexity.[10] In *Maru*, Head negotiates "identity politics" into a situation that could be socioracially explosive but is saved by unusual individual identities, unbelievable though they seem. The reality or impossibility of a paramount chief desperately wanting a matrimonial alliance with a Masarwa is not the point of engagement for Head. I believe that she uses the class-race difference between Margaret and the two men who want to marry her as a reminder of the trope that determines racism in every society, be it entirely Black or entirely White. It is the existence of so fundamental a racism in every society that horrifies her, especially after she left the apartheid state. Her short-lived romance with an exile's nostalgia for "Old Africa" was not yet over, and since she was loath to offend the Batswana, she made her story "beautiful and magical," one in which everything "apparently" works out. However, her purpose is much more serious. The fairy tale is a red herring to examine whether minority discourses can merge with national discourses; and even though for Head the answer is yes, she is unable to be convincing.

There have been several scholarly articles about the impossibility of a Batswana chief deigning to marry a Masarwa, without addressing the issues that concerns Head most, namely, the possibility or impossibility of marginal people belonging to national discourses. These articles suggest the opposite interpretation, that is, Maru as anti-fairy tale. A paper by a Batswana scholar, Rasebotsa Nobantu, is interesting in its determination to ignore the fundamental premises of Head's narrative. Nobantu wanted to prove the literal and sociological impossibility of such a mismatched marriage. She implied that since the premise of the book, the marriage between Maru and Margaret, was impossible, scholars could not take the novel seriously. Her conclusion and others like it are based on, to say the very least, very dubious grounds, which insist on examining Head's novel as a realistic piece. However, even though one can empathize with Nobantu's attempt to save the aristocracy of Botswana from the disrepute of such an idea, I do not believe that Head's purpose is the opposite. And I also believe that Nobantu is picking up a very important strand in the novel, which is the failure of the authorial desire for the possibility of the merging of dominant and marginal discourses in a hierarchical and phallogocentric nation or society like Botswana. What Nobantu ignores is the possibility that Head deliberately used the marriage between the two characters as a device to show the Batswana precisely what it irked them most to see. By slipping this into her novel, she gives certain ideologies even more impact since the overt challenge lies elsewhere. A Motswana would be led to attack the incongruity of the marriage between a Masarwa and the paramount chief rather than examine the patterns of historical racism. I believe that Head's message is transmitted through this ruse and her strength as a writer lies in this sly, yet seemingly innocent, organization. Nobantu's position ignores the real challenge that Head raises. For Head, the two discourses of margin and center are incomplete without each other and therefore must be merged. The question remains: Can such a merger dispel exile and translate into a sense of belonging for peoples inhabiting margins as well as those in the center?[11]

The reason that the remoteness of a marriage between an actual paramount chief and a flesh and blood Masarwa remains largely unimportant is that Head herself remains disinterested and detached from its reality. Indeed, the authorial interest wanes after the "unlikely" marriage takes place. Maru and Margaret are banished from the "common" view of nations altogether. Rather, given the realm of actuality, Head chooses the most implausible of possibilities because it is precisely the shock value that interests her, and through that she brings about the narrative dialogue of her novel to fruition. Like Nobantu, the Batswana would be shocked, just as the Masarwa would be shocked, at a marriage between Margaret and Maru. The question that remains enduring and provocative is, What does Head want her readers shocked out of, and what does she want them shocked into? In order to absorb the shock value this marriage would evoke, she deliberately devises the fairy tale genre in specific ways to weave a trope that addresses the issue of cultural racism in Botswana. Head's usage of such an extreme device tends to distract the actual subject of her engagement, that unless the dialogue between the dominant and the dominated takes place there cannot be a nation-state, even a decolonized one. In order to merge the experience of the oppressor and oppressed into national discourse one has to see these two opposite poles of the same political ideology not so much in revolutionary, but in dialogic combat with one another.

Nonetheless, if we call *Maru* a fairy tale, with a happy ending, are we exempt from taking it seriously in yet another variation of Nobantu's thesis? Head's second novel evades the convenience and simplicity of the semiautobiographical trends pervasive in her other novels. Head told Lee Nichols that "a whole portion of it [*Maru*] was myself, my African background. It's easy for me to put myself into the shoes of Basarwa (Bushmen) people you see."[12] But it is fairly clear that this novel is not overtly about Bessie Head at all. The character, Margaret Cadmore, is absent and present in the novel in the same way that female characters in other well-known fairy tales are. Usually the definition of fairy princess limits rather than liberates our protagonist. Margaret is always somewhat remote and silent in her responses to others. Her desires are presumed rather than real. In other words, we are never told that Cinderella wanted to be the prince's wife just as we are not told that Margaret wants to be Maru's wife, but we assume she does. In the Disney versions of both Cinderella and Snow White the young women are constantly dreaming of the handsome prince but not aggressively. In fact Moleka, Maru, and Dikeledi's responses to Margaret are far more defined and rife with expectations compared to those of Margaret, who does not expect anything from anyone. Perhaps she is a mere receptacle of stray desires. We do find out that she was scared of her own capacity for violence when she nearly strangled the disruptive student in her class, but again she stopped herself. Except for the very occasional tear from the corner of an eye she does not seem to be emotionally aware of what is happening around her but is preoccupied by the experimental function of living her life, which was completely designed and implemented by her benevolent, adoptive colonial m/other-fairy godmother. It seems that it is not the function of her life to be experimental but rather that she is the experiment. .

Another extreme reaction to Head's second novel is dialogically more fruitful. Daniel Grover says that *Maru* "depicts love as a magical force from a fairy tale that overcomes insurmountable obstacles and unites people of different cultures and classes."[13] And this is precisely where the gender betrayal takes place. Grover reinforces the earlier refrain of the mismatched marriage, though, this time it is posed as a possibility only if it can be couched in the structural framework of a fairy tale with "happily ever after" thrown in. Both Nobantu's and Grover's criticisms seem phallocratic in terms of their meticulous attention to the "romantic" structure of Maru and Margaret's elopement given the difference in their class background and not enough stress is laid on how Margaret has entered another, and this time, gendered bondage. The question of the possibility of this marriage is not as relevant to the discussion of this novel as the idea that this marriage suggests a fairy tale ending for Margaret.[14] The fairy tale–like quality of this novel reasserts Head's desire to construct *Maru* as a children's story. She tends to tease serious questions into existence but does not incorporate them into her discourse.

The question raised by this novel is whether Head says anything meaningful about "Black on Black" racism in Botswana. Given the complex institutionalized encouragement of Black on Black racism in apartheid South Africa, she is understandably horrified to find the same determining factors in Botswana. Both the Masarwa and the Batswana are Africans, the latter having enslaved the former; Head successfully explicates and complicates this issue. She assumes that an analogy can be made between the racism encouraged by apartheid among "Coloured" and Black people, and the racism that exists among the Khoisan and other Black Southern Africans. However, another aspect of the same question remains unanswered: does Head believe that her argument about the merging of marginal and national discourses in the context of her novel remains an illusion or does she ultimately shy away from awkward questions of race and gender as they remain outside the dominant national discourse? I differ from Zoe Wicomb, who thinks that, in *Maru*, Head successfully accomplishes "the stealthy negotiation of race and gender."[15] I believe that issues of race and gender become hopelessly confused with the fairy tale aspect of *Maru* and never become part of the dominant discourse of nation. The "apparently" happy marriage the protagonist has with Maru emerges as the only important aspect of the novel.

The Basarwa are economically disenfranchised and banished into occupational slavery just as the untouchables are still delegated to cleaning other people's toilets and floors in South Asia. Of course there are always exceptions but generally speaking they cannot do anything occupationally that is not limited to the general Batswana expectation of what the Basarwa people are capable of. Head points out appropriately in the passage just cited that racism and prejudice are tied to the objectification of a given people without dialogic collaboration with them. "How do the Batswana know that the Baswara cannot think?" Head asks. They certainly have not asked them or even tried to find out for themselves whether the Basarwa think or not. Perhaps these differences, from a sociohistoric standpoint completely arbitrary, are necessary to the continued existence of a sociopolitical hierarchy that the Basarwa contribute to but had no part in forming, and to date, did not have a chance systematically to dismantle. Even though Head is willing to throw this benevolent mantle on the Batswana, to her, they still represent power and control over the Basarwa.

These questions inform Head's desire to write about the kinds of exile that affect people—in this novel, the women of the underclass and men of the elite. Exile in *Maru* is suggested not so much by leaving a place where one belongs, even though that is never absent, but rather by exclusion. Maru and Margaret's desire to marry each other, and become one with the other's group, is indicative of their primary motivation—which is "to belong." What Head wishes to suggest simultaneously is a possibility of merging the dominant with the marginal discourse. Indeed, in Head's case, the dominant seems incomplete without the marginal, for it is only in the reality of the marriage that there is a resolution of opposites. Head does not view this dichotomy as one of binary opposition but rather as two aspects of the same discourse desiring to merge in order to form a whole, out of a natural national instinct. She is concerned, here, with the sense of belonging that is usually nurtured by the community out of which one emerges, to which one owes primary allegiance and the one which recognizes that same sense of belonging as legitimate. In his essay on exile, Edward Said assumes that all exiles have a sense of belonging, but for a Black South African this inherence must always be extremely problematic and unclear. For Said, exile would seem to suggest a sense of nonbelonging and nonallegiance to the community one is born into or finds oneself in, as well as a nonrecognition of one's legitimacy in exercising that very same sense of belonging.[16]

Racism can function as the exilic force that disrupts a sense of belonging. It functions well if the victor and the victim can easily perceive the boundaries between them. A disregard or even a critical examination of these arbitrary yet deliberately fixed boundaries upsets the precarious sociopolitical and economic balance set by the dominant segment of the hierarchy. Ignoring social boundaries, as in the case of interracial marriage, can be perceived as a lethal threat to that same balance. Bessie Head writes, "They all have their monsters. You just have to look different from them, the way the facial features of a Sudra or Tamil do not resemble the facial features of a high caste Hindu, then seemingly anything can be said and done to you as your outer appearance reduces you to the status of a non-human being."[17]

In *Maru*, just as in *When Rain Clouds Gather*, the narrator assumes an interesting omniscience. This omniscience is used in order to create an idyllic atmosphere in Dilepe, reminiscent of the one in Golema Mmidi, though Dilepe does not seem to experience economic hardship in the same way that Golema Mmidi does. However, the omniscience which was pervasive in her first novel is not entirely overwhelming in her second. More or less everybody was a part of this idyllic village life in *When Rain Clouds Gather*. Even the goats contributed to this utopia. Similarly, in *Maru*, the Queen of Sheba and Windscreen Wiper, a mother goat and her kid, are more integral to village life than the paramount chief himself. In *Maru*, the people in the village are neither broad minded nor do they contribute to an idyllic atmosphere of goodness. In fact, quite the reverse happens in terms of the common villager. When people find out that their paramount chief has married a Masarwa, "they had only one alternative: to keep their prejudice and pretend Maru had died."[18] This is synonymous with saying that the marginal discourse of the Masarwa is forced back into marginality and the possibility of its merging with the dominant discourse was a good but short-lived idea.

After *When Rain Clouds Gather*, the conceptual structure of good and evil changed dramatically in *Maru*. The identity spaces that individuals and power structures inhabit, and in turn use to define themselves and to manipulate others, within national constructs, shifted considerably from Head's first novel. There are pockets of good people and their goodness is problematized, since they are not entirely good, and there are people who are petty in their evil actions. These people are not evil incarnate, as Chief Matenge was, but rather terrified of making any structural changes in the existing patterns of power structures that privilege their own identity discourse. These are the people who cannot tolerate a Masarwa colleague or a Masarwa teaching their children. These same people are responsible for and desirous of exiling others who can claim "birth right," like the Batswana schoolchildren who assaulted a six-year-old "Coloured." The center perpetually fears the consequences of what could happen if the structures were dismantled, made less rigid. These people are not "evil" as such, but are capable of petty evil in the form of prejudice. And even though one can claim that racism is a form of prejudice—prejudice seems a lot milder in comparison. If one is able to understand the fear behind prejudice, then it is easier to feel compassion and harder to condemn those people. Thus, culturally subversive identities are tied to both dominant and marginal discourses of nation and there is a tension created between them in the individual. As a result a happy marriage between them becomes almost impossible. Is Head implying that the exile's consciousness remains impenetrable?

As a child whose mother dies directly after giving birth, Margaret is the archetypal example of experimentation, exile, and colonialism. She is cut off, utterly, from her own people after birth and is taken over by an individual, by a colonial administration, by an experimenter, and also by a set of differently expressed prejudices. Ebele Eko has designated Margaret Cadmore Senior as "her foster mother's programmed alter ego." The program, however, excludes rather than includes Margaret Junior into any one reality. Her identity is always defined as separate from, rather than belonging to, anything or anyone. And even though we are told several times that "her mind and heart were composed of a little bit of everything she had absorbed from Margaret Cadmore. It was hardly African or anything but something new and universal, a type of personality that would be unable to fit into a definition of something as narrow as tribe or race or nation."[19] Margaret is a woman and a Masarwa. Even Margaret Cadmore Senior was not just "everything" but rather a something, that is, a British missionary and, very important, a colonial. As a child, Margaret Junior's discourse is filtered through to her from the colonial woman's perspective. It comes straight from the English metropole down to the colony. The movement is always from the center to the margin. This pattern is duplicated after she marries the nation, that is, Maru. Margaret's subjecthood consisting of "a little bit of everything" remains strangely unconvincing. Head wishes to advertise Margaret Cadmore Junior as a sociopolitically cosmopolitan citizen of the world, but what she succeeds in doing is inculcating total passivity in a "bush woman," a passivity that is inculcated in the culture through the same oppression she wishes the Masarwa to critically overcome.

Cadmore Senior has charged her with, "'One day, you will help your people.' It was never said as though it were a big issue, but at the same time it created a purpose and burden in the child's mind."[20] The enactment of this burden lies outside the pages of this novel. The only act that she is willing to undertake is to make the unpopular and difficult statement, "I am a Masarwa!"[21] There is a sense of dignity about claiming her identity back from the malaise that has surrounded her identity traditionally, but she is extremely passive, like a fairy tale heroine, in terms of everything else that happens to her in the course of the novel. Even Cadmore Senior's training of her is absorbed with great concentration and with a curious yet reserved obedience. She never rebels but rather becomes a perfect Cadmore product, and later she brings the same perfect obedience as the pupil in her relationship with Maru. Surely this liberates her neither as a Masarwa nor as a woman.

So when Margaret correctly or incorrectly assumes that she has been rejected by Moleka, she suffers passively, and we learn that she has even expected such an occurrence. The only explanation for such acceptance of what is loathsome to her comes from her recognition that he would never think of her. She accepts the suit of Maru in a total state of shock, stupor, and perhaps gratitude. Is that the only reigning emotion in her life, then? Gratitude for being "rescued" by her adoptive mother? Gratitude for the paramount chief deigning to marry her? Gratitude for being "rescued" by and for a "double colonization"? Gratitude for being allowed to paint pictures that are immediately stolen from her by her best friend? Doesn't her attitude, i.e., her Masarwa-like obedience and gratitude, bring about the wrath and outrage of Nobantu or Head herself, and others?

I believe that Margaret Cadmore remains the perfect victim of racism and sexism throughout this novel. At the end of the novel, after Maru has eloped with her, Head writes, "When people of the Masarwa tribe heard about Maru's marriage to one of their own, a door silently opened on the small, dark airless room in which their souls had been shut for a long time. The wind of freedom, which was blowing throughout the world for all people, turned and flowed into the room. As they breathed in the fresh, clear air their humanity awakened. . . . the horror of being an oddity of the human race, with half the head of a man and half the body of a donkey. . . . They started to run out into the sunlight, then they turned and looked at the dark, small room. They said: 'We are not going back there.'"[22]

Even though her marriage to Maru has been responsible for that "wind of freedom," blowing into the darkest corners of Masarwa oppression, it is not *her* actions that have done that but rather her passive acceptance of somebody else's actions, which always remain external to her. And surely the nexus of Masarwa struggle is not to accept charity but rather to enter consciously into the new definition of a nation. By remaining passive Margaret does not provide a dynamic model for her people—people that she never meets either as savior or as fellow sufferer. She is not even aware of what her marriage has affected in terms of Masarwa rebellion. She remains tied to a variation of the contented life of "happily ever after," which is where the novel opens. Or does it? Her marriage to Maru remains invisible—he becomes "dead" to his people, and Margaret, who has known a little notoriety because of her racial identity, gets taken to a place of "yellow daisies" much like a no wo/man's land, perhaps of fairy tales—always ridden by the emotional gestalt of her husband, the paramount chief without portfolio. The discourse of the nation, through which the relationship of the oppressor and the oppressed would be forced out of the closet and into the foreground of national definitions, goes into spaces inhabited and reaffirmed by exilic consciousnesses. Both Maru and Margaret become exiled from the national public sphere into the personal private sphere of individualized emotional economies.

Lloyd Brown's critique quite accurately privileged Margaret as an "artist" occupying a "central position," and later Zoe Wicomb corroborated by reconstructing her into the artist *par excellence*.[23] The latter she may not be, because she does not project her dreams on to her husband. Rather he uses her to substantiate his own desires while marginalizing hers. Wicomb writes, Margaret "paints her dream, which, in fact, is a projection of her powerful suitor's desire, and which later, when he sweeps her off into marriage, is translated into reality." I believe that Margaret remains the inarticulate "school-teacher, painter, and woman."[24]

Much like a fairy princess, Margaret has been banished into another exile just as she was emerging from one exile. There is a suggestion of a possibility that the oppressed might uninhabit the private sphere and enter into the national discourse when Maru first announces his intention to marry the Masarwa schoolteacher, but that "dream" is soon dissipated when both the paramount chief and his Masarwa wife leave the well-defined boundaries of their nation in order to live among the "yellow daisies." Maru chooses and lets Margaret follow him to a place where the myths of daily life are defined by individual interactions and not where the national myths collide with the discourse of oppression.

When Margaret consents to leave with Maru, her life becomes defined and hyphenated by that same exile. Her relationships with the school-children, with Moleka and Dikeledi, have been quickly and irrevocably cut off for the "paradise" of yellow daisies. She walks into the picture she has created—dreamed—earlier like a passive Dorian Gray and only at the controlled promptings and encouragements of Maru and Dikeledi. Margaret walks out of a dream in order to enter into the experimentation commenced and planned by her future husband. She becomes frozen in that same picture, reflecting and being reflected in the tempestuously extreme moods of her god-husband-chief. Margaret remains defined but never defines herself. She continues as the stunted identity she has always been. She remains both gendered and exiled. Both Margaret Cadmore, the missionary, and Maru, the paramount chief, define her but do not let her define herself.

Further, it is Dikeledi, the chief's sister, who becomes pregnant with another chief's child. It is Dikeledi and not Margaret who is about to provide Dilepe with the future chief. Margaret remains barren, her marriage to the paramount chief notwithstanding. There is no possibility in the future for Margaret to even vicariously enjoy the fruits of leadership through a son or daughter. She disappears with her husband into another margin, accomplishing little. The pregnancy of Dikeledi announces the sexual engagement between Moleka and herself, Maru and Margaret's engagement seems altogether nonsexual.

Head problematizes Margaret's marriage to Maru even though it is peripheral to the larger subject of this novel, and it appears only in the beginning and at the end. We are told that she never stops loving Moleka who has reversed personal and political history for her. The quiet resistance she shows is in loving Moleka even after her marriage to Maru. Head writes: "There were two rooms. In one his wife totally loved him; in another, she totally loved Moleka." [25] Moleka seems not to react to her as he has to all the other women in his past but, instead, is willing to take his "heart out of the secret place" in order to give it to her. Though Moleka is a very sexual person, even the possibility of their union seems nonsexual. Masarwa Margaret's perceived asexuality is very problematic in terms of gender, class, and identity discourse. It seems a bit overly convenient for her to be completely above sexuality, for then she is not a threat to the status quo at all and can continue to be half Masarwa and half fairy princess.

Moleka makes a great show of publicly eating from the same table and utensils as his Masarwa slaves, all the time hoping his sleepy, unaware fairy princess would hear of his love and his heroism. Margaret steadfastly remains utterly unaware of any act of external love, for liberation is like a gift for a member of the underclass. As good slaves, they certainly do not expect such a gift, and, unfortunately, Margaret epitomizes such an expectation. Even though she remains unaware of these gestures, often because they are sabotaged by Maru, she absorbs the taciturn love that Moleka has directed toward her and returns it upon several occasions in the novel.

One recurrent accusation against Head's creation of Margaret is that she is the "Bushy" who "was hardly African or anything but something new and universal, a type of personality that would be unable to fit into a definition of something as narrow as tribe or race or nation."[26] If Margaret is "hardly African," as we are told, then what is she? Is being non-African a definite value? How does being "hardly African" inform postcolonial identity politics? And surely part of the question that Head is trying to raise is, if the Masarwa are not African, then what are they? If being "hardly African" is a value, then this is a curious sort of value for an African woman writer in exile to be peddling, her cool reception by the Batswana notwithstanding. Is it even understandable for Head the exile to be writing about "narrow" definitions "of tribe or race or nation"? When one examines the bitter history of the Khoisan in Southern Africa, then one sees that they suffered a similar fate under Afrikaans and British rule. The colonials, being unable to manipulate the nomadic Khoisan people, paid money for anyone bringing in a severed Khoisan head, and the rationale they used was exactly the one Head uses for Margaret, that the "Bushmen" were not African but Chinese. Surely Head is falling prey to exactly what feminist and minority discourses are prey to? If one is to create even one exception, which is not to say that people are not exceptional, the conscience is somewhat appeased at the cost of any real change. The status quo determined by hierarchies and traditional dichotomies within nations continue to flourish.

Head tends to want to liberate her protagonist from the narrow boundaries to which she perceives other people exiling her, but often she does the reverse. She wishes to release Margaret from the limitations of her oppressive birth right, but in doing so, she leaves her without any identity or quest for one, and thus denigrates the idea of having a Masarwa identity. In the last analysis, one might well ask whether Head is able to release Margaret Cadmore at all. Perhaps she merely succeeds in rescuing her from her innate subjective identity, which, I argue, Margaret is never able to claim in this novel, let alone, reform. Head, unwittingly tends to objectify her even further. As I have mentioned earlier, Margaret never reaches beyond the experiment that she becomes for a number of people. Thus, she remains at best a fairy tale princess, or at worst, a willing object for merciless experimentation—a guinea pig. Feminist readings of fairy tales, such as "Sleeping Beauty," often imply that the fairy princess is objectified through her extreme passivity. Both elements—experimental object and passive fairy princess—are innate in Margaret Cadmore. Even though Margaret says any number of times that she is a Masarwa, the analysis and recognition of her identity goes no further than that. Why is Head at great pains to make her into a nothing? And even Head, after whitewashing her personality into something that is "unable to fit," is unable to rescue her from the larger expectations of passive acceptance preeminent for a Masarwa slave. As Trinh T. Minh-ha would have it, Margaret is unable to assimilate the "inappropriate self" that resides in every "I" and continues to respond as a being without "status."[27] Her stature as Maru's wife seems identical to her status as a Masarwa. And it is not that Margaret is "unable to fit" because she is a revolutionary, but rather because she fits into nothing and has to be taken deeper into the dream or fairy tale to which she belongs. Margaret, in the last analysis, does exactly what has been chosen for her by others: her education, her employment, and her marriage all fall into the realm of other expectations of an extremely successful experiment, one that has created a mannequin, not a human.

The problematic areas of Margaret's character notwithstanding, she does tend to evoke great pathos. Like Makhaya before her, she tends to want to take the dubious road toward "peace of mind." Head has an enduring interest in taking her protagonists to the brink, "one road leads to fame and the other to . . . ," usually peace of mind. In *Maru,* "a little brown, dusty footpath turned away from the roaring busy highways of life. Yellow daisies grew alongside the dusty footpath and danced in the sun and wind."[28] Head always rewards the people who take the little "dusty footpath." The picture that haunts Maru is the same one that has haunted Makhaya earlier: "There was a busy, roaring highway on one side, full of bustle and traffic. Leading away from it was a small, dusty footpath. It went on and on by itself in the distance. 'Take that path,' his heart said."[29] The yellow daisies on that dusty path are always reserved as a reward for the exiles. This reward comes after resisting the worldly merits and demerits of a public life. But exiles always remain exiled from the discourse of nation that continues to be a problem in this novel. Head makes her main characters choose the road that leads to peace of mind. I believe that this consistency informs her concept of exile from a very particular part of the world, namely, South Africa. Head herself turned away from the corrosive apartheid in South Africa toward a country with enormous "food production" problems, where she remained stateless for over a decade, and her protagonists choose the same destiny. Of course, it is the "turning away from" that defines the exilic identity.

The desire to escape to a peaceful, well-ordered life of daily work and leisure precludes the relentless, all-encompassing racial hatred that Head's characters flee from. In some ways, Margaret manages to escape, and in others she simply cannot escape from racial hatred because even Africans can call her Africanness "un-African." It is almost as if apartheid is unendurable at a fundamental human level for her. Even to fight would require monumental reserves of strength and energy—energy that could conceivably be put to more progressive use—and all of Head's protagonists choose the latter. However, even though Makhaya could escape to a peaceful, nonracist Golema Mmidi, there is no racial peace for Margaret in Dilepe. She has to be removed from the realm of national social interaction altogether because she carries her "apartheid," her exile reality and identity, close to her, and it chases her relentlessly to every corner of the South African globe except the wilderness Maru chooses for her domicile.

Margaret reaches the personal, political, and social exile of her own nightmare time. She has certainly painted herself into a picture, dream, and nightmare. There is no place for her in Dilepe. She can only reside in the "loathing" of the people of Dilepe. She continues to live within the marginalized discourses, first as a "special" Masarwa and then as wife, interchangeable roles. She never enters into the dominant discourse of nations and their laws. Despite her marriage to Maru, she lives in a never-never land of a nightmare and even the "yellow daisies" seem to fade. Head writes, "In fact, until the time he married her she had lived like the mad dog of the village, with tin cans tied to her tail."[30] I would go so far as to suggest that the cans never come off because she is very quickly removed from a world where the tin cans would rattle and draw attention to themselves. An interesting Pakistani proverb comes to mind: "What does it matter if a peacock dances in the forest: no one can see its beautiful plumage." Human presumption aside, Margaret along with her talents is banished to a forest, in exile from the nation-state, where she can be admired in tyranny and isolation, never being aware of Moleka's love, or seen as a Masarwa with clout, among the people of Dilepe. The isolation of Margaret evokes the picture of the fairy princess in need of rescuing from the monster who guards her and keeps her all for himself, as Maru does. Her story is like a fairy tale that never ends. There is no awakening. Is she still waiting? One can only imagine that this time she wants to be rescued by Moleka.

Margaret has been personally and politically disenfranchised and later neutralized by her segregation from other Masarwa. She has no sense of a Masarwa identity because she has never come into contact with them at any except the most peripheral level. We are told that the wind of freedom has blown into the Masarwa consciousness, which was previously contained in a dark room. Yet, if Margaret was a symbol of that freedom then surely she would not retreat willingly to a prison of someone else's making, hyphenated by the same dark exile that has been her people's lot for generations.

Her private life before she marries Maru is a mirror image of what happens to her later. There is no change or development in her character. Head writes of this picturebook marriage: "So quietly did he enter the house that his wife looked up *fearfully* from her work of preparing the table for the evening meal. He sometimes had vicious, malicious moods when every word was a sharp knife intended to grind and re-grind the same raw wound" (emphasis mine).[31] "Fearful" of a loved and loving husband? Why? Head is quick to add that Margaret suffered a perpetual amnesia in regard to "previous suffering." But surely even if she is "quite mad and drunk with happiness" inspired by Maru, she is still the object of Maru's every whim, just as she was to her educator before him. She tends to suffer a constant nervous tension. When she is going about her "work" of laying the table, she "looks up in fear" to anticipate the paramount chief's mood—as his Masarwa slaves would, not his equal. Her happiness seemed to depend entirely on him, as it had before on the approval of her teacher who drummed even the notion of "lake water lapping against the shore" onto her arid country; she is the one who needs the lake water on her perpetually arid country. She needs to be filled but, after her marriage, comes out quite empty herself. What does that say about the Masarwa? If only all of them were this empty they could be sent to reeducation camp! Perhaps this view is a bit cynical and Head certainly did not have the imminent bondage of Margaret in mind, but rather the liberation of the Masarwa people as a whole and Margaret as the part belonging to the whole.

For Margaret, even though "the days of malice and unhappiness were few and far overbalanced by the days of torrential expressions of love,"[32] they were still not dependent on the training she had received as an educator, her love for painting, or her love for Moleka. Indeed the "torrential expressions of love" sound just as oppressive as the "days of malice." Even if one is to assume that love is the biggest liberating force and therefore the most revolutionary, Maru's love for her is still binding geographically and emotionally. In fact, her days as an artist are over and were used by Maru so that she could realize something about the possibilities of her aesthetic life, but only as that vision was to become linked with his own. Her paintings and thus her thoughts are colonized by the patriarchal hierarchy as it is aided and abetted by her closest woman friend, Dikeledi, who steals her friend's treasures in order to appease the same patriarchy that disconcerts her as well. Dikeledi, by giving her paper and paint and taking the paintings away for her brother, exercises power over a Masarwa; Dikeledi is able to give and to take away.

However, the extreme infatuation that Margaret experiences in Dilepe is puzzling. The fact that all "good" and powerful people in Dilepe seem to fall in love with her is problematic in the extreme as well. Maru, Moleka, Dikeledi, and many others seem to reach a higher spiritual plane when they come into slight contact with Margaret, and as a result they fall madly in love with her. Their love seems as racist as their hate did earlier. If indeed the love of these "good people" is directed toward her oppression then it is sick indeed. And it certainly seems to emerge as a reaction to her oppressed Masarwa status.

These people who represent dominant national and social forces tend to "love" the idea of Margaret rather than the reality. The flesh and blood Margaret is exiled a second time into oblivion after her marriage to the paramount chief, her beauty notwithstanding.

The betrayal of the exiled Margaret's identity is twofold. She is never allowed contact with her people but is allowed to call herself by their name. Any humanity that she has is colonized into the private domain of Maru just as the humanity of his other Masarwa slaves is fettered. This happens without any muttering of protest from the individual Masarwa, Margaret. It is curious and pathetic that even though the nation of the Masarwa can liberate themselves because of Maru's marriage to a Masarwa, she cannot liberate herself in the same way, because with the marriage she becomes the god's anointed and must respond appropriately to her new position, which she dons with equal equanimity, that is, silence, exile, and invisibility.

Does she become, then, a princess in a fairy tale who must forever be the passive, half-asleep tool of patriarchal aggression as well as affectionate control? Does Maru's fear of losing her inform her status in any way? He is nervous about one day giving up Margaret to the greater love of Moleka. He has recognized Moleka's love for her omnisciently but she herself is unaware of the reciprocity of that love. Perhaps Moleka would have to abduct her, Maru-fashion, like a sleeping beauty, in order for such an eventuality to take place. Or perhaps the very purpose of an unbelievable "happily ever after" is to remove problematic temptations from the path of the fairy princess altogether, so that that disconcerting emotional space, that is, a place in the national discourse, which would make her conscious of the many layers of her exile, never encroaches on her "happiness."

Zoe Wicomb has commented on Margaret's success as a woman and as a Masarwa. I find her reading of *Maru* extremely enticing but unconvincing. It is true that "both the heroine's relation to representing as well as to being represented" are problematized by Head, but in the final analysis, the character is unable to distinguish between her dream, desire, identity, and that of her powerful husband's. If her first two exiled states are her status as a Masarwa and her status as a colonized subject, her third is that of wife. Just because she is able to paint several paintings denying the "unity" of his desire does not mean she is able to "disrupt the realization of his dreams" or "resist total subjugation through creating a space in which she could insert inventions of her own."[33] Those inventions are suspect because they always remain in the private rather than national spheres of her destiny. In other words, her subjectivity, which is being built up as a national model in the beginning of the novel, falls far short of the earlier promise.

It seems that it is much easier to negotiate the "Masarwas' racial liberation" than it is to resolve Margaret's "identity as a woman," for it is always tied to the dominant national patriarchal discourse. Even though the Masarwa are dependent on the marriage for their liberation—or so we are told—this marriage does the opposite for Margaret. She is never allowed by Maru to function as a "knowing" being. He never tells her of Moleka's love or allows her room for that love, whisking her away from all reference points at a weak moment in her life. She is the fairy tale princess but one that will never be awakened unless there is a radical change in her prescribed role, perhaps as a leader of a nation.

Upon turning toward the male counterpart of the fairy princess, Maru, one runs into extremely problematic analytical constructions. He too, is exiled, though in his case it is voluntary and eludes understanding. Head creates a complex scenario for his exile: "The man who slowly walked away from them was a king in their society [of three or four people]. A day had come when he had decided that he did not need any kingship other than the kind of wife everybody would loathe from the bottom of their hearts. He had planned for that loathing in secret; they had absorbed the shocks in secret. When everything was exposed, they had only one alternative: to keep their prejudice and pretend Maru had died."[34]

Curious as it is, Maru reemphasizes his people's racial prejudice toward the Masarwa, but he does even more. He solicits the "loathing" for his wife by everybody and somehow wishes to become a pariah himself. Why must Margaret suffer for Maru's sadomasochistic tendencies? There is, however, another interpretation of his disappearance. Maru himself becomes a messiah figure through his turning away from worldly kingship, toward a Buddha-like engagement with an unpopular, inward journey into the soul. Out of this problematic journey came "a vision of a new world that slowly allowed one dream to dominate his life."[35] And this private dream, for which he needs Margaret's oppressed Masarwa insights, is to be introduced at some point to the national discourse, but again even in that introduction Margaret remains peripheral, marginal, accidental. If indeed the "new" national, postcolonial discourse continues to function as a result of Margaret's exclusion, then obviously the postcolonial nation has let more than half of its population down. It is not the actuality of oppression that Maru seems to want to incorporate into the national discourse but rather his own private understanding of oppression, which in the last analysis may or may not help liberate oppressed people within national boundaries. And we know from his ways that he is far more at ease with thinking than he is with acting.

Why does a paramount chief need to be loathed in a society that is eager to proclaim him king and god? How does such an occurrence inform the "vision of a new world," Head's discourse on the status of exile, and "universal brotherhood"? For Head, exile becomes an inherently disruptive force and necessitates the creation of "a new world," which constitutes a constructive force. For Head, one of the functions of the state of exile is thus completely revolutionary. However, Maru is neither "dispossessed" nor is he an exile, even though he does not "belong."

This is where Head's narrative weakens. Head seems on the brink of deciding whether the character Maru should, in his renunciation of wealth and power that the nation has bestowed on him, serve the cause of oppression, and thereby actively give birth to the new world he dreams of, or retreat into the personal world outside time and place. Do these two worlds stand in contradistinction to one another? He tends even to leave the "metropole" of Dilepe to be governed by Moleka and Dikeledi, both of whom are not as remote as Margaret and Maru. So much for the idea of philosopher kings! It is very hard to be convinced of Maru's goodness when he takes the bed away from one Masarwa because all his other Masarwa slaves would clamor for beds as well. Is he really interested in any one Masarwa's liberation, outside of what he designs for himself through Margaret? His motivations are usually selfish and tyrannical.

It is probable that Head intended to soften the blow of racism perpetrated by one African on another by using this "magical" tale, complete with the fairy godmother, Margaret Cadmore Senior. Whereas she does not wish to deal with race as a problematic issue between Whites and Blacks in *When Rain Clouds Gather,* she deals with Black on Black racism somewhat evasively in *Maru.* Racism between Whites and Blacks in

South Africa is stark enough, and in Botswana or Dilepe, Head tries to overcome the problem by giving a "political agenda" to Margaret and Maru. But the tools she uses, like their marriage, fall far short of a serious fictional analysis of relationships between geographical and social space within the national discourse. The problematics of the situation remain the same: the Masarwa are in the last analysis given a very dubious liberation and certainly continue to remain outside the national construct. At the end of the novel they come out of "the dark room" of their oppression but when they are in the light they can only look back at that room. The step toward claiming the nation by force is never made within the boundaries of this novel.

Similarly, Maru seems utterly disinterested in Margaret's social status, at first. What interests him is the status of her beautiful "oppressed" soul, with which he, among many others, is in love. We never clearly see this beautiful soul except if one harks back to her personality, which was something "new and universal," though hardly African. But "new and universal" is always external to national geographies. The theme of "universality," as it stands in contrast to the national discourse, which began as a particular construct in her first novel, is further elaborated in her third novel, A Question of Power. What seems to constitute the "beauty" in this new universal mind is that it cannot locate itself anywhere and cannot be located in historical time by others. Head intended to liberate her discourse from national constructs through this device, but she really ends up severely curtailing the theoretical functions of her universalist characters. For Margaret cannot belong anywhere except in the wilderness of the "yellow daisies." At the same time, the man she marries and the man she falls in love with both represent the dominant forces in the nation. And there is something, as Edward Said has told us, akin to "modern tragedy" in not being able to belong anywhere—in being "dispossessed." Perhaps Head has not quite thought out what a universal personality would do, and this identity that craves to belong even in the wilderness does have fragments of goodness and power. But the desire itself for "universality" functions as a reaction against belonging that "homes" and "unhomes" the exile from the nation she uninhabits. Is Margaret, then, the epitome of a "modern" tragic heroine, a status that Edward Said gives to his twentieth-century exile?

Maru, in spite of his omniscience and his spies, does not seem to belong naturally to his chiefdom. He is constantly ill and everybody seems to be waiting for him to die because he simply cannot cope with the business of falling in love or governing Dilepe. He later obliges everybody by disappearing entirely, and people pretend that he has died. His evil brother, Morafi, gloats over all the diseases Maru seems to contract and waits for the day when he will be deposed through death. The implications that Head draws from this strange and unchieflike behavior is that there are two distinct worlds for Maru: one, where the time and place belong to the public, and the other where you give yourself over entirely to matters of the individual "soul."

Maru ties Margaret to a part of the inner non-national life to which he finally retreats. In the time and place of the social-national world she is the mad dog with tin cans tied to her tail, and because of that incapacity it is impossible for him to stay as chief. Since he has always exulted in the inner life, she forms the right excuse for him to retreat from one world into another. For he can continue to be king in the new world but she remains fixed to her own "bushy" identity. He never thinks of untying the tin cans from the mad dog's tail. And it is "tragic" to note that these two worlds are never able to coexist in this novel even though the desire for that coexistence is the fundamental premise of this novel. Margaret is the one who marks the end of his journey in one social time and embarks on the inner time. In one sense she remains instrumental but her own psyche and its complex needs are never prioritized by him or the author. Implicit in this retreat is that Maru can always return to his nation but it will probably be without Margaret.

Maru forces one to wonder whether it is necessary to be rejected by the social world of the nation and its discourses so completely, as Maru orchestrates, in order to achieve the rewards and sanctuary of the inner life. And if indeed the people decide to keep their prejudice and "pretend that Maru had died," what has he accomplished? Is his power only manifest over Margaret? Head emphasizes her own questions: "But did it end there? Was that not only a beginning?"[36] There seems to be too much reliance on one large gesture, the marriage between a paramount chief and a Masarwa, to sort out the generations-long problem of racism and oppression. It is, at one level, quite understandable that this grand gesture becomes the foundation for the discursive analysis of this novel. But it seems that this factor is what the whole narrative ties itself to. Though, for clarity, one needs to specify that the emphasis is on this marriage only as it becomes a political act. The very nature of political marriages is the public purpose that is being sought through such an alliance.

Even after this marriage takes place, the Batswana continue to loathe the Masarwa and to pretend that Maru has died, but the Masarwa are liberated and we are told that "people like the Batswana, who did not know that the wind of freedom had also reached people of the Masarwa tribe, were in for an unpleasant surprise because it would be no longer possible to treat Masarwa people in an inhuman way without getting killed yourself."[37] Thus, racism goes underground, much as Maru and Margaret have done. Even though grounds are constructed for the liberation of the Masarwa people and it appears that everything will be fine, there seems to be a storm brewing at a personal and political level.

And, even though Maru has convinced Margaret of his love, there is impending danger of her surrender to the greater, voluntary love of Moleka. The marriage between these two rests on very precarious foundations, always threatened from the external world from which they banish themselves. Head writes that "there was nothing he could invent to banish the other room. He seemed to be its helpless victim and it was not much to his liking as jealousy was almost an insanity in him and the inspirer of it was nearly his equal."[38] Can the validity of this marriage only be understood outside the national boundary and in internally exiled circumstances? Can a fundamentally social institution, like marriage, exist in isolation? Their marriage contains strife simply because the internal reality of a marriage always reflects the external conditions of a sociohistorical milieu.

Moleka is part of that externality at a very threatening emotional level, like Margaret's identity as a Masarwa. Just as the Masarwa are external to the nation-state yet threaten its carefully constructed economies and hierarchies, the public sphere threatens the private life of Maru and Margaret. Maru's greatest fear is Moleka's prior claim to Margaret's love. And even though they never consult her except in Maru's hasty "rescue," he fears that "perhaps his heart was wrong and a day would come when he would truthfully surrender his wife to Moleka, because he had decided that Moleka's love was greater than his own."[39] There is a disturbing language of siege, surrender, and gender objectification here. One might well wish to know what the surrendered Margaret may want to say about it. This militaristic and gendered language is the backdrop of a marriage which can only exist on exilic, non-national ground, that is, in a displaced space. Thus this exile, in which both characters passively and actively collaborate, takes on a curiously sinister mood and seems only to be explained by a danger from the external material and emotional conditions prevailing in Dilepe, in the form of Botswana and Moleka.

The dichotomy of the external political reality of the conditions of the Masarwa and their internal liberation follows the same sort of pattern that Maru and Margaret's marriage sets up. Inner harmony and resolve of the Masarwa are being threatened by the hegemonic racist ideology of the Batswana. The possibilities of these potentially eruptive situations do not make for the promised harmony of the yellow daisies, except briefly and in total isolation and exile. But that aspect of the threatened harmony is not something that Head problematizes. Instead she makes the format of *Maru* as close to a fairy tale as she can possibly make it, in order to table any discussion of the problematics of the situation she creates.

Head may succeed in making this novel "so magical and beautiful" that even the author would want to read and reread it, but only on the surface. The moment this novel is examined as a novel about a certain kind of "prejudice," we see that only the surface is being skimmed and that the rest lies undiscussed, unchallenged. The possible marriage between Moleka and Margaret could have been extremely problematic because Moleka would never retreat from his position as a leader and totem of Dilepe. Maru, as Margaret's jealous husband, is always infuriated with Moleka. He thinks, "What did he want with a woman who meant nothing to the public? . . . Moleka would never have lived down the ridicule and malice and would in the end have destroyed her from embarrassment."[40] But at the same time Moleka would never have removed Margaret from the national public sphere that dominates his life and perhaps should have dominated hers. Perhaps that is the reason that such a marriage would have served as the symbol of liberation for both the Masarwa as well as the Masarwa woman, Margaret. The public sphere occupied by such a union would force the Batswana to examine their own prejudice. Maru, on the other hand, takes his pariah wife and, tail between his legs, disappears from view forever, much as an individual social tradition would demand.

Head steers away from the eventuality of Moleka and Margaret battling their love and traditional status publicly, which such a marriage would necessitate. She refuses, at any level, to make Margaret into an active sociopolitical national being within a sociohistoric context. The character Dikeledi is part of the foil created to banish Margaret from her social and political surroundings, the boundaries of which she is just managing to assess. Dikeledi also loves Moleka—and of course everyone has to be happily married off. Dikeledi's pregnancy is carefully orchestrated in order to neutralize Moleka's catatonic, nonsexual ardor for Margaret, because Maru demands that his sister be treated with more consideration than his rival's other mistresses.

The relationship between Moleka and Maru is the only real rivalry in the novel. Even though they have been friends and Moleka had always willingly given up the women who attracted Maru, in the name of friendship, Moleka's generosity dissipates as soon as the unsuspecting Margaret comes on the scene. They both try to outwit each other, but since Maru has far more patience and a very efficient system of spies, Moleka does not stand a chance. It seems, however, that Moleka was always the generous one in that relationship and not Maru. Maru never gives up anything for Moleka and is selfishly gleeful when Moleka spends the night with his sister.

What does this lack of generosity show about the character who is compared to a god and loved like a god, even though that love is never real? Maru seems to have an invalid's personality, which is demanding and does not tend to give anything back in return. He seems to fall under the category of his own criticism, "People who had nothing were savagely greedy. It was like eating endlessly."[41] He does seem to need a great deal of protection, and his spies and his friend Moleka want to "protect a personality too original to survive in an unoriginal world."[42]

The problem with that portrait of Maru is that, like Margaret, he is mythologized to such an extent that he does not remain a real god or chief or even a man. And it is only men and women, not myths, who inhabit national spaces. He seems to act at the most mundane level of petty jealousies, spies, and show of power over a Masarwa employee, Margaret. He seems to be competing with Moleka as any ordinary man would. He sees the effect that Margaret has had on Moleka: "It was like finding inside himself a gold mine he's not known was there before." And he immediately decides that he does not want Moleka to have this gold mine but wants it for himself. Head's choice of a metaphor for Margaret's soul pertains to the mercantile world and the allusion to gold mining is surprisingly unfortunate. Given the colonists' bloodthirsty tradition of the gold mines just across the border from Botswana, a South African writer could not afford even an innocent reference to gold. Yet, images of possession, ownership, and economic exploitation tend to dominate relationships in this novel.

Maru seems to be parasitic at yet another level. Sinister things happen to the women he has loved and left; they seem either to disappear altogether or go entirely mad; moreover, he is physically debilitated from his numerous loves. We are told that "those he wanted or loved became the slaves of an intensely concentrated affection."[43] This affection seems to bind the innocent victims of his attention tightly in a prisonlike, airless oppression, reminiscent of the airless room inhabited by the Masarwa. Of course, one can argue that his affection would be very flattering and healing for a young Masarwa woman who had received no affection from her guardian and only negative attention from her social status as a Masarwa. However, the question of whether his affection is any less negative remains a question posed metafictionally rather than as part of the narrative—by Head herself through implication. Even though it is implied that Maru and Margaret are a match for each other, one cannot help thinking that she might follow the same history the rest of his romantic connections stumbled into.

However, he does marry Margaret. How does that relate to his messiah status? Messiahs are generally revolutionary figures at a fundamental level, as is Maru. He is not like any paramount chief in the experience of the inhabitants of Dilepe. He is not enamored of his position though he takes full advantage of it. But his messiah status is more problematic and obviously of more interest to Head. When he first sees Margaret, who is shocked by the propensity for cruelty emanating from someone who looked like Dikeledi, he has a vision of taking a "dusty overgrown path" as opposed to the busy highways of life, highways that certainly would not cross Dilepe.

It seems as if that is what he has always needed in order to embark on his revolutionary career. His revolution is a private one because it entails rejecting the kingdom of public national social power for a kingdom of the "soul," where he can welcome the "new world." It takes a woman like Margaret, unsuspecting or otherwise, for Maru to recognize the bankruptcy of national social power. It is strange that he courts the social loathing he receives after his marriage: "He had planned for that loathing in secret," in order to be able to retreat into the realm of the mind because he suspects that it is richer than the one he is leaving.[44] Again, the private world of the mind simply cannot coexist with the world of social expectations. It seems to me that if he were preparing for a private life of the mind, then surely, much like Buddha, he should have renounced his link to all existing political and social institutions rather than escaping to a world where he continues to exercise his mastery over Margaret's slavery. If he is rejecting the social-national world, and that choice is often privileged in this novel, then the whole discourse of Masarwa oppression and liberation is unnecessary, for liberation can only take place within national and gender constructs.

Why Maru must evoke the loathing of his people is unclear, but his unhappiness and illness in the external national and social world, which delegated him power, speaks for his special visionary abilities. Head writes, "Previously . . . the reply had always been disrupted by people. People were horrible to him because they imagined that their thoughts and deeds were concealed when he could see and hear everything, even their bloodstreams and the beating of their hearts. If they knew all that he knew, would they not have torn him to shreds some time ago, to keep the world the way it was where secrets and evil bore the same names?"[45] Not only is Head introducing the idea of a pervasive evil in her paradise but Maru is presented as someone who needs to be protected from human pettiness. Moleka and all the others tend to defend him because they suspect his uncommonality in their midst. Head seems to elaborate messiah characteristics of knowledge beyond the visible. People seem to want to punish the kind of knowledge that Maru has. They wish to continue with their blindness about themselves and prejudice toward others. The connotations are that any disruption of tradition makes the rabble violent. Thus, Head is privileging the discourse of nation by focusing on Masarwa oppression usually ignored and initiated by chiefs. But she is also criticizing and minimalizing the same nation by underscoring the pettiness of all the individuals who are responsible for Masarwa oppression perpetuated by chiefs as they represent the Batswana nation. The commoners seem to be worse because even their leaders have to flee in order to "save" themselves from their people. Why would any Masarwa want to belong to a nation of pettiness and evil?

Maru is curiously aware of his role as savior: "Maybe some blot of human wrong had to happen to force Maru to identify himself with the many wrongs of mankind."[46] But, surely, in the light of his one political act, his marriage, this altruism is not sociopolitically viable, because it is debatable whether this public "political" act is not just a private one, especially after the perpetrator's disappearance.

He may have left the site of the loathing because he, along with his Masarwa bride, would have been "torn to shreds" had they stayed. All he is able to do is make a gesture, albeit one that is unusually belligerent against tradition, and he then escapes quickly to private and nonnational safety. Maybe Head has succeeded only in creating a figure who can cry "Wolf!" There is a suggestion that knowledge of unpleasant facts, like racist oppression, can alienate and exile people from their own cultural heritage. Maru acts on such knowledge and exiles himself before he is destroyed, but the Batswana pretend that Maru has died after his marriage because he is no longer a threat to anyone in Dilepe. Surely the pretense of his death neutralizes the one political as well as personal gesture that he makes in the entire novel.

Thus, does Head imply, through the narrative events, that racism can only be overcome at a personal level, never a political one? This marriage between a paramount chief and a Masarwa becomes privatized in the extreme after they leave. They do not even remain in the minds of people; the Masarwa use it as a politically liberating force but never really have any recourse to it because the newlyweds disappear immediately and seem to dwell forever in the land of "yellow daisies." Have racism and gender oppression really been overcome, even at a private level? Their marriage is never one between equals. Hasn't Margaret become the virtual and literal slave to Maru's affections as well as to his malicious manipulations, of which one sees an overabundance in his earlier dealings with Moleka and Dikeledi?

Isn't Head saying something grim about humanity that she does not say in her first novel, *When Rain Clouds Gather?* The implications that humans do not wish to be reminded of their evil is an accurate but dismal view. Head may have needed the stark contrast of good and evil that one generally finds in a fairy tale. But her choice of where that good and evil reside is interestingly different from her first novel. In her first novel, both goodness and evil could reside within national boundaries, and not in exile; for above all Makhaya wanted to "belong." Does Head mean to imply that exiles are always exiles no matter how circumstances are changed? Both Margaret and Maru remain exiles of one sort or another in spite of the unifying gesture of marriage.

It remains unclear why Maru leaves Dilepe. In a fit of passion he confronts his sister when she reminds him that he is paramount chief: "Has it not occurred to you that I might despise, even loathe them? Three quarters of the people on this continent are like Morafi, Seth and Pete—greedy, grasping, back-stabbing, a betrayal of all the good in mankind." [47] So it is with a knowledge of the identical loathing that people have for his difference, that he leaves. But his character certainly gives us pause because there is also something quite anarchic about him. Head writes, a little further on, about the voices of the gods that he hears; in turn, they enlighten him as he responds to them and thinks about the connotations of what they say to him. "That they were opening doors on all sides, for every living thing on earth, that there would be a day when everyone would be free and no one the slave of another? People no longer needed chiefs and kings and figureheads who wore dazzling garments." [48] His leaving may be a political decision stemming from the voices of his gods who told him that being a paramount chief was becoming obsolete, or so Head implies; like a deposed monarch, he goes off to a comfortable place, watched over by Pete, Seth, and Margaret.

The character of Maru is closer to the characters Head created in her third novel, *A Question of Power*. He seems to be a combination of good and evil, "half of him was a demon," coexisting with the godlike visionary who wants to "create a new world." This complexity, when Dikeledi is teasing him about proposing to the Masarwa schoolteacher, makes him state with perfect equanimity, "As for proposals, who else do you think would want to marry her, besides myself?" [49] This is at once a claim that only he is capable of seeing the beauty of her soul as well as an assertion that no one else, particularly not of his stature, has the gumption to take a socionational risk of that kind. *Maru* is a circular novel. Its beginning is the end of the dramatic action. Head writes, "He needed a puppet of goodness and perfection to achieve certain things he felt himself *incapable* of achieving. He could project the kind of creative ferment that could change a world, but he was not a living dynamo. She was. So was Moleka. All he wanted was the freedom to dream true dreams, untainted by the clamor of the world" (emphasis mine).[50]

Maru lacks the dynamism of a Margaret and a Moleka and needs them in order to dream his dreams, though "puppets" they remain. In Margaret, who "was a shadow behind which lived another personality of great vigour and vitality," Maru sees someone who would ensure "that I am never tempted to make a public spectacle of myself."[51] But as a gendered Masarwa being, Margaret would have no compunction about donating her vitality to him. He delegates the task of not being tempted, not to himself but to his wife's Masarwa status. Problematic as it is, Moleka's vitality seems to be tied to physical and social strength, whereas Margaret's is tied to being a Masarwa. Maru uses the energy of Moleka and Margaret in order to harness it for the good of *All*. At least that's what Head wishes to project. However, what happens is that Maru binds the two characters who are dynamic to his own needs and requirements and they are never able to explore the world without his interference. Moleka and Margaret are never allowed to confront each other about their love and Margaret is banished—exiled to a remote space much like a grateful Masarwa slave, subject only to the whims and fancies of the paramount chief, Maru.

Head seems to express ambivalence toward the idea or reality of slavery and racism. She tends to have no problems looking at Masarwa characters, or expressing their strength and dynamism, though she tends to imply that their greatest strength is in their oppressed status, which is almost an argument for the continued oppression of these people rather than their liberation. However, when she comes around to the actual lesson to be learned from the fairy tale, she seems to be as much on the outside looking into the oppression of the Masarwa as someone who is part of an oppressed group. This is how Head saw Margaret's role and often said so in her letters to Randolph Vigne.[52]

The characters in large part remain one-dimensional, especially Margaret who never comes off the page with the qualities that the author professes she has. Margaret does exactly the opposite in terms of her "consensual" exile into a place where she is forced to act out Maru's natural inclinations of leadership and not her own. If she is so dynamic, surely her strength is wasted in exile and her only reason for being there is the racism she has been formed, created, and invented by Head to combat. It is not far-fetched to assume that her only reason for going is to become a sort of a slave to yet another kind of classism. This time, she virtually becomes her husband's slave, who congratulates himself for marrying someone with "cans tied to her tail like the village dog." The assumption he makes—and perhaps Head does too—is that Margaret is useful only to him, not to herself or her own community. It is he who must make use of her as his kind have always made use of the Masarwa, much like the colonial White woman earlier made use of Margaret even though she raised her, and for want of any imagination she gave the girl her own name or identity. Head's ambivalence at yet another level becomes clear. She takes her heroine away in order to provide a peaceful life for her with a god, outside national constructs, but Margaret never chooses that. Maru and Head do. If my assumption is correct, it is ludicrous to talk about liberation from boundaries of "tribe, race and nation," because in the final analysis, those very boundaries remain unchallenged and monolithic in *Maru*.

If we are to regard Margaret as a useful instrument, then we have to examine the godly side of Maru's personality. The godly side of his nature is tied to the liberating revolutionary and messiah figure. The need for Margaret in Maru's life is linked to his growing awareness of the oppression of the Masarwa. Through her, he becomes aware of the nature of oppression and the consequent liberation. As Head writes, "But the conditions which surrounded him at the time forced him to think of her as a symbol of her tribe and through her he sought to gain an understanding of the eventual liberation of an oppressed people. . . . He had already awoken to the fact that mistreated people are also furious people who could tear him to shreds."[53] In the new order that Maru wants to bring about, his marriage to a Masarwa, a political act of another kind, would be an entirely positive affair. Perhaps the Masarwa woman to whom only he wishes to be conjugally linked will save him in the new proletarian order, the existence of which is imminent, as both Maru and Head imply.

But Head's interest in racism, in spite of her clear, volatile feelings about apartheid, remains entirely academic. Rather, hers is a general sweeping discourse: "How universal was the language of oppression! They had said of the Masarwa what every white man had said of every black man: 'They can't think for themselves. They don't know anything.' The matter never rested there. The stronger man caught hold of the weaker man and made a circus animal out of him, reducing him to the state of misery and subjection and non-humanity."[54]

Couldn't the same argument be made about Maru and Margaret and the national power structure implicit in that relationship from the start? Doesn't he exile her to a status very much like a circus animal's, with an audience of one, even though he takes her away from the hostile racism of the people of Dilepe? I do not believe that Margaret's complicity in Maru's design is any indication of how Maru plans to use her or whether she would be complicitous in that specific usage of her social status.

Even though, as Head points out, the language of oppression is universal, the national particularities cannot be undermined. The Masarwa, by Head's own admission, are economically handicapped. But she offers no analysis of what that means in the Botswana of today. Further, if economic viability is crucial to the liberation of oppressed peoples as they take their place in the nation, then Head's ambivalence becomes clear when she takes Margaret out of the job market and into, even a very advantageous, marriage. Margaret's exit from the economic marketplace is a setback for women in general and the Masarwa in particular.

However, there is a very hazy consciousness, on Head's part, of the can of worms that she has opened up. The more she tries to make this novel "magical and beautiful," the more glaringly problematic it looks. What Head relies on is her ambivalence toward the sleepy peace that a fairy tale (of a prince marrying a ragged Masarwa) evokes. She does not wish to look at the fact that if you belong to a minority you are exiled from national and gender discourses. Thus, "racism," as Head tries to suggest, does not only rely on the "lack of communication between the oppressor and the people he oppresses," though that is certainly a part of it, but rather it relies on the maintenance of economic and social dominance, that is, excluding the oppressed from nation spaces.

To imply that if only the Batswana knew that the Masarwa could "think" and "know," everything would be clarified, is part of the larger ambivalence that Head expresses toward the notion of racism in African societies. So, even though she says that the Masarwa would have to "fight" in order to overthrow the yoke of slavery, the way that fight is enacted is only at a personal level through the marriage of Maru and Margaret. Head wants and does not want to recognize the existence of racism in Dilepe. I believe that the question remains academic for her because she is never really able to slip "into the skin of a Masarwa person," as she claims she can. The validity of her novel comes from the wish fulfillment that a fairy tale potentially evokes.

Head usually talks in generalities of the oppressed people of the world and cites examples from the Hindu caste system. She speaks of what the Masarwa in general are being awakened to. But, we never hear what is happening in particular to the Masarwa community. One can plead for Head that this is a fairy tale; therefore generalities are enough. But when Head writes of Margaret, she fails to slip inside her skin. Margaret recedes into never-never land, a displaced non-national space where doubly exiled pariahs cannot live.

When Head talks about the reaction of the Masarwa people's response to their own liberation, at the end of the novel, she is very much the outsider looking in. She is looking at these odd people who are at last scratching their heads in wonder because they believed that they were half human and half donkey and now discover to their own and everybody's amazement that they are all too human.

But it is important to emphasize that this novel is remarkable in the questions that it is able to evoke in the postcolonial milieu about nations, leaders, laws, and oppressed, gendered peoples within those constructs. Perhaps Head's greatest contribution in this novel is a critique of the postcolonial nation as it is unable to have an equal society where oppressed voices can come to inhabit exiled space.

4

WOMEN'S IDENTITY AND A QUESTION
OF GOOD AND EVIL

To raise the question of identity is to reopen again the discussion on the self/
other relationship in its enactment of power relations. Identity as understood
in the context of a certain ideology of dominance has long been a notion that
relies on the concept of an essential, authentic core that remains hidden to
one's consciousness and that requires the elimination of all that is considered
foreign or not true to the self, that is to say, non-I, other.

—Trinh T. Minh-ha, "Not You/Like You"

IN HEAD'S novel, *A Question of Power,* about a protagonist going "mad," I
would like to invoke, for the purposes of my analysis, Michel Foucault's traveler, mad wo/man, and exile *par excellence.*[1] Traditionally and
historically "mad" men and women have always been believed to have
a deviant sexuality. Insanity often implied not being able to distinguish
right from wrong actions, including sexual actions. Insane women
were often thought to be nymphomaniacs. This idea is exemplified by
Head's exile, the madwoman and mother Elizabeth. In this autobiographical novel, Head tests the idea of how a colonized being with an
unfixed identity, an identity out of its normal mental and geographical
sphere, or what I have called the exilic consciousness, can "belong" to
evil institutions, such as apartheid.

For Head, questions of sexual identity, in relation to good and evil,
were integral to "dispossession." Even though, in large part, apartheid
determines the ultimate "Evil" for Head, what is interesting is the point
where individuals and the hierarchies they represent manifest evil de-

sign and intent. It is curious also that even though the exilic consciousness, which is Head's point of engagement, was privileged and was above reproach in both *When Rain Clouds Gather* and *Maru*, in *A Question of Power* she does not spare even the exile from what she has called a "workout" of the soul. She explores in this, her most important novel, the interiority of the exilic consciousness. In order to link the exilic consciousness to the collective consciousness of "universal brotherhood," the author tests the psychosexual foreground of Elizabeth's biographical reality. Head interlinks and interfaces questions raised by, of necessity, Janus-faced exilic identities with questions of evil and power, with the latter often used synonymously. For Head the ultimate issue is, How can an identity, committed to a profound humanism, come to belong to herself, to a community, and to the nation in which she is an exile?

Head's protagonist, Elizabeth, has been too hastily exiled to a nonplace by readers because her life seems to resemble the author's. I wish to argue that Head orchestrates the relationship of the author to the protagonist in order to discuss certain aspects of women's identities under patriarchies and apartheid. For example, Elizabeth's personal biography has brought the insider/outsider dialectic, which apartheid creates between White and Black South Africans, directly into the mechanisms of her psychosexual identity. For Head, this insider/outsider dialectic epitomizes the exilic principle and the evil in *A Question of Power* is balanced by this dialectic—the exilic principle. As Arthur Ravenscroft has perceptively, if unpopularly, stated, "The movement here . . . is into the vast caverns of interior personal experience. . . . But there is no confusion of identity between the novelist and the character."[2] It is important to remember the distinction made by Ravenscroft because, as Arlene Elder has pointed out, there is always imminent danger for women writers in general, especially Third World women writers, to be considered less serious because they are writing themselves—their autobiographies. My interest here is unrelated to issues of autobiography raised by Arlene Elder, Françoise Lionnet and Bella Brodzki and Celeste Schenck.[3] Instead I wish to develop the discourse on exile, which has been undermined by dismissive arguments about women's autobiography. Bessie Head herself tends to regard this novel in a specific socioautobiographical context and has said, "My third novel, *A Question of Power*, had such an intensely personal and private dialogue that I can hardly place it in the context of the more social and outward-looking work I had done. It was a private philosophical journey to the source of evil. I argued that people and nations do not realise *the point at which they become evil;* but once trapped in its net, evil has a powerful propelling motion into a terrible abyss of destruction. I argued that its form, design, and plan could be clearly outlined and that it was little understood as a force in the affairs of mankind" (emphasis mine).[4]

In Head's ideology there is no distinction to be made between the experiential agonies of political and personal biography. Even though *A Question of Power* is blatantly ambivalent about the notion of personal or political good and evil, it tends to inform Head's idea of the place of the individual in society as well as that same society's responsibility in regard to that individual. This dialogic phenomenon of interchange between the society and individual is particularly problematic when the individual exile represents consciousness in the process of trying to create a sociopsychological home within the boundaries of recognizable displacement, in short, trying to "belong" to another place at another time.

Elizabeth manifests great discomfort at her inadequacy in dealing with Batswana greetings. The disappointment she evokes in people because she is the only one who does not have "six hundred" relatives is felt poignantly by her as well as the person with whom she wishes to share a greeting. The evil in *A Question of Power* is balanced by the insider/outsider dialectic or the exilic principle. In other words, being an exile or outsider means that one must experience "dispossession" as an evil. Thus, it is no surprise that the novel opens with Elizabeth's discomfort with Batswana greetings. An African exile from a particular sociohistorical milieu, upon finding herself in another country which is not familiar psychologically, is sometimes the overt victim of racism and is the most likely candidate for mental breakdown. In addition, social behavior patterns determine and are indicative of a society.

One of the first things Elizabeth observes is her "outsider's" place in the scheme of the Batswana greeting: "It seemed to Elizabeth that it took people half an hour to greet each other each day. It took so long, they said, because Motabeng was a village of relatives who married relatives, and nearly everyone had about six hundred relatives. . . . People often looked at Elizabeth with a cheated air."[5] This is the kind of folkloristic information usually given to an outsider—an outsider who simply does not understand the social function of a particular culture's greeting. Head uses these devices so that the outsider has the possibility of understanding something that the members of that society have no need to explain to each other, if indeed there is an explanation handy. However, for Elizabeth the information becomes sinister because the language of exclusion distances the exile and exteriorizes her culture, language, and customs—the very components that make up her identity.

The sociopsychological effect on Elizabeth is puzzlement at first, but later it becomes part of the marginally alienated way in which an exile must learn to live. It must be odd when one cannot greet someone casually in the morning, especially another African, who may look a lot like oneself, without leaving them feeling cheated. Even though Head is using humor to describe a trivial situation, the results of this alienation are not so benign. Elizabeth does "go mad" and starts screaming abuse at her hosts and insisting that she is not like the "Bloody, Bastard Batswana."[6] The need to substantiate oneself as the exile by heaping abuse upon the society that excludes one and challenges one's sense of belonging has an adverse effect on Elizabeth. This cumulative psychological effect of exile is precariously balanced by Eugene, a minor character in *A Question of Power*. He tends to "help" other exiles like himself overcome the alienation by engaging them in the cottage industries project, which eventually becomes a form of political commitment for Elizabeth and saves her from total alienation.

The insider/outsider, reality and nightmare, phenomenon is intensified by the characters in this novel. They provide the interlinking between the society and the individual that makes the Sello and Dan of Elizabeth's imagination identical to the corresponding Motabeng characters who in actuality existed and who had a specific social standing. As Ravenscroft has stated, Dan and Sello form a polarity much like the Maru/Moleka one earlier. "Bessie Head makes one realize often how close is the similarity between the most fevered creations of a deranged mind and the insanities of deranged societies."[7] The echo of madness is always present. The characters who are based on real village people lend the narrative poignancy and immediacy which would not have been the case had they been entirely fictional.

In *A Question of Power*, there are three interrelated problems that

Head wishes to work out: sexual identity, personal and political questions of good and evil, and madness. In this chapter, I will show how these aspects are related to the exilic consciousness.

Sexual Identity

IN THIS novel, sexuality is part of an identity discourse determined by the exilic principle but the character of Medusa stands outside the bounds of recognizability in the Motabeng situation, as Dan and Sello do not. She represents Elizabeth's fear of her own sexuality and, thus, she is part of Elizabeth's sociosexual consciousness. The first set of confusions in Elizabeth's mind is related to the dichotomy between sex and language. Even though Medusa, in Elizabeth's nightmare, is the symbol of overabundant African exclusivity and sexual power, she is much more. Head evokes Medusa for her hypnotic charm, her harridan's power, and her mythological connection to her own and other women's sexuality; perhaps she is even the mother incarnate for her illusive yet seductive connection to Elizabeth's mother's deviance. She is the femme fatale. She first appears as the consort of Sello, but seems to be in perpetual competition with Elizabeth at all kinds of levels, constantly threatening the latter's sense of belonging and place as well as the space inhabited by her sexual identity. She tells Elizabeth in one of the nightmare visions:

> "We don't want you here. This is my land. These are my people. We keep our things to ourselves. You keep no secrets. I can do more for the poor than you could ever do. . . ."
> The wild-eyed Medusa was expressing the surface reality of African society. It was shut in and exclusive. It had a strong theme of power-worship running through it, and power people needed small, narrow, shut-in worlds.[8]

It is obvious in this passage that Elizabeth's greatest fear is one of not belonging socially or sexually as an African among other Africans; added to that is the fear of not being wanted or claimed by other Africans as Medusa suggests. Charles Larson's dated oversimplification of Elizabeth's sexuality in A Question of Power is sexist and reductive rather than illuminating. It is not that Elizabeth is "disturbed about her physical appearance . . . [and] fears that men are not physically attracted to her," or that the "failure of her marriage also contributes to her . . .

sexual guilt," but rather she is afraid of her own sexuality.[9] After all, Medusa is a creation of her own mind.

For somebody whose land has been taken away by other colonizers, Elizabeth is very sensitive about the land issue, and that is a real enigma for her because it directly confronts the problem of an identity that cannot belong to a geographical place or to her own subjectivity. For Head the materiality of "land" coincides with sexuality and identity. Even though she is afraid of the "surface reality" of Africa she is sufficiently threatened as an outsider to feel exiled in the new community. She feels very ambivalent about not belonging in the "narrow, shut-in worlds," with whose magical allure Medusa constantly tantalizes her.

Gradually Medusa's attacks on Elizabeth become more sexual and more personally corrosive, bridging the gap between the personal and political identity. Head writes,

> She had some top secret information to impart to Elizabeth. It was about her vagina. Without any bother for decencies she sprawled her long black legs in the air, and the most exquisite sensation travelled out of her towards Elizabeth. It enveloped Elizabeth from head to toe like a slow, deep, sensuous bomb. . . . Then she looked at Elizabeth and smiled, a mocking superior smile:
> "You haven't got anything near that, have you?"

This experience is overwhelming in the quality of its seduction and in terms of its rejection of Elizabeth. She describes the experience as "falling into deep, warm waters, lazily raising one hand and resting in a heaven of bliss."[10] This is obviously a very pleasant kind of sexual experience for Elizabeth and birthing images are used, without the violence of expulsion, to describe the sensual feelings. In "Stabat Mater," Kristeva would imply that it is through this birthing that Elizabeth's sexuality allows her to become one with the mother, but of course in her case this fundamental right becomes an elusive luxury since the mother's sexuality is defined by absence.[11] Here, Elizabeth chooses an African mother to birth her, even though in reality her mother was White, but later it is the same African mother who betrays her and gives birth to her. For Elizabeth, betrayal and love coexist in any manifestation of sexuality. Both Elizabeth and her mother seem to be lovers and competitors as well as mother and child. The "sensuous bomb" seems orgasmic in proportion. Here, Head's writing is very reminiscent of how Hélène Cixous exhorted women writers to "Write! Writing is for you, you are for you; your body is yours, take it. . . . Your body must be heard."[12]

Head seems to participate in the explosion of women's awareness of themselves and does what Cixous counsels women writers to do. Her protagonist is living through her body and sexuality in order to understand the connection that is denied to her by both Medusa's and Africa's rejection because she is Coloured. For Medusa would not deliberately remind her of her alien status if indeed the boundaries were not being gradually eroded by the discovery that Elizabeth experiences through her body and the connection of that body to that of the mother or Medusa's African body. This process presumes a reclamation which in my analysis of *A Question of Power* never takes place. The desire to reclaim the banished woman's body and identity grows in Elizabeth who is slowly becoming aware of her problematic connection to Africa as well as her own African body. Elizabeth is not a "voyeur," but rather one dispossessed of her own body and sexuality who experiences in passivity—but experience she does.

When Elizabeth's psyche experiences Medusa's rejection at a sexual-lingual level the whole process of an exile's reclamation begins. Prophetlike, Cixous counsels women: "Women must write through their bodies, they must invent the impregnable language that will wreck partitions, classes and rhetorics, regulations and codes, they must submerge, cut through, get beyond the ultimate reserve-discourse, including the one that laughs at the very idea of pronouncing the word 'silence,' the one that aiming for the impossible, stops short before the word 'impossible' and writes it as 'the end.'"[13]

Medusa forces Elizabeth into the process of an exile's urgent need to reclaim her body through language in order to seek her lost, primary fundamental "home." Thus Elizabeth follows her birthing mother to madness. Cixous's "impregnable language," in Elizabeth's context, can only mean a language that has been spoken through the "Third World" woman's body and sexuality and which can be applicable only as it demands and is in process of searching for that sense of identity and belonging. For this language invites itself to be appropriated, through inclusion in discourses that define and communicate Elizabeth's relationship to African languages and African sexuality. Audre Lorde has spoken about the power of the erotic, and, for Elizabeth, Medusa is terrifying because she confronts Elizabeth with her own erotic power and desire. Thus Elizabeth's exchange with Medusa, competitive as lovers are competitive, also suggests the beginning of the definition of discourse for the sexually and socially exiled woman.

When Medusa shows Elizabeth her vagina it is also a way of showing Elizabeth a dimension of her own sexuality which seems shellshocked after her primary and secondary sexual relationships are destroyed through taboos enforced in apartheid South Africa. Elizabeth's mother's sexuality, and here I assume that the sexual connection between a mother and especially a daughter is implicit, becomes an icon for her own.[14] In her "journey," Elizabeth has discovered that her White mother had had a deviant sexuality, as her own husband does later. There are strong implications of "unnatural" promiscuity when sexual relationships between Whites and Blacks are mentioned, which the Immorality Act presupposes. One sees the same sort of promiscuity in Elizabeth's husband. His is manifested through both homosexual and heterosexual contact with countless partners. In fact he seems to have sex with anyone who is willing and suggests it to people who are unwilling.

Her withdrawal from and fear of her mother's madness and sexuality and her husband's promiscuity is perhaps understandable, but it does sit festering in her psyche. When Medusa approaches her in a homosexual gesture, she experiences great pleasure and her sexuality is "reborn," even though it is rejected because her own vagina is "nothing" compared with Medusa's. And, as psychoanalysis tells us, the primary sexual focus is always on the mother. For Elizabeth, Medusa is both mother and lover. Later, the same sort of experience occurs when Dan's heterosexual gesture makes her feel like an "ancient goddess of love." She is overwhelmed, but her craving for primary sensual and sexual pleasure in the context of love is never fulfilled even by her own mother. It is only through a physical and lingual reclamation that she can hope to experience primary sexuality first as a craving felt through Medusa's attack and then through Dan's seduction. Even though she has experienced acute pleasure and knows mentally that it can exist in the context of love ("Love is two people mutually feeding of each other") she herself is never to experience it simultaneously.[15]

What is important is that she is able to negotiate a language of sexual pleasure within the confines of love through interiorizing her external experience.

Later, she does, however, experience the nonsexual love of Tom, Birgitte, and Kenosi and the sexual, if extremely threatening and problematic, attentions of Dan and Medusa. Even though Medusa rejects Elizabeth's sexuality, she introduces into Elizabeth's sexual discourse a possibility that haunts her through out the novel. Elizabeth, however, continues not to give the sexual part of her identity any immediate credence or space, constantly denying its importance in spite of her sexual nightmare. Head writes as an explanation after Medusa's attack, even though in the context, her response is unbelievable: "But it was not maddening to her to be told she hadn't a vagina. She might have had but it was not such a pleasant area of the body to concentrate on, possibly only now and then if necessary."[16]

Here we see Elizabeth's great reluctance to become engaged with the experiential discourse of her sexuality, but obviously the effect this has on her is devastating and "maddening." Elizabeth admits that when she was told about her own and Medusa's vagina in its relationship to African languages by the latter, she "had her first mental breakdown." Head writes,

> But Medusa's next assault pulled the ground right from under Elizabeth's feet. She fell into a deep hole of such excruciating torture that, briefly, she went stark, raving mad.
> Medusa said: "Africa is troubled waters, you know. I'm a powerful swimmer in troubled waters. You'll only drown here. You're not linked up to the people. You don't know any African languages."[17]

Even though Elizabeth can dismiss the sexual assault and rejection, often not with the greatest impunity, she cannot disregard the utter alienation and exile into which Medusa's sexual-lingual attack thrusts her. It is no accident that the threat of linguistic and geographic banishment comes right after the sexual rejection. Both of these seem to be such vital components of any understanding of one's identity—an identity constantly misunderstood and threatened in exile, almost as if the facts connected to an identity, Elizabeth's identity, are deliberately kept at bay.[18]

Sexual displacement entails a theoretical recognition of how crucial the discourse of sexuality is to the formation of one's identity and how imperative it is to understand the exilic in that context. Thus the reclamation of an exile's sexuality into the identity spaces, which she is bringing into being is an incorporative "gesture of belonging." Monique Wittig, with some concurrence and some criticism from Judith Butler, has claimed that subversive sexual identities, such as lesbian sexual identities, do not fall into the categories of the heterosexual exchange. Therefore lesbians cannot be said to have a "sex," since that gender category is defined through heterosexual divisions. However, Butler and many other feminists have claimed a place for the subversive within the "norm." Given the sexual politics associated with the Immorality Act, and Elizabeth's and her parents' sexual history is no exception, the subversive—the exilic identity—tends to fall into a social "norm" even if it is the norm only in minute part.[19]

As one perceives in *A Question of Power*, even though Elizabeth constantly undermines and refuses to recognize its importance, sexuality is tied to her exilic identity and keeps cropping up in different forms. Her motherhood, which is perhaps the only aspect of her sexuality that is most readily acceptable in Motabeng, is problematic also. Since she is a single mother, she cannot have a nervous breakdown without first making sure that Shorty is well taken care of. Her own mother was sent to an insane asylum and simply could not claim her motherhood as Elizabeth is able to do later. This is one of the places where the White "privileged" mother and the Black outcast child can meet, that is, in their capacity as mothers. For Kristeva, female desire to incorporate the maternal identity can be realized through either poetic language or through becoming a mother oneself. Becoming a mother in its fullest sense is a very difficult task for Black mothers and mothers of Black children to accomplish in South Africa. Both Elizabeth and her mother have to struggle to be mothers. The White mother can be a mother only as a taunting absence, whereas the Black mother, Elizabeth, can claim her motherhood only through great mental and emotional turmoil. Thus, the mother's sexual identity becomes the most problematic part of this novel and keeps reemerging even though Head steadily tries to submerge it. In my analysis, that evasion is indicative of Head's view of her protagonist's sexual identity and Elizabeth's need to escape it in exile. The problem of sexuality is never resolved through acceptance of subversiveness but rather through Elizabeth's rejection of the self which manifests sexuality. Thus the idea of sexual "pleasure" both hetero and homosexual *jouissance* are abruptly negated by the "gesture of belonging" instead of being incorporated into it.

Elizabeth's own immediate biographical and historical existence is riddled with the problematics of sexual relations between races intensified by apartheid and the power structures it tends to nurture and in turn to pathologize. In Elizabeth's case the psyche tends to link madness and sexuality, for her mother is punished with madness when she expresses a deviant subversive sexuality. The consequences of such an act, considered socially unacceptable, leaves enormous amounts of power in the hands of a society responsible for meting out judgment and punishment. Society could take away your womanhood as it is an affirmation of your sexuality and/or motherhood. The discomfort Elizabeth feels is different from the punishment meted out to the mother and to the "nonexistent" father. She is looking back, however, at the actions of her parents, which predetermined her own historical biography and later, in exile in Motabeng, her sexuality and motherhood as well.

First, the Black "stable boy, who was a native," disappears completely from the consciousness of the reader and the writer's novel. It is odd that the myth that a racist society would inculcate is nurtured by Elizabeth as well, for she never looks for her Black father. It seems that her father's disappearance argues a nonappearance of the male factor, which denies Elizabeth's mother's sexuality, in a way, forcing her to give "virgin birth" and making the presence of the "stable boy" superfluous. The absence of the father is reinstated by Elizabeth's lack of interest in him—the Black father made absent through apartheid. Elizabeth's birth ties her as a daughter to her mother's absence more than to a presence of an African father in the past. He becomes invisible whereas the White mother becomes a symbol of bravery even in her absence and perhaps because of it. Elizabeth is tied to her mother's sexuality and madness much more than to the existence of an African father who was perhaps forced to disappear without knowing that he was to become a father.

The silent disappearance of the Black African father is part of South African history that is interrupted and forgotten, which informs Elizabeth's concept of her exiled sexual identity. Her unwillingness to engage in the constantly reemerging challenge of the sexual-lingual discourse imposed on her by Medusa testifies to the grave discomfort she feels at being forced to confront issues related to her exile's sexual identity. How is it that the child of an African father can be attacked in Africa for a lack of connection to African people? Why is it that she speaks no African languages? Her own position in this regard is nebulous. The connection with the White parent, which is the most economically and psychologically enduring, is the very aspect of her identity that alienates her completely from the people she wants to claim in Motabeng. The lack of any spoken African languages, with which Medusa taunts her, is again the accidental reaffirmation of only one part of her parentage and does not include the other.

Later, she embodies Medusa's rejection and says to the nurses in the hospital, "I'm not an African. Don't you see? I never want to be an African. You bloody well, damn well leave me alone!"[20] When under emotional pressure, Elizabeth tries to annihilate her identity completely from the African part because it is too troublesome and generally comes with enormous expectations which she does not think she can meet. She does assume Medusa's compelling suggestion, for she thinks that her denial is going to absolve her from her responsibilities as an African. This never happens and the more she tries to run away from this crucial aspect of her personality the more it tends to confront her. Interestingly, she is restored to sanity the moment the White doctor sees her as a "comrade racialist."[21] This abruptly brings her back to an acceptance of her loyalties to Black South Africans and, by extension, the Batswana.

After Medusa is expelled from the nightmare life of Elizabeth, though the entrances and exits are never explained or predictable, an even less benign figure takes her place in Elizabeth's consciousness. Dan seems to be excess incarnate, but again his seduction is sexual and subtle, just as evil is supposed to be seductive, without anyone, least of all the subject, identifying it as evil. Head writes,

> He bent right down to the floor and kissed her toes. As he removed his mouth a warm glow remained on the area he had touched. It changed the atmosphere drastically. . . . More than anything, the extreme masculinity of the man instantly attracted her . . . no one personally loved her

or touched her in a way as to invoke physical sensations. The man placed his mouth on her hand. The most exquisite sensation passed from him to her . . . it was a heightened ecstasy.

She debated a moment with herself: "I ought to find out more about this." . . .

He kissed as firmly and decisively as the way he had grasped her around the waist. . . . He made a woman feel like an ancient and knowledgeable queen of love.[22]

Elizabeth's seduction is physical and sexual. It provides Dan with a carte blanche access into the interiority of her "deranged," derailed mind. Her sexual awakening in this passage is testimony to the "journey" she is taking from being an exiled identity to an individual who is aware of all aspects of that exile and is coming to a realization of how halting a place that must be. When she says she "ought to find out more about this," the "this" refers to her capacity to find and experience pleasure or, as Kristeva would say, "jouissance." She takes the plunge in spite of her past experiences, which alienated her from her sexuality as well as the sexuality of both White and Black South Africans.

In the scheme of her "insanity," the desire for understanding "the point" where things become evil subordinates Elizabeth's discourse on sexuality while remaining an inherent part of it. Sexuality often becomes the vehicle for understanding one's identity and has obvious allure for identity discourses. Which is precisely why it formulates a part of Elizabeth's breaking down process. Sociohistorically, societies have been often recorded as becoming corrupt through an examination of the sexual practices which were prevalent at the transitionary periods. Thus, sexuality itself takes on excessive proportions and nightmare qualities, but sexuality also becomes a vehicle for understanding individual and societal "insanity." Inherent to Elizabeth's "journey" is the foreground of her parents "subversive" sexuality. Dan, or as Elizabeth learns later, Dan as a guise of Satan, permeates her life with perverse sexual contact with his "nice time" girls. She cannot participate, but even as just a witness she is overwhelmed and remains for a long time a passively outraged bystander to his numerous sexual encounters. In spite of his onslaught and her weakened emotional condition she tends to regard some of the characters in the drama he imposes on her with great sympathy simply because they are "sad"-looking women. Or as Margaret E. Tucker has stated: "Head disarms the abject by making everyone, including the reader, a part of it." Elizabeth's sympathies for Dan's "nice time" girls are very insightful especially from someone who is taken up with her own turmoils. Her observations are interesting in terms of the discourse about female sexuality and solidarity. Tucker further adds, "He [Dan] seems to be asking her both to see herself reflected in these women (woman as womb, woman as whore) and to see herself as lacking something that they have, sexual power possession of Dan."[23] It is clear that the scenes with Dan and his many women are not about women's sexuality, but only about his overabundant power and prowess and as he represents evil.

The quality of the nightmares themselves are linked to sinister aspects of human evil. For instance in Dan's transition from God to Satan, there is an introduction to the most nightmarish topic for mothers, that of child molestation. The emergence of this particular evil is somehow related to the idea of Elizabeth's precarious motherhood and is thus integral to her sexuality. The fear of being abandoned as a child is linked to the very real possibility of abandoning her own child because of her periodic illnesses, and, thus, to what seems like the exaggerated fear that Elizabeth seems to manifest toward her own and other people's sexuality.

Further, it is important to realize that it is her sexuality and the seductive relationship with Dan that keeps Elizabeth in a situation that disallows her, for a long time, to identify the "point" at which her relationship with him turns visibly from good to evil. Head writes about this seduction: "When he talked of love to her there was a pathetic appeal in his tone. His love was exclusive, between her and him alone. They ought to be silently wrapped up in it, with no intruders. The pathetic appeal had a corresponding appeal in her. He'd flung a hook right into her pain- and feeling-centre."[24] Elizabeth's first contact with Dan and his later reaffirmation of the earlier seduction leave her entirely confused in regard to her own sexuality. He offers exclusivity in a tone of "pathetic appeal" which she can never resist because it meets a similar "appeal" and need in her and this also keeps her mesmerized and controlled by the sexual punishment he deliberately inflicts on her. The "corresponding appeal" in her, for him, is identical to what Head says about power in relation to governments and individuals. The process always begins with a desire for change which later turns into desire for power over the individual and thus becomes corrupt and evil. The punishment, which Dan starts inflicting on Elizabeth, begins by his putting the phonograph records on in her head and also by bringing on an enormous variety of women into her house, her very bed. There is a corresponding level of intimacy that Elizabeth develops with his and his entourage's sexuality, for it occurs relentlessly as she tries to sleep in a bed she can no longer call her own. He lets her know that these women are sexually more appropriate for him than she could possibly be and that each of them has a specific sexual characteristic that he needs in order to fulfill his own overabundant sexual needs and desires. However, he keeps Elizabeth hooked on his love and that is one of the major delusions that she has to work through during her "insanity" in order to come to terms with the questions related to good and evil and to resolve the dichotomies of her exilic consciousness. Elizabeth does figure out, almost in spite of herself, the sinister aspect of Dan's seduction: "If Dan hadn't been such a hard spitter (he spat with glorious contempt at things he dominated) she might have permanently made excuses for the other side of his song. As it was, she said: 'I might have died under the illusion that I loved him.'"[25]

Ultimately he is more sinister and destructive to her psyche than Medusa, because the latter was clearly aggressive from the start, and knowing one's enemy helps one not to be seduced by any mirage. But Dan, on the other hand, offers everything ambiguously, first pretending that he "loves" her, with an extremely seductive gesture, and then indicating various promises that he almost immediately contradicts by humiliating her sexually through his bevy of women and his exclusive sexual, rather than love, interests. Medusa is not the "other." She inhabits part of Elizabeth's consciousness as a manifestation of "self-loathing" or "self-contempt," and in Elizabeth's case it is loathing and fear of her sexuality, connected to her mother and to her past. Medusa also represents the erotic power that Elizabeth shies away from. Dan is the other, his sexuality is different from the object of his seduction, Elizabeth. Therefore the discourse takes on a separate hue from the first one. Perhaps the life-and-death struggle between Elizabeth and Medusa is more dismissable, at one level, than the one she has with Dan simply because she fears patriarchal betrayal more than a betrayal springing from the matriarchy as represented by a very contemptuous mythical female figure—the archetype of seduction and betrayal. Medusa is the first to tease out the possibility of a sexual-lingual dialogue between the terribly betrayed exile and the male betrayer, Dan, one whose betrayal Elizabeth expects yet whose support she craves.

The connection between Head's discourse on sexual and exilic identity is in the "gesture of belonging." In Elizabeth's extreme reluctance to expel Dan from her mental dialogue with her identity is the desire to belong—to belong sexually to someone; especially as that is an extension of belonging to a community. And, as we have seen earlier, his seduction of her is complete. She is the "ancient goddess of love." For someone to "belong," at last, to even a stereotypical sexual image of herself, projected by an "African" man, is extremely alluring. It is through the acceptance of this African man that she hopes to be "African," and for a long time does not realize that he is also instrumental in her losing ground completely in order to regain it completely in that last "gesture of belonging." For it is through her seduction by him that she becomes witness to unspeakable sexual evil. In Head's context real belonging can occur only after gaining knowledge of both good and evil.

Medusa becomes a symbol of the division between Elizabeth and her mother and manifests that unified yet divided sexuality, problematic as it is. She is also indicative of m/other Africa who betrayed her children through colonialism, but that too falls in the limit of Elizabeth's internal comprehension. However, when Dan brings other women into Elizabeth's bed and mind and constantly uses them to betray her, that act of betrayal is sexually and socially external to Head's protagonist and thereby harder to negotiate into her conscious identity. As Tucker states, "Fragmenting her [Elizabeth's] mind is much like dissecting her body; both deny her wholeness and any sort of power."[26] After all, Medusa shows her her own vagina whereas Dan shows her the sexual capacities of innumerable women, thus objectifying Elizabeth's own sexuality. She has not remained the "ancient goddess of love" but has instead become a symbol of sexual inadequacy and abuse. It is interesting and perhaps part of the historical discourse between men and women that even though she expels Medusa, a woman, she is unable or unwilling to expel Dan till the end of the novel. The difference in betrayal emerges out of "herstorical" female consciousness. This consciousness is connected both with the female body and traditional historical patriarchal betrayal of female sexuality.

It is interesting that Elizabeth goes through both kinds of "journeys" and the bisexual consciousness that emerges from this journey is partly an evasion of sexuality and a craving for fulfillment in the context of exclusive sexuality and love. This desire for exclusivity, as I will show, later translates into what Head develops as "universal brotherhood," after rejecting certain kinds of manifest "politics." The movement is toward a final rejection of Dan and the key to her sexual identity that he pretends to hold. This earlier desire for love is replaced by a higher desire for love as it can exist between people devoid of sexuality, like her love for Tom and Kenosi.

Thus, when Medusa exteriorizes Elizabeth's sexuality, exiling her from her place of residence, Botswana, the battle is clear to Elizabeth. Medusa taunts her about her physical and linguistic un-Africanness and exiles her sexually and linguistically from Botswana, where she wants to belong. These sorts of exile are based on semifacts. She has no way of claiming that what Medusa and later Dan are attacking is really a pseudoconsciousness and does not realize that she "belongs" till the end of the novel. Dan and Medusa manipulate her insecurity about "belonging" to Africa. It is, however, true that Elizabeth is not linked sexually or linguistically with anyone in Botswana, which exacerbates her exile, her dispossession. At the same time she knows that she is not linked up to the people of Botswana in those specific ways. But when Dan seductively offers to change that by giving her exclusive sexual attention and love and then takes it away in increasingly nightmarish cycles of giving and promising and professing and then snatching it away and humiliating her, she is completely hooked and does not want to see his initial betrayal. He is villainous only in that he represents subjective polarity, the "inappropriate other in every I."[27] She is physically debilitated and going "insane," which makes it hard for her not to hope passively that his earlier promises would not resurface immediately. Ultimately he erodes her sense of self or identity, which is linked to her desirability as a woman, her status as an "ancient goddess of love," and as a dispossessed "member" of a culture which was not her birth right.

Elizabeth's response to this abuse seems to follow the pattern of research done on battered women who often assume that the violence would stop or was caused by external pressures and would not occur if conditions were better or if they were better wives and mothers.

Elizabeth keeps hoping to get back to the earlier point in Dan's seduction where "love is two people mutually feeding each other" and not one torturing the other relentlessly. She is unable to escape Dan's inflictions because he is seductive but nonetheless a phantom of her mind, and phantoms, by definition, are inescapable. When she was unhappy in South Africa, after she married, with the promiscuity of her husband, she took her small boy and left for Botswana, but she is incapable of escaping Dan even in an asylum six hundred miles from Motabeng, where he first starts persecuting her. He seems to be "of" her, belonging to her, phantomlike, just as she belongs to him.

It is, however, possible that Elizabeth suffers from delusions, especially after Dan starts tampering with her mind. Head writes, "He'd pick on people she met in daily life, always introducing a vivid, indelible fact about their sex lives, so abruptly, so unexpectedly that her daily contacts were reduced to that one fact. The persistent picking on people she met in her daily life totally demoralized her."[28] These delusions manage to control her contact with friends, acquaintances, and strangers but she is so debilitated by this onslaught of seeing the world as "evil" that for a long time she does nothing about it and later describes this period as an exploration in the heart of evil. For instance, part of her nightmare phobia is a paralytic fear of homosexual men. Head's own attitude to male homosexuality is never clear but Elizabeth describes her experience in finding out about her husband's homosexuality. For her, her husband is manifesting social perversity and promiscuity, and then later she has a vision of homosexual men dying en masse. This vision is "prophetic" given the AIDS virus which it predated. But when Dan starts saying that her friend Tom is potentially homosexual, she is jolted into asking Tom his feelings on the subject while carefully watching his reactions. Part of her "insanity" is not being able to count on the predictable "goodness" of those around her, and it is clearly irrelevant what the specific unpredictability is. Thus, in the scheme of her insanity, Tom's supposed homosexuality or Mrs. Jones being a procuress for her daughters is relevant only in that they are, for Elizabeth, manifestations of "Evil."

Her fear of homosexuality is as great as her fear of her own sexuality because she engages in that discourse obliquely and only as it relates to her understanding of good and evil. Toward the end of the novel, she dismisses her sexuality and seeks another kind of "belonging." Earlier, in an ironic twist, without seeing the implications, she tells Kenosi that if she were a man she would marry her. But she can say that because she is making this offer without the connotations of sexuality, although many readers in the 1990s believe that they can perceive homophobia in *A Question of Power*. As I pointed out earlier, there does seem to be fear and sexual ambivalence on the part of the protagonist in this novel about several questions relating to sexuality and language as it informs primary emotions, aspects of which remain unresolved till the very end of the novel.

The discourse on "perverse" sexuality is not entirely separate from Elizabeth's relationship to sexuality in general. Even though Medusa and Dan introduced her to the possibility of experiencing pleasure, she was never wholly comfortable with that aspect of her identity and later simply terminates the dialogue partly because it has been so brutal but also partly because she is unable or unwilling to trust an expenditure of any energy on the erotic, which has let her down. However, the power of the erotic is the journeying ground for her exteriorizing individual and institutional good and evil in Southern African society. But, ultimately, Elizabeth only interiorizes that dialogue and instead of having a somewhat coherent discourse on female sexuality as it subverts and is subverted by good and evil manifestations of power, we have an author's reluctance to extend the subject. Thus, even though there is a ground-breaking scenario of Janus-faced interrelations drawn between sexuality and the power of good and evil, unfortunately the discourse on sexuality gets eliminated from the question of power.

At the end of the novel, the resolution of the problematics of sexuality are wound down, in this explicit novel, in a disappointing way. After Elizabeth comes out of the mental institution, Tom suggests that she find a husband to protect her from her solitude. Tom's solution is one-dimensional in its patriarchal implications but her reply is characteristic. She tells him that "it's not part of my calculations." On the next page, she rejects her sexuality entirely: "The model stood up and turned to face Elizabeth. They were identical replicas except that what stood before Elizabeth was a demon of sensuousness. She had thick, swollen, sensual lips. She rolled her eyes with mock innocence. . . . She oozed horror and slime."[29] What she is rejecting is the extreme, such as Dan's sexuality, and she does not distinguish it from perversion. Even though Dan has tried to make the real Elizabeth superfluous in order to destroy her, in her rejection of Dan as Satan, she also rejects her own sexuality because it has never been allowed to exist except as an adjunct to Dan or earlier to Medusa. In making him superfluous in her life, she has to terminate the dialogue she began with her own sexuality because it had become polluted by his pervasive and perverse desires.

In *A Question of Power*, the discourse on sexuality goes only so far. It is as if when the dialogue gets interesting, Head withdraws her own earlier interest in it. One can say that this is understandable given her ambivalence about her own sexuality and its sociobiographic inception, but that would be simply settling for less, as Elizabeth does. The sensuous and erotic aspects of her identity begin to terrify Elizabeth. When she realizes that she wants to be sexually fulfilled, she is repulsed by her own desires, ultimately rejecting part of her identity. This rejection becomes another part of the gendered exilic consciousness and it is this same consciousness that negotiates a place of "belonging" but never without a heavy price. For Elizabeth the price of belonging to a community erases the possibility of belonging to the sexual aspect of her identity. Precisely in her longing to belong, she dispenses with any aspect of what she perceives as individual or social disharmony; for sexual desire suggests disharmony to her. The model for sexual desire must be rejected because it represents individual excess. It is almost as if Elizabeth has either absorbed patriarchal obtuseness about women's sexuality or is too threatened to implicate her own identity with any aspect of tumult. Even though Head wishes to incorporate female sexuality as part of the mechanics of belonging to self and community, she withdraws at the eleventh hour.

Personal and Political: Questions of Good and Evil

SIMULTANEOUS with the desire to throw the doubly oppressive yoke of being a colonized African and a woman aside is the enormous sexual and social guilt at belonging in part to the White oppressor. After all, Elizabeth had a White mother and no "African languages." Medusa informs her, "'You see, that's what you are like,' she said. 'That's your people, not African people. You're too funny for words. You have to die like them.'"[30] Identity, thus, is reduced only to a question of belonging and does entail, despite our earlier suspicions, a question of exploration. Suddenly finding herself in a position where she had to defend herself against this onslaught, Elizabeth starts apologizing in a guilty way for being a Coloured from South Africa: "'I'm not like that. I've never been a racialist. Of course I admit I'm Coloured. I'm not denying it. I'm not denying anything. Many people who are Coloureds are quite nice too, just like Africans.'"[31] This engagement is indicative of Head's intense desire to be part of a universal personality so she can get away from definitions that pigeonhole her. She is acutely aware of the political condemnation of Medusa. She is paralyzed and goes "mad" because Medusa, her harridan mother, challenges her desire and ability for doing "good" in Botswana, for she has tainted blood. Elizabeth embodies not only un-Africanness in her heritage but the racism of the mother's family. Sello's Africanness is also described on the first page of *A Question of Power*, as "almost incidental," that is, accidental but not of crucial importance. For Elizabeth, a question of belonging rests on a desire both to appropriate and disown her Africanness at the same time.

As Head does not make too clear a distinction between communal and individual suffering, it is not surprising that in the foregoing passage she tends to use those two categories interchangeably. Societies and nations "do not realize the point at which they become evil," and for Head, individual and social madness ensues from this inability for self-criticism and perhaps self-knowledge, what Paulo Freire has called "critical consciousness," which, in the last analysis, can and does in Elizabeth's case lead to what Head termed "a terrible abyss of destruction."[32] Elizabeth's critical consciousness is manifest in her awareness of the individual self as it relates, belongs, and is responsible to the community but is dismissive of the self that seeks to be fulfilled as a sexual woman. She can accept the self that grows beautiful vegetables for the Motabeng community and not the other, for it seeks to understand and fulfill just itself.

The "point at which they become evil" comprises Head's most profound engagement with individuals and hierarchies. These individuals and institutions are responsible for the evil of imposing exile—a state of nonbelonging on others. She explores such a "point" where the personal and political coincide. In *A Question of Power*, internal madness, especially a nervous breakdown, is in some way linked to external societal madness. As Ravenscroft has pointed out, Head shows us the close similarity between "a deranged mind and the insanities of deranged societies." Head's understanding of personal and psychological turmoils comes from her knowledge of social ills and the individual's relationship to those power structures, which informs her analysis of power. Head's main concern is with exclusion as an evil phenomenon. For her apartheid was such an exclusionary evil. As Linda Susan Beard has remarked, "With an idiosyncratic omnidexterity that has rendered her writing anything *but* transparent to those who have read her work, Head's revisionary prose undermines the binary madness—the formulaic antitheses—that long centuries of *de facto* apartheid begat long decades of *de jure* apartheid."[33]

Foucault positions power in terms of social institutions, exemplified by his famous asylum, both enacting and representing control and oppression of the individual. The asylum is a very important icon for Elizabeth. She is to discover only as a schoolchild that her mother was put in an asylum, the same one she passed on her way to school as a little girl. Like Foucault, Head recognizes and distrusts institutional power in its relationship to the individual. Foucault, however, often overlooks individuals as participating agents and sees them only as victims. Head, on the other hand, perceives evil as inherent in both individuals and institutions. She perceives individuals and institutions functioning in conjunction with one another, often at the cost of both institutions such as governments and individuals living under apartheid regimes.

A Western feminist reading might locate *A Question of Power* in the literature of women's madness. Novels such as Sylvia Plath's *The Bell Jar* (1971), Charlotte Perkin Gillman's *The Yellow Wall Paper* (1973), and Penelope Mortimer's *The Pumpkin Eaters* (1962) all come out of a specific tradition. I am not concerned with the legitimacy of such a claim about Head's third novel. Such a claim for the Western novels seems far more appropriate because they paint various aspects of the middle-class female anxiety of purpose. On the other hand, Head's novel is concerned with profound questions of good and evil in their relationship to power and how the answers affect individuals who wish to be responsible members of their communities. In the Western novels, all three heroines tend to go mad because patriarchal society refuses to let them have a sense of purpose within their own context of desires; men impose traditional arbitrary purposes and desires on them. It is out of a resentment of this imposition, and here I am simplifying for my own argument, that they go "mad." Elizabeth's case is somewhat different. She has to be involved in economic-occupational activities because she has a small child and no economically viable husband to support them both. She cannot escape to a room of her own because there is none into which her madness does not follow her. Her "madness" emerges from her dialogue with the gendered sociopolitical world, which she cannot help but feel part of, that is, her part in the apartheid reality. Head has said in an interview that

> in *A Question of Power* the work-out is so much more subtle. It shows how the narrator, Elizabeth, *with good intentions,* is so broken down—the whole process of break-down and destruction is outlined there. A person in the grip of such a process has very little to say. I felt that I had overcome that tendency in me to moral preachiness. The question is left so open. There is a line that forms the title of the book—if the things of the soul are really a question of power then anyone in possession of power of the spirit could be Lucifer. That is, I might in my essence then symbolize Satan. I'd lost, in *A Question of Power,* the certainty of my own goodness. The novel was written under pressure. I was alarmed [emphasis mine].[34]

Later, on a less personal note, Head pursues the idea of good and evil in their relationship to power:

> If you feel that you have moved into another world where no human decencies are observed and basically you are a normal, decent human being, there is this high alarm. The book was written with that high alarm. . . . But then my argument is that when people are trapped in death situations they really don't know what's killing them. Is it that evil has a coherence of its own? Even if the broad proposition that this is about God and the devil is true—the work-out there of God is at the centre where all the horror happens. . . . I cannot help feeling that a type of book like mine has so much validity because it comes *from Southern Africa.* The whole world is aware that the situation here is so awry. My book has been shaped in such an abnormal way and with such a fierce work-out of good and evil where goodness itself can be questioned [emphasis mine].[35]

Head is making several propositions here, and her inclusion of South Africa is not a coincidence. She is interested in "the culture of hate" because South Africa tends to provide the perfect model for individual and social evil, or, as I have said earlier, the insider/outsider dialectic pervades every aspect of life in South Africa. What is the point at which innocuous suburban White Southern African housewives continue to train in shooting galleries and acquire guns as part of the normal course of their life? Even though Head does not talk specifically about that particular evil, she does talk at length about where the apartheid madness in South Africa springs from and what it constitutes. According to Head, and she implies this over and over again, most of the evil in South Africa is connected in some way or another to the idea of human, racial hatred premised on economic fear, ignorance, and avarice. These phenomena always emerge from the insider/outsider dialectic, which the exile faces. It is the White South African, the outsider who brutally colonizes the insider, the Black South African. And again it is the South African exile, Elizabeth, who cannot negotiate Batswana culture and language.

Elizabeth's personal biography can never be wholly extricated from apartheid or from that "point" where societies and humans become evil often without "knowing" it. This quality of interiority and exteriority manifested by every evil practice is not surprising. Head's interest in this "point" especially since her own biographical consciousness and thus, her identity, is determined by the point at which evil occurs in *A Question of Power*. Margaret E. Tucker describes the dichotomies in this novel as "splitting of inside from outside."[36] Head's personal biographical consciousness later draws on an acute understanding of several sociopolitical evils and then sketches connections between individual and institutional phenomena. For Head, the effect of good and evil on individuals and societies and vice versa is potentially a vortex out of which one cannot emerge.

Elizabeth's and her mother's madness in its relationship to their sexuality has been misunderstood. A phallocratic, yet "kindly" criticism would be to imply that Elizabeth is frigid as a woman because she had terrible experiences with men. This kind of "critical analysis" creates a wasteland, however, refusing to see the subtle negotiations between sexual-lingual exile and sociohistoric identities in this novel. I believe that it is important, if not crucial, to analyze Elizabeth's madness in relation to her sexuality. But it is equally important not to reduce her sexuality to one function. There is certainly an evasion of conscious sexual discourse on Elizabeth's part but that discourse goes underground. I do not wish to belabor the point of the subconscious, because one does not need to here. All one has to do is to examine the content of Elizabeth's nightmares to see that an intense dialogue between the African identity and the Coloured sexuality is occurring, and that it is simultaneous and interdependent with the dialogue between good and evil.

The insanity emerges out of a rejection of one aspect of her identity—her sexual self. But the sanity is restored once she emphasizes her "concentration" on society, or as Head would say "humanity in general." It is curious what event leads her back into the unreal, the insane. Earlier, it is precisely because reality and nightmare merge that the characters who inhabit the insane part of her mind are not distinguished from the characters who live around Motabeng in jeeps as Sello does. In *A Question of Power*, the point at which things turn evil coincides with the point where reality and nightmare become indistinguishable, causing madness. The racist doctor in the mental institution, probably much like the one her mother went to, who sees her as a "comrade racialist," abruptly restores a portion of her sanity. She poses the existence of goodness in the doctor in a problematic way. He is not only a quack but a racist. Yet he loves children. He suddenly has great regard for Elizabeth, who would be undistinguishable from other patients to him except that she tends to think about her son, Shorty, and is concerned about not being there on his birthday. This strikes a note of sympathy in the doctor, who is then no longer just a racist but becomes "a good father" in regard to his own children, and as a result he is considerate of other parents. It is these "points," which blur the quick and absolute decisions that politics in South Africa must necessitate, that in turn engage, confuse, and result in Elizabeth's madness.

This duality and ambiguity of the possibility of good and evil in the doctor and herself is part of the struggle for sanity, and belonging is at the apex of this construction. For Elizabeth, and more particularly for Head, the problem of good and evil is tied to the politics of identity, which are both personal and political. Head does not necessarily wish to save the "racialist" doctor from being considered evil but rather she is interested in a complete picture, one in which one can look outside and inside. When she talks about her own propensity for this evil, to Birgitte, she includes the rest of humanity. Elizabeth says,

"My destiny is full of doubt, full of doom. I am being dragged down, without my willing, into a whirlpool of horrors. I prefer nobility and goodness but a preference isn't enough; there are forces which make a mockery of my preferences. . . ."

"I imagine a situation in some future life," Elizabeth continued. "I imagine my face contorted with greed and hatred. I imagine myself willfully grabbing things that are not mine. And in this darkness of the soul, you will one day walk up to me and remind me of my nobility. That will be my magical formula. I'll hear you and turn away from the darkness.[37]

The "whirlpool of horrors" is synonymous with the "madness of not belonging," to which Elizabeth descends in the two breakdowns she experiences over the course of this novel. She becomes evil in her disparagement of the Batswana during her "insanity." Elizabeth's inability to rely on a simple preference for "goodness and nobility" as lifelong maxims for her actions startles her into the horror of "madness." And she enters a "nightmare time" which is anarchic and renders her powerless. She talks about "forces which make a mockery" out of her preferences for goodness. I believe that this is a comment on the helplessness of the forces of change determining any society, revolutionary or not. The power structures render us helpless as well as complicitous in ways that Elizabeth is aware of in her own psychic time and space. The "whirlpool of horrors" is also the "point" at which one can no longer decipher what is "Good" and what is "Evil." This point manifests an imbalance which can tip one into insanity, which it does.

In the passage just quoted, the face she recognizes as her own inhabits the "darkness of soul." The mere preferences for "goodness and nobility" could not be entirely superfluous because she can be saved by the "magical call" to her own goodness. Head is interested here in the areas and capacities of good and evil in individuals as social beings. The "lesson" this novel inflicts on us is that both good and evil can be chosen by each individual even if these phenomena are not intrinsic. For her, the important question is, How far does a society or an individual, on both sides of the power divide, absorb an evil such as individual or social apartheid?

In her plea to Birgitte, Head emphasizes the dialogic relationship of two individuals who make up a community and the responsibility they might have for each other's survival in the social world. Birgitte does not hesitate to say "I will," when Elizabeth asks her if she would give her a hand to pull her out of the "darkness of the soul." In this gesture there is emphasis in the revolutionary cross-cultural aspect of dialogue between two women who have decided what is important in terms not only of their relationship to each other, but also in regard to the question of good and evil. In addition, this episode is noteworthy because the predominantly enduring and good friendships in Head's novels are usually between women. Even when Dan shows her one of her nightmare women, Miss Sewing-Machine, Elizabeth is able to feel immense commonality with her: "She always looked at Elizabeth as though she knew what friendships between women were really like." [38] The longing in that statement is a precursor to the longing Elizabeth felt for her absent mother and by extension a harmonious community of women.

In this novel the apartheid evil is consummated by the more general evil which may include individuals even as unsuspecting as Elizabeth. The most remarkable factor about this novel is that it conveys what an enormous impositional and liminal force apartheid really is. She is limited by it even as she escapes it—she can only be the madwoman, the exile *par excellence*. Apartheid becomes that most unconciliatory sort of political essence that Elizabeth finds unnegotiable in and outside South Africa. In writing about Elizabeth's response to the "never to return clause" in her passport before she leaves her home country, Head says, "She did not care. She hated the country. In spite of her ability to like or to understand political ideologies, she had also lived the backbreaking life of all black people in South Africa. It was like living with a permanent nervous tension, because you did not know why white people there had to go out of their way to hate you or loathe you." [39]

But in her "host" country she discovers that she simply cannot escape either because she, Elizabeth, is the unwitting "reincarnation" of that same evil. Her biography, which she has neither made nor chosen, is part of the Janus-faced reality of the South Africa that traps her. Thus, it is not simply the mad mother but rather the obscure White mother with an unacceptable, unreconcilable sexuality and the remote Black father with an equally dubious sexuality who embody in Elizabeth all that is contained in the apartheid evil that she tries to escape and, in the last analysis, simply cannot, "the gesture of belonging" notwithstanding.

I have noted the exile's relief at being able to write herself in Botswana as she was never able to in South Africa, for the institutional systems of silence and "loathing" do not make room for such expression. As soon as Head went into exile in Botswana she wrote prolifically. Likewise, when she got to the country of her "chosen" exile, she was able to express her anxieties, which were kept carefully in check, perhaps for purposes of sheer survival in South Africa. But the thought of not being able to belong drives her into insanity. The precarious balance of her "sanity" was toppled because there was room and dire need in Motabeng. Elizabeth's nervous breakdown occurs because she finally stops running from all the evil and devils of the past biography and turns around to take account of human and personal biographical connection to the evil so that she can turn away from it "whole," exorcised and with a sense of sexual-historical awareness. It is through this interiority and exteriority of experience that she can ultimately but precariously "belong," in Motabeng. The peculiar construct of Elizabeth's nightmares and their violent expulsion from her brain conveys the sanity of belonging to humanity, to Motabeng, and by extension to the universal "brotherhood of mankind." Ravenscroft has suggested, "I do not believe that Bessie Head's novels are offering anything as facile as universal brotherhood and love for a political blueprint for either South Africa or all of Africa."[40] Her picture of what that brotherhood entails is not only complex but aims to examine the longings of a postapartheid era.

Even though Birgitte is not there to fulfill her earlier promise, it is Tom, her other very close friend, who will not give up extending the hand she needs to pull her out of the mire. He seems persistently good, in spite of the brutal message she sends him after he travels six hundred miles just to see her. Their relationship is as intellectually profound as her relationship with Kenosi is sacred at another level. She continues the dialogue about "universality" with Tom—a dialogue she had begun with Birgitte earlier.

For Head, both good and evil, belonging and nonbelonging, are ideas determined by the exteriority or interiority of individual psyche's in particular geographical places. There are interesting interconnections between the idea of good and evil in its relationship to exile. It is possible to interpret the cause of her breakdown as springing from her exile, and certainly Elizabeth is extremely antagonistic toward the Batswana. She hurls abuses at them in the mental institute and assures them she is not one of them. This counterattack is evident partly as a defense mechanism to preserve interiority of the exile's identity against people with whom she knows she does not share a common heritage. Even the Eugene man seems to understand her situation in a particular tradition of the exile. He tells her, "I suffer, too, because I haven't a country and know what it's like. A lot of refugees have nervous breakdowns."[41] In this century, there is a profusion of testimonies from South African exiles. As mentioned earlier, Nat Nakasa said, before jumping from a multistory window, that he could never get used to the police not hunting him down in New York, thousands of miles from South Africa. Thus, certain sorts of exile can be regarded as unbearable at the level of the human psyche, which also experiences simultaneous relief at being away, as Elizabeth did upon escaping from apartheid.

What is the pain of not having "a country"? A South African exile is exiled by the minority White government, which usually does not allow her to come back to the "homeland." In postcolonial, postmodernist discourse, the notion of home has become dubious, indeed. Edward Said remarks that "exile is strangely compelling to think about but terrible to experience . . . a condition of terminal loss."[42] Does this loss drive one "mad?" What is this loss? Is it loss of land or is it the connection between one's identity and land, language, and culture that evokes belonging? Elizabeth's life was begun in loss and determined by loss. She lost a place in the world outside the asylum because her mother was "mad" and she lost her mother because she was a White woman with a Coloured child in apartheid South Africa. At the end of *A Question of Power*, Elizabeth raises her hand over the "land in a gesture of belonging." This "return" to South Africa is integral to Head's idea about universality, which anticipates and informs the postapartheid era.

At the time that Head published *A Question of Power*, she had been in Botswana for nearly ten years, and the patterns of exile and the "evil" of "non-belonging" emerged in curious patterns of interiority and exteriority to overwhelm her. She had used the escape route from South Africa—a South Africa that through apartheid became another sort of exile for Black people and did not seem to sustain her emotionally and intellectually any longer. But leaving implied that Elizabeth had to understand the extremes of good and evil in both the individual and society. She does not have a choice about being able in grand, mytho-logical terms to determine the course or limitations of this journey. It hits her in the form of an invasion of her soul, body, and mind.

A very real anxiety faced by South Africans and others in voluntary or involuntary exile is a tremendous guilt at not being part of the revo-lutionary struggle at home. Time and again, the whole question of the meaninglessness of life in exile crops up. Part of this dilemma is related to a sudden lack of political identity and the other part consists of a desire to be part of a political milieu. Head and most of the protagonists she creates tend to turn away from politics and that is not a popular position for a South African exile. For Head, the task of politics is to fight in order to procure, in the simplest possible terms, livable human conditions for everyone; and in this way she is political in the most profound sense. When she is talking to Tom, whose understanding of politics is a popular leftist one of cheering the separatist ideology of the Black movement in America, Elizabeth is furious and tries with tears in her eyes to explain the goal of political struggle as an understanding of humanity rather than race or class, or any other specific interest group. Her position is unpopular because it appears as if she is not supporting the voice of the marginalized individual, especially in South Africa where the complete land disenfranchisement began and ended brutally for the entire Black population. But in Head's analysis, even though these realities are accountable one must go further than the justified political outrage of the liberal, Tom. She tells him: "Once you make yourself a freak and special any bastard starts to use you. That's half of the fierce fight in Africa. The politicians first jump on the band wagon of past suffering. They're African nationalists and sweep the crowds away with weeping and wailing about the past. Then why do they steal and cheat people once they get into government. . . . Any heaven, like a Black-Power heaven, that existed for a few individuals was pointless and useless."[43]

For Head "universal brotherhood" was simple human existence for all and not just for a few. Her South African experience makes her extremely wary about inhabiting anyplace as a freak in a specialized group. Perhaps Elizabeth's only recognition, given her sociopolitical re-ality, is that she is a Coloured. With the Janus-faced identity of a Col-oured she can see clearly how you cannot only "belong" to one group, for often, as in South Africa, that group is manipulated into a buffer zone—a no man's land. In order to belong profoundly an individual must join the entire human race. I do not believe that Elizabeth thinks it unworthwhile to fight for individual or group freedom, or for identity in its connection to specific geographical space, which colonialism steals. After all, Elizabeth herself is engaged in a battle of enormous proportions between the forces of good and evil, so she is not opposed to an overthrowing of oppression as Head's novel *Maru* exemplifies. What is hard for her critics to absorb is that her political stand is an unpopular one, simply because it insists on employing Head's own foresight about short-term political activity. She has claimed over and over again her interest in change for all humanity, not in larger idealistic terms, but in an immediate sociopolitical way. Her interest in "universality," often confused with whitewashing differences of culture and race, is an all-encompassing political idea. However, Head does not problematize the idea of universality through implicating a serious analysis of race and class oppression. Even though she does it in other contexts, her concentration is very consistently on humanity in general and not on special pockets of people. In fact she sees a grave problem in making or calling anything special, in terms of interest groups, righteous or otherwise, and no doubt her South African apartheid experience informs that suspicion; for in South Africa the ideology of the Dutch Reform Church, another special group, was directly responsible for stealing the land from the Black population because the anointed White population had "special" rights of superiority over Blacks, land, comfort, and economic stability.

It is, nonetheless, appropriate to suggest Head's profound political engagement with South Africa even though she left. Elizabeth continues to address her political ideas to the somewhat befuddled Tom:

> "There is some such thing as black people's suffering being a summary of everything the philosophers and prophets ever said," she said. They said: "Never think along lines of I and mine. It is death." But they said it prettily, under the shade of Bodhi trees. It made no impact on mankind in general. . . . Black people learnt that lesson brutally because they were the living victims of the greed inspired by I and mine and to hell with you, dog. Where do you think their souls are, then, after centuries of suffering? They're ahead of Buddha and Jesus and can dictate the terms for the future, not for any exclusive circle but for mankind in general."[44]

Even though she recognizes that that suffering has made Black people, in potential, more spiritually advanced than a Buddha or Jesus, they should not demand a special place, for even that demand can be subverted by hegemonic power structures more easily than if the same demands are made for "mankind" in general. The interior/exterior implications of Elizabeth's proposition are clearly universal, uncategorical socialism where political power itself is understood as evil and unnecessary. There is, however, another equally important concept of power in *A Question of Power*. This second sense deals with the innate moral goodness of each individual, whether she is an exile or not, who in turn constructs a society. This is where power and goodness come together, dispelling the enticement of evil as it is manifested by political power. Head's ideas about good and evil in their relationship to power come directly out of the influence of Buddhism and Hinduism and the Indian communities she lived in while she was still in the Cape. In her desire to take humanity away from the "I and mine" market socioeconomy, she makes the most profound statements about political direction. For her, the notion of Black Power exists not so much in the raised fist, as Tom suggests, but rather in emulating the historical sufferings of all humankind of which Black people are a part, not a whole, even though they have been excluded by power structures.

Head's critics have often claimed that she is "apolitical" or even "politically ignorant" because she tends to be very nervous about definitions.[45] This criticism is far too simplistic because what her protagonist tries to come to terms with is an identity that has been exiled socially, sexually, and biographically. Elizabeth neither chose nor can she cope with the history that haunts her. The knowledge that her mother "was insane," and that if she is "not careful" she would "get insane just like her," becomes the whole point of her personality, for which there is no compensatory emotion. She cannot overlook the "silent appeal of her mother," and when none of the prefects will listen to "her side of the story," especially when she has been in a fight, it is her mother's words that haunt her: "'Now you know. Do you think I can bear the stigma of insanity alone? Share it with me.'"[46] Even as a child she is being asked by the adult world that wrecked her childhood to share the space of their misfortunes with her. Perhaps because of their absence, she can not escape either her mother's insanity or her father's oppressive traditions and lives, years later in Botswana, under the yoke of both her parents' exile from "their own" society, from their role as parents and from their right as humans. Suddenly, the simplest aspects of human life, such as parenthood and marriage, are stolen from this White woman and Black man just as motherhood and fatherhood are taken away from so many Black South African families through apartheid.

Head's third novel has overtones of her second novel, *Maru*. When Sello appears in the first line of the book it seems crucial to Head to point out that "it seemed almost incidental that he was African. . . . And yet, as an African he seemed to have made one of the most perfect statements: 'I am just anyone.'"[47] Head is deliberately negotiating a dual problem into existence here. It is important to recognize one's Africanness, but at the same time recognize the oneness with the rest of humanity even though the rest of humanity may have wanted to deny that fundamental component throughout history. It is the wrestling of power, not from the strong in order to give to the meek, but rather as a recognition that individuals constitute the whole of humanity and that political power as it is a sickness can pervade all of humanity, not just its parts.

In *A Question of Power*, Head is ready to take on larger problems, such as the relationship of good and evil to power. Whereas in *When Rain Clouds Gather* and later in *Maru* she has talked about economic solutions, and those solutions are always tied to the immediate needs of the individual in question who in turn is always based in her society, in her third novel every aspect and configuration of the individual affects the global and national. Elizabeth is described as a prophet, at first possessing the "arrogance of innocence," which is torn from her completely in the individual struggle against good and evil, but is reinstated in a surprising "gesture of belonging" at the end of the novel.[48] The novel constitutes a circular understanding of the elements of power as they are related to the good and evil in individuals and societies.

Head's notion of good and evil is somewhat unclear for different reasons. Is Head implying a Manichean division of the world by using the traditional distinctions between good and evil? How does she relate this idea to the individual and society? The implication of power implicit in the notion of good and evil in their societal application is far more comprehensible than the division of good and evil in Head's dialectic. How is Elizabeth's "breakdown," which is integral to her sexuality, tied to implications of good and evil power?

It is not always clear why Elizabeth embarks on the journey that she does, even though one can detect enormous strength and humor while she is in the depths of despair. Head writes, "Journeys into the soul are not for women with children, not all the dark heaving turmoil. They are for men, and the toughest of them took off into the solitude of the forests and fought out their battles with hell in deep seclusion. No wonder they hid from view. The inner life is ugly."[49] A journey often implies choice in regard to the intended exodus from one place and time to another, but perhaps only for someone without an exit visa. Given her psychological reality, this particular freedom of choice is further denied to an exile from South Africa. In Elizabeth's case there is no choice about this journey into an individual's exilic consciousness. And this consciousness is intrinsic to Black South Africans whether they are in exile or not. She and the characters who enter into her psychic life assume that she must fulfill the demands of the journey to the "heart of her darkness," no matter how painful it may be.

The interiority and exteriority determining this journey—madness—concentrates on the "point" at which individuals and societies become evil and in addition, on what sorts of incentives they have in regard to that nonchoice. In *A Question of Power*, evil and good coexist, forever facing each other and away from each other, Janus-faced, sometimes in confrontative combat and sometimes one completely displaced by the other. The imagery is very Christian and, thus, often Manichean. Head always pits God against Satan, even though the names Dan, Sello, and Medusa do not immediately evoke the Christian dialectic. However, what is crucial to Head emerges when both Satan and God, Dan and Sello, become interchangeable and no one can tell, especially not Elizabeth, which one is good and which one completely evil. This loss of clarity is integral to the complexities of power relations.

For Elizabeth, a constant changeability of the "truth" in regard to people's supposed essences becomes the material for that madness resulting in her nightmares. This madness results in shifting expectations. Elizabeth's nightmare vision starts to interfere rapidly with her social connections when she is awake, which is ultimately the reason she is put into an institution. The radical switching of "the truth" sends Elizabeth's exilic consciousness into mental contortions. When she attacks old Mrs. Jones and calls her a procurer for her daughters, there is a breakdown in the demarcation between interior and exterior reality for everyday reality becomes mixed up with her nightmare visions. She can no longer keep them separate. The nightmare life tends to echo the real life of Elizabeth and she cannot distinguish between the two, just as she cannot distinguish between Sello who is not consistently good and Dan who is not consistently evil.

Sello's creation in her mind is never questioned. Why, for instance, does he appear to her? What precisely does she need to work out through his appearance in terms of personal and sexual betrayal? Is she, in the last analysis, successful? Foucault suggests an interesting premise to his important work on madness and civilization, which I believe relates to Head's preoccupation with the "point" at which things turn evil. This "point" is of course subject to interpretation in Foucault's analysis, but in Head's frame of reference it is the possibility of institutional and individual weakness for assuming evil postures and actions that constitutes the area of major concern to her. Whereas Foucault's frame of interest is in the social archaeology of reason as opposed to insanity, for Head the insanity comes from amassing power which in turn corrupts to the point of making both society and the individual evil.[50] And further, unless individuals who are especially equipped to do so explore the point at which individuals and institutions turn into instruments of evil, then apartheid becomes a real possibility in any society. Wilson Harris thinks that phenomena such as apartheid indicate a death wish of a particular society. He claims that when members of a society pass by a homeless or starving person, they are wishing the death of their own society.[51]

Madness

ONE OF the most crucial ingredients of *A Question of Power* is madness in its relation to exile. Foucault makes an interesting comparison between the exiled fools in the trope "ship of fools" and the exile. He writes, "It happened that certain madmen were publicly whipped, and in the course of a kind of a game they were chased in a mock race and driven out of the city with quarterstaff blows. So many signs that the expulsion of madmen had become one of a number of ritual exiles."[52] The asylum has, in "civilized" society, replaced expulsion. But the decision about assessing who is mad and who is not has something to do with what is socially accepted behavior and what is not. Head's mother was exiled out of an established social position and coaxed into insanity within an asylum; it has never been clear whether she did exhibit "mad" traits or just socially unacceptable ones, if one is ever able to make such a distinction, which Foucault doubts. Indicative of this exile is a desire by "normal," homogeneous, usually bourgeoisie society, the mainstays of power, to dispel the influence of "insane" people from its midst. It would be socioeconomically very dangerous for daughters of upper middle-class White English families, or indeed any White families, to start producing Black children in South Africa, even in the post-apartheid era. Therefore, it serves the interest of that particular group to call such behavior "mad" or immoral. Thus, the fear that Elizabeth has of becoming mad like her mother, which is first teased into existence, is not far-fetched in the least. After she hears about the sociopsychological deviance of the mother, she expects to relive the same legacy, which of course she does in exile many years later, in Botswana. But in Elizabeth's case, the "madness" and the asylum are not entirely imposed on her. Whereas her mother does not seem to have any choice about recovering from her madness or being released from her asylum, except through death, Elizabeth does, for she leaves the asylum. This perhaps is the only privilege of the Black child over the White mother under apartheid.

The idea of coexisting madness in exile seems to be a prevalent component in her relationship to Medusa with the added complication of her mother's and her own death. She is constantly threatened with death and even her child's life is threatened because her son Shorty is like her, an exile, a Coloured and thereby unacceptable to "real" Africans. Both madness and death seem to be linked to her exile and to her mother's actions in life and in her suicide. Elizabeth's madness seems to be the most lucid insanity recorded by somebody who was in the "passage," the "journey" of madness herself. Here one has to recognize the license not of the fool but rather of the person declared "insane." Foucault makes very clear analogies between the exile and the mad person which are relevant to the understanding of A Question of Power. He calls the fool the "passenger par excellence" because he has become the "prisoner of his own departure," always "kept at the point of passage."[53] Madness, a quest of one's sexual identity, perpetual journey, homelessness, and exile thus become synonymous with one another. Exile too, perpetually keeps Elizabeth at "the point" of belonging and not belonging.

Elizabeth talks about the journey or the passage from not belonging to belonging to the place of her exile, though whether it can be implemented is extremely questionable. Like the fool, Elizabeth is kept at the brink of departure, frozen in timeless bondage, because of the history imposed on her through apartheid, its attending madness, and the Batswana reminder of her foreignness. Her breakdown is an affirmation of her remaining forever in passage, in exile. This exile, however, does enlighten her about certain forms of "truth." Foucault writes,

> The passenger . . . has his truth and his homeland only in that fruitless expanse between two countries that cannot belong to him. . . .
>
> At the opposite pole to this nature of shadows, madness fascinates because it is knowledge. It is knowledge, first, because all these absurd figures are in reality elements of a difficult, hermetic, esoteric learning. . . .
>
> "Wisdom, like other precious substances, must be torn from the bowels of the earth." This knowledge, so inaccessible, so formidable, the Fool, in his innocent idiocy, already possesses.[54]

Edward Said, in his essay on exile, expresses the tragedy of being caught in the "fruitless expanse between two countries that cannot belong" to the exile.[55] Madness is the fruitless exile between sanity and insanity. It is from out of her madness that "learning" and "wisdom" emerge and enable Elizabeth to make prophetic pronouncements about the world and her own sense of "dispossession." Here, as in Shakespeare and Foucault, the wise man and the fool are combined because of their special insights. When she has completely lost the distinction between her private hell and the one outside, she leaves a terrible message in Motabeng, on the post office bulletin board for everybody to see, about the real man, Sello, mistaking him for the one in her nightmares. It is precisely at this stage that she creates a scandal as her mother did before her, reaching a "point" between reality and nightmare, and she is immediately dispatched to an insane asylum.

What possible "truth" and "knowledge" does she manifest in terms of her insane reality? Perhaps Foucault's fool already possesses a knowledge through his unselfconsciousness about the difference between reality and dream. When Elizabeth cannot distinguish between the reality and nightmare, she becomes an embarrassment to be hidden away, the scandal to be hidden, like her mother. The "truths" that affect her life and the prophecies that come out of her madness tend to be the most lucid part of her "passage." Her pronouncements about the teleology of politics are prophetic and profound. She wishes to carve out a sociopsychological space for human beings of all races and not for one race or another. Perhaps that is why her view is problematic for militant Black groups because they see her giving away what has not yet been won by the Black race and certainly not yet—not completely—in South Africa. But Elizabeth is presuming postapartheid liberation by calling upon equality for all. Given the current politics of South Africa, this is not such a far-fetched desire.

Head has been criticized for taking on the position of the prophet because her protagonist, while "insane," tends to become the self-appointed conscience of the people of Botswana. She does this in several ways. One possibility is that she uses her madness to assert herself "at home" in exile by making pronouncements about African politics and social figures in Motabeng. She criticizes them, because she assumes she is at home and has freedom to talk about what concerns her. The other possibility is that "insanity" is the only format for her to resolve and articulate some of the sociopsychological problems she faces in being an exile and a woman who is having enormous problems struggling to keep her head above water. The third possibility is the one pointed out by Medusa, that she is trying to survive her outcast status as a Coloured in Botswana through her counterattack while asserting the difference that obviously exists between her and the other Batswana who know and are related to each other, through language and social conventions.

The prophecies are the most problematic, in terms of narratology, because they are tied to both her sanity and insanity. The prophecies represent the interiority of her recovery from madness. She recovers because she is able to find that goodness within herself, the goodness that she spoke to Birgette about earlier. If she can find goodness in herself she can find it in humanity. Somehow, it is revealed to Elizabeth by Dan and Sello, both good and evil, that she is part of the prophecies that become integrated into her life as soon as she arrives in Motabeng. What these prophecies mean is not clear until right at the end of the novel but they certainly have something to do with her "insanity" or knowledge exhibited by the "passenger par excellence." Fairly early in the novel Dan tells her about Sello, the God character: "He never gets born without the prophecies. They included you too."[56] The connection between Sello or God as a representative of goodness, and his protégé, Elizabeth, becomes clear, in regard to the prophecies when at the end of the novel she says: "There is only one God and his name is Man. And Elizabeth is his prophet."[57] The prophecies form the mythological substance of Elizabeth's interiorized agonies about good and evil. And the prophecies become related to how she defends herself from mental abuse and physical onslaught. According to popularly held ideas about madness, one could easily assume that Elizabeth is suffering from "delusions of grandeur." But I do not believe that this is the connection between Head's purpose in introducing the prophecies and working them out during the course of Elizabeth's madness. I believe that the "prophecies" comprise wisdom from having experienced and resisted the onslaughts faced by an exiled and gendered identity.

The prophecies culminate in "God . . . is Man. And Elizabeth is his prophet," a formula resembling the first pronouncements of Islam. There is, no doubt, a sense of simplicity and grandeur about this statement, and the driving force comes from someone who has emerged from a battle where her own goodness was questioned and destroyed in ways that unnerved her totally. Elizabeth is someone who sees clearly that "the dividing line between good and evil is very narrow."[58] The possibility of merging good and evil is transformed into the question of power, which is debated with more vigor especially after the discourse on sexuality is abandoned.

For Elizabeth, the question of good and evil had commenced in South Africa along with the ambivalence toward questions of sexual identity. In South Africa the only reality lies in a "vehement vicious struggle between two sets of people with different looks; and, like Dan's brand of torture, it was something that could go on and on and on."[59] This apartheid reality with its implications of evil is ultimately the one that Elizabeth has to use as the point where her "journey" begins and ends. Sello and Dan are the mode of dialogue and individual sexuality the testing ground that Head develops in order to make Elizabeth's body and mind the stage for the enactment of that good and evil which she needs to come to terms with. She is always warned by Sello to maintain her "own mental independence." The dialogic conditions she sets for herself through Sello are never easy in the least. Sello says,

> "You have an analytical mind. You must analyze everything you see." She failed to heed the warning, and the day he abruptly pulled away *the prop of goodness* she floundered badly in stormy and dangerous seas.
> "You must have suffered a lot in South Africa," he said. . . . "But you are not to hate White people [emphasis mine]."[60]

It is the simple belief in her own goodness, what Head calls the "arrogance of innocence," which dupes her into thinking that she is untouchable at some deep core. That idea is toppled, but it is exactly this faith that also saves her from suicide. In this regard she, unlike her mother, gets out of the asylum, lives, and writes. However, when that fundamental understanding is shaken, then she loses her sense of goodness and her sexual self and Dan can take supreme hold over all aspects of her life. In *When Rain Clouds Gather,* it was understood that the exilic consciousness is above evil intentions; but now Head problematizes her own earlier assertion in *A Question of Power.* The entire dialogue consists of relentless questions posed to the outsider, the exilic principle, but the resolution comes from the final "gesture" of belonging and not the dialogue itself.

The enactment of this drama of good and evil is indicative of the question of power that individuals resolve and choose just as much as societies and institutions do. And as I have argued, for Head questions pertaining to sexuality are also linked to questions of good and evil power. The exilic consciousness Elizabeth represents has to approach the point where she either rejects evil and can "belong" to Motabeng or forever becomes an exile—a madwoman. In rejecting evil such as Dan's sexual perversities, she also rejects her own sexuality. And again, for Head the entire issue of power has to be resolved, both individually and collectively, before it can be translated into her doctrine of "universal brotherhood." One discovers at the end of the novel that Head's narrative was always going in the direction of her "universalist" interests. She is not interested in the "I and mine," which justifies her antipathy toward her own sexuality. The status of Elizabeth's exile is substantiated because there is no such recourse to the resolution of good and evil in terms of power in the South Africa she left. However, the possibility of a "world of love" compels Elizabeth to make a metaphoric and literal "journey" toward understanding the "point" at which individuals and societies become evil, and the lessons she learns are again simple and profound. Head writes:

> It was the kind of language she understood, that no one was the be-all and end-all of creation, that no one had the power of assertion and dominance to the exclusion of other life. . . .
>
> There were many beautiful things said at that time, because an awakening of her own powers corresponded to an awakening love of mankind.[61]

If it is the case that even White people in South Africa are not the "be-all and end-all of creation," as their economic, political, social, and religious ideologies have indicated, what kind of political possibilities does that raise for the oppressed Black people? This is the direction that Head's narrative tends to take, a direction that makes the conceptual reality of postapartheid a dialogic possibility. In this way she resists not only the demons of personal "madness" but also the horrors of political madness, namely, apartheid. I believe that Head's notion of "universality" is contained in that possibility which has a great deal to do with the postapartheid settlement even though her discourse is not explicitly about South Africa but, rather, about a woman *from* South Africa. The political and the biographical aspects are coexistent in questions posed by the exiled identity.

The affiliations that Elizabeth makes are a direct result of her recovery and only after she has fulfilled the prophecies she was employed to execute. She accomplishes this recovery by understanding that even one individual's enactment of good can dispel evil. It is through this dialogue that her faith in her own goodness is restored. Head writes: "She had been thrown a powerful life-line, as though by turning inward she had found that the centre of herself was still sane and secure, and that the evils which had begun to dominate her mind had a soaring parallel of goodness."[62]

When Elizabeth can restore faith in her own goodness even though there is always a possibility for evil, she can see good restored in society as well, which is why the novel can end with "a sense of belonging." However, this transition from confusion about the goodness of humanity, because that is how I would define her "insanity," to a restoration of harmony is problematic in terms of the notion of exile. This recovery is problematic also in regard to the complete switch from "insanity" to the "love of all mankind." One of the questions Head scholars frequently ask is, Is this complete and abrupt switch from suffering to "belonging" plausible?

It is the ambiguity of good that enrages Elizabeth at first. She recognizes evil in all shapes and forms because she has a thorough grounding in the kinds of evil that can coexist within each psyche. But when she turns her reliance toward manifestations of good and those very symbols turn evil right in front of her eyes, she finds herself filled with bewilderment and rage. The exilic consciousness seems to be rooted in uncertainty yet desires to rely on stable definitions. When Sello, who has been compared to Buddha and always appears as the quiet thoughtful monk figure, allies himself with Medusa and treats Elizabeth as incidental, she develops "a deep, black rage" against him. It is as if Elizabeth experiences the state of goodness in all its ambivalence. Goodness is represented by the monk figure of Sello and not the Sello in the brown suit, though often, because of the ambivalent nature of good, Elizabeth herself is confused by the two personas. She calls a belief in goodness her "life-line." Sometimes it is thrown at her and she can save herself and at other times it is taken away from her, leaving her floundering in the evil manipulations of Dan and Medusa.

The violence with which she reacts to the keeper of goodness, Sello, is very different from her guard against Medusa and her subservience to the seduction of Dan; even her response to perceived good and evil is distinct. She is angry with Sello but helpless before Dan and Medusa. She can only "belong" after learning that any power that springs from evil motivations, even if it is Black Power, is bad. Only when she is entirely lost can she no longer answer the questions that this novel engages:

> What is love?
> Who is God?
> If I cry, who will have compassion on me as my suffering is the
>   suffering of others?
> This is the nature of evil. This is the nature of good.[63]

Her images and emotional needs for love constantly delude her into drifting further away from the answers that she so desperately needs in order to overcome the evil of exile that has made her psychologically helpless and troubled by her alienation. The "universality" she invokes is a defense against the alienation of her exile. If one could transcend, as Head counsels numerous times, "class, race, and nation," then the problems of exile and territoriality would dissipate considerably.

The other part of her "universality" constitutes an acceptance of humanity at a fundamentally simple level, where interests of race, class, and nationhood do not disappear altogether but they do not determine human interaction. "Universality" is contained in the acceptance of a generalized humanity through which the individual can accept her position in the social milieu, even of her exile's surroundings. The "belonging" that comes out of her recognition as a person who is tied to and sustained by the abilities of the growing nurturing land is also indicative of a completed search for her own psychosocial purpose in Motabeng—which is at once home and the site of exile.

However, her release from her madness is still unaccounted for. In terms of the narrative, it is a let-down because suddenly almost without any explanation Elizabeth is well and ready to join her friends and her son in Motabeng. There are several instances that force her to confront her own exile. When she realizes that the quack doctor in the sanatorium thinks of her as a "comrade racialist," that marks the beginning of her recovery. Her attitude changes. At first she screams at the Batswana nurses to leave her alone because she never wants to "be an African," later she participates in the institutional activities. The other instance that coaxes her back to "sanity" is the desire to be with her son Shorty again. Interestingly enough, both these activities reaffirm her affiliations with others. She realizes both that she is not a racist and that she is a mother, two crucial parts of her identity systems that assert belonging to a material world. These realizations also wrench her away from individual malaise toward social placement and acceptance in the small community in Motabeng.

Her sanity is restored, not just through external circumstances but through some of the discoveries she makes through her dialogue with the half-mythical, half-real characters of Sello and Dan. Sello, she finally realizes, shows her the complete goodness that humanity is capable of. Head writes, "Sello made me believe that mankind had now acquired the soul-pattern I saw on the face of Buddha. Lots of people looked like him in their souls. I was so exalted those days I simply took a wild mental leap. I thought: Mankind will awaken to the wonder in their own souls. Poverty will be solved overnight; there are so many magnificent people alive."[64] But just as quickly as he shows her the possibility of "human goodness," which is reminiscent of Makhaya's desire to make everyone a millionaire, Sello takes it away, warning, "'You're wrong about one thing,' he said seriously. 'You're wrong about this mankind waking up business. I hope they never do. I don't trust them. Once they see something they'll use it to kill each other. Everything that could be useful, like atomic energy, they use for death. If they get an idea that they have inner powers too, can you imagine what they'd do?'"[65]

Sello's warning seems to contradict all the lessons that Elizabeth has learned through the course of her "insanity." Sello seems to continue his task as someone who is constantly bringing Elizabeth's inclusion of humanity and "universalism" into sharp relief. He does not think that all of humanity is ready, as Elizabeth is, to bear the fruits of inner truth. Here again, the Buddhist and Hindu influence on Head is quite pronounced. Sello indicates that people who have not experienced the "workout" that Elizabeth has at a personal level can never understand what it means to value inner knowledge without abusing it in order to seize power over the rest of humanity.

But to return to Elizabeth's notion of self-grandeur, it is curious that *she* is chosen for this "workout" and comes to accept what Sello tells her: "Then we said: Send us perfection. They sent you. Then we asked: What is perfection? And they said: Love."[66] Later she speaks of herself as a "prophet." What, then, do these prophecies indicate? Is Elizabeth really insane? These realizations occur at the point when she is ready to come back to Motabeng—the Motabeng she had rejected—only when she is ready to belong. She comes back with a clear sense of and desire for belonging which had been absent before. And it is through her status as a prophetess who belongs that the exilic consciousness is restored to its privileged position in the hierarchy of Head's interests.

Elizabeth tends to take her task as a "prophet" rather seriously. She comes back to Motabeng to all the tasks that had become unbearable for her; isn't it the task of the prophet to come back to the society that forsakes her in order to fulfill those prophecies? Kolawole Ogungbesan writes in his article in *Présence Africaine* that the Cape gooseberry is synonymous with Elizabeth, in that both desire to take root in a foreign country in an organic way.[67] The communal symbol of the Cape gooseberry becomes the individual's totem of not only belonging but returning to fulfill all the ideals nurtured in a state of exile. The prophecies have to do with Elizabeth being chosen to come to Motabeng and adopt the land as she wants the land to adopt her. Her "destiny" which was full of doubt suddenly is aligned.

Her relationship to the land and to her own dispossession becomes the only grounding activity that brings her back to sanity every time her nightmare life threatens to take over. And it is exactly this type of belonging that the exilic consciousness craves. Sometimes it is Kenosi who warns her that she really has to come and take care of the garden and sometimes it is the sheer necessity of taking account of all that keeps on growing in a garden that restores her; using the berries to make jam as soon as they are ready brings order to her life. This relationship between work, growing things, land, and belonging does account for Elizabeth's coming back to sanity in part, but not entirely. What reverses Elizabeth's "soul death," is, as I have indicated earlier, a let-down. Sello, in telling her about Dan's power over her, says: "What he showed you was all that he had in his heart. There was nothing else. He saw the opposite in you. He saw the monk. He thought you might not fall in with his plans. That's why he took you on, to remold you in his own image. I gave him a free hand because I wanted to study, completely, his image. And I thought you needed the insight into absolute evil. I'm sorry it was so painful." [68]

Even though the passage seems to make Elizabeth the dupe of the great yet whimsical patriarchal manipulation, one cannot forget that Sello is really her own personal creation, just as Dan and Medusa are. And the lesson she learns is twofold; first, she "had no illusions left about god or mercy or pity," and, second, she experiences "a slow, upwelling joy and happiness." [69] This ambivalence is identical to the one she experienced in the beginning, before her "insanity." What then is this journey that Sello and she both proclaim to have completed? I believe that her victory, which is really only part victory, is a personal one, even though the lessons are communal. The let-down comes when all that is absolute evil, like Dan, just disappears in a cloud of smoke and to take its place another equally dubious wisdom that signifies absolute good toward humankind appears. This aspect of Head's realistic novel seems to be the riskiest. If everyone is to live happily ever after, another kind of novel is required.

To add to the simplistic lessons learned, Elizabeth projects, or rather Sello projects for her, that "torture and evil became irrelevant," and just after this he shows her the "incandescent light" that signifies the "brotherhood of man."[70] I suspect that Head is unable to gracefully end a complex novel especially after the protagonist's sanity is restored. She too is an exile who had several nervous breakdowns, like Elizabeth, and needs to resolve them in order to have a considerably happy ending. But Head gives her novel this ending at a price.

The "happy" ending, even though it does not detract from the "workout," comes somewhat abruptly. The resolutions seem a bit simplistic. The exile's desire to work is understandable; when she says simply to Kenosi "I've come back to work. . . . Let me see the garden," the restorative part of her life is asserting itself.[71] But the resolution of the madness and "soul death" is another matter altogether. Head can only talk about that aspect of Elizabeth's recovery in Christian platitudes: "David's song arose in her heart once more, but this time infinitely more powerful and secure: 'I have been through the valley of the shadow of death, but I fear no evil. I shall dwell in the house of the Lord forever.'"[72]

And even the devil incarnate, Dan, with whom she is seeking a confrontation especially after she has seen through his seduction and the very narrow "dividing line between good and evil," becomes a force of deeper realization in her life. Head writes, "But Dan had blasted her to a height far above Buddha; he had deepened and intensified all her qualities. He was one of the greatest teachers she'd work with, but he taught by default—he taught the extremes of love and tenderness through the extremes of hate; he taught an alertness for falsehoods within, because he had used any means at his disposal to destroy Sello. And from the degradation and destruction of her life had arisen a still, lofty serenity of soul nothing could shake."[73] After she has learned good even from perpetrators of evil, like Dan, *A Question of Power* is resolved as a novel, even though many questions of another kind remain unanswered.

Upon wondering why it is part of the expectation of a reader of this novel to look for answers, one has to examine the dialectics set up by Head herself. The problematic ending is certainly a testimony to Head's inquiry into the nature of power in its relationship to good and evil. She does provide some clues in regard to these problems but falls short of the grand design. Her collaboration with Sello to bring about universal goodness in the microcosm and by extension the macrocosm of societies remains unfulfilled. In the last analysis Elizabeth has found solutions not for Elizabeth the prophet or Elizabeth the savior but rather for Elizabeth, Tom's friend, the Elizabeth who works diligently with Kenosi and stuns the people of a dry land with luscious vegetables, and finally the Elizabeth who is constantly pulled back into belonging to a community and to an identity because she can never forget that she is Shorty's mother or Kenosi's partner.

So even though she remains an exile, it is through the dissipation of that exilic principle that she can "belong." It is through what Linda Susan Beard has called the "recovery of the ordinary" that her sanity is restored, and that recovery sends the exile back through an experience of her exilic consciousness toward a sense of belonging.

5

"WOMEN TALK":
A Dialogue on Oppression

The Collector of Treasures recreates Wole Soyinka's "dome of continuity," con-
necting the past and the present. The volume, by its very existence, is an articulate challenge to the axioms of white South African historiography, that too-
oft-repeated gospel about the imposition of Christian civilization as a slavific
solution to the interminable, internecine tribal conflicts of the region.

—Linda Susan Beard, "Bessie Head's Syncretic Fictions"

BESSIE HEAD'S collection of short stories was undoubtedly written over
a longer period than her novels. The stories were written after she had
found a home in Botswana, "where the African experience is continuous and unbroken" and while she observed life lived by women there.[1]
It is evident that she did not even intend to write these stories for a
specific collection because many of them were published by various
journals and magazines before the publication of *The Collector of Treasures* in 1975. On the surface, these stories tend to be simple pictures
of women's village life in Botswana, sometimes interspersed by the
author's sporadic commentary. As Head herself said, *The Collector of
Treasures* is "like a resume of 13 years of living entirely in village life."[2]
But upon a closer examination of the range of ideas and images that
Head incorporates in this work, it becomes clear that these "straightforward" pictures of village life are not just that but rather a complex
dialogue between women and sometimes between women and men,
about women's experience of society, culture, and their own roles in
that milieu. What is prevalent in these portraits primarily of women is
what lies under the surface of women's actions within and without

171

societal norms or what constitutes Head's subtext. In other words, Head's expertise consists of a subtle insistence that what one sees on the surface of women's lives is not the complete picture. There is always a "story," occasionally articulated by the women, that translates into a dialogue they struggle to realize with other women and themselves. In each story, one is left to wonder whether there is a truth behind the truth of the events taking place in the narrative. In the story "Life," for example, one wonders whether there is another truth behind Life's fun-loving urban ways or whether that is a given fact that has to be absorbed whether it is true or not.

These stories chart women's oral culture and the experience of that culture. The delicate subtlety of the subtext constitutes women's "herstory," or what Françoise Lionnet has called the "geographies of pain." Michael Thorpe has authenticated the relationship of Bessie Head with the mainly oral village storyteller in *The Collector of Treasures*. He notes that the "subtitle, *and Other Botswana Village Tales,* indicates her kinship with the village story teller of the oral tradition. Hers are rooted, folkloristic tales woven from the fabric of village life and intended to entertain and enlighten, not to engage the modern close critic."[3] Yet this modern critic, among others, is fascinated by the complexity inherent in the women's dialogue which is at the root of this collection.

I shall not discuss the stories that have been published elsewhere, except when the focus of my argument necessitates. What is fundamentally interesting about this dialogue between women is that one can perceive quite clearly that, through fictional explorations into gendered sociopolitical identities, Head is coming to terms with the exiled position that women inhabit and experience in most societies.[4]

It is not so much that these explorations are new, but rather that Head's implied analysis of women's experience becomes a very important part of "Third World" feminist discourse. In her portraiture of women, she describes and critiques the narrow framework of women's lives and the constant negotiations and renegotiations that women with personal and political identity agendas are willing or compelled to make.

The nature of Head's explorations is feminist in political sympathy and ideology, her disavowal of feminism notwithstanding. These stories are woven into the sociohistoric framework of women's lives and draw heavily on the actual lived history of tribes in Botswana, linking the two together in unorthodox fashion, simultaneously contributing to feminist colonial discourse. Even though Head feared identification with groups and always claimed she was "not feminist," she tends to base her discourse on what Zoe Wicomb suggests as the primary task of the Third World feminist critic: "We might as well start on the level of nomenclature," she writes.[5] Head attempts to accomplish this through a specific focus on women's lives in Botswana. Part of the "naming" encompasses taking Third World women out of the context in which they have been too readily seen, that of victimized "other" forever suffering a triple colonization. It is not my intention to negate the victimization or pretend it never happened but rather to unfreeze the "viewed" victim from under the microscopic focus of the viewer and examine not only the pockets and modes of resistance that are apparent in their lived experience, but also the subversive dialogues they have with each other about them. A close textual analysis of *The Collector of Treasures,* especially as it addresses issues relating to women's dialogue about their experience, accomplishes this. This analysis illuminates yet another aspect of women's consciousness. This time the dialogue is about their own exilic identities and commences as a result of the emerging consciousness about the sociopolitical and historical spaces that women uninhabit.

The communication of these specifically feminine areas of discourse emerge out of two dialogues, one that the women characters have with each other and the one that Bessie Head communicates to her readers. Both fall into the realm of what I call "women talk." The second, where the author directly communicates these areas of women's discourse to the reader, are of particular interest. Head is doing at a sociological and literary level what Kumkum Sangari and Sudesh Vaid do at a sociohistoric level in their book *Recasting Women: Essays in Colonial History.*[6]

As reviewers have noted, Sangari and Vaid draw distinctions between the "study of gender in colonial societies . . . locating it . . . within existing forms of inequality (class, caste, etc.) and the interrelationship of contest and collusion between indigenous patriarchal norms and those held by British administrators."[7] These distinctions are important to Third World feminist discourse because they help locate specific areas of women's oppression without scattering its lessons amid the macrocosm of postcolonial discourses.

Head, very consciously, goes much further than the distinctions made by Sangari and Vaid by drawing yet another conclusion. She adds another qualifier to these discussions, by stipulating areas of discourse, where patriarchal structures existing before colonialism were, especially in terms of the Southern African family structure which left a large majority of men "without resources," more prone to reconfigure the damage done by colonialism to traditional values. Rather, African men became the "victims" of colonialism but continue to practice traditional patriarchal superiority over the women without taking the responsibility that tradition designated. For instance, polygamy becomes a subject for intragender debate, but most of the men who are responsible for the postcolonial version of polygamy often refuse to enter that debate. Head compels the women to enter the debate through an examination of their sexual and economic experience under the shadow of polygamy. It is through this entrance into the minute intimate details of women's lives that she forges an "authentic" Third World feminism.

Bessie Head told Linda Susan Beard in an interview conducted shortly before her death, "Most of the stories there are based on reality; they're not inventions. They happened; they are changed."[8] This interest in the actual historical pain of women's experience coincided with her obsession about the misrepresentations of colonial history. As she does elsewhere, Head could have used her active imagination to create "purely fictional" accounts of women's lived experiences in Botswana, but she does not. Instead we have a conjunction of "herstory," truth, and a critique of patriarchal structures of government, out of which what I call "women talk" emerges in all its multilayered complexity.

Along with the process of "naming," Head inquires into the root of women's experience of suffering in Botswana and, by extension, in Africa. The portraiture of the women in the context of their various narratives is extremely poignant. They seem to leap off the page in haunting verisimilitude. Women are portrayed as grandmothers, young and old lovers, wives and mothers. There is in all these portraits a subtle, noncondemnatory dialogue on women's experience of their sexuality and their desire for socioinstitutional and moral power. In her discussion of women's sexuality, Head is unafraid to introduce the subject of old women as sexually "liberated" beings.

The absence of commentary on women's lives as a lived, not an observed, experience is a feature of African literature that such writers as Head, Ama Ata Aidoo, Buchi Emecheta, Flora Nwapa, and others changed completely. Head, like her African women colleagues, does tend to begin at the level of "nomenclature." What does this mean? Surely women's experience is "named, called and often classified" as "gender oppression," in several feminist discourses. Does the discourse of the "other" or "difference," as it both is and is not separate from feminism, really contribute to the African postcolonial context, or does the woman's marginality simply get dispersed in the malaise of general racial as well as colonial oppression?

I believe that Head makes a case for the distinct struggle that Botswana women are engaged in, at this point in history, as it is separate from and as it coincides with colonial oppression which they shared, as women, with the men. Their struggle coincides with the South African woman's plight as well. Whereas in Southern Africa, the White woman "having identified the traditional place of female veneration—the home, motherhood, the family—as the very site of their oppression, sought their liberation outside of the home," apartheid, and in Botswana losing men to the mines, enabled the same notions of motherhood, family, and home for Black women, to be "characterized by desire" to find a home, which often remains unfulfilled.[9] At this juncture, the analogies with slavery in the United States and other places, especially in the writings of Toni Morrison and August Wilson, can be made quite literally.[10]

The women who appear in the obviously historically inspired tales in *The Collector of Treasures* are "others" only in that they are the reason why men, especially important chiefs and kings, disregard tradition. Head wants to argue that since women are not the natural pillars of tradition, they are able to challenge it more stridently than the men, as well as demand the same from their men. In "The Deep River: A Story of Ancient Tribal Migration," only one possible cause of the patterns of migration in Botswana is traced.[11] In a society where men and women are considered to be veering away from and discarding tradition if they fall in love, Sembembele and Rankwana's love for each other seems to handicap them, but the social blame seems to fall entirely on the woman because she is the cause of Sembembele's one "weakness." As reported after the event, even the old men who don't seem to remember much can say that "they lost their place of birth over a woman. They shake their heads and say that women have always caused a lot of trouble in the world."[12]

In a footnote following the tale, Head assures us that "the story is an entirely romanticized and fictionalized version of the history of the Botalaote tribe." Head is aware of the irony of "actual recorded fact." She adds, "Some historical data was given to me by the old men of the tribe, but it was unreliable as their memories had tended to fail them."[13] Even though this is an "entirely romanticized and fictionalized" version, it still constitutes the folk "history of the Botalaote tribe," and some "historical data" was given to her by eyewitnesses. Her recording and recoding "herstory" sums up the problematics of postcolonial and gender dichotomies. Just as Head's histories, *Serowe: Village of the Rain Wind* and *A Bewitched Crossroad*, seek to decolonize or envision the past, this tale of ancient migration tends to exonerate the love that Sembembele and Rankwana have for each other. The story has a bias in perceiving them as lovers and companions rather than as destroyers of tradition. This tale, further, presents Rankwana as not the only one responsible for breaking up the tribe. She is portrayed as somebody who knows her own mind and not somebody who can be led mindlessly by what is designated as "her womanly role" in her traditional society. She wants Sembembele to acknowledge the love they share as well as the product of that love, their son, and anything short of that, she is willing to die for. She refuses to be herded from man to man for the convenience of short-sighted patriarchal demands and traditions.

The old men who provide the "historical data" for Head do not tell her anything about the bravery and steadfastness of Rankwana. She makes that up in her own "imagination." But, would not an entirely patriarchal society governed by tradition do much the same to women's discourse that the White racist colonials did to African history? Head tries to negotiate women's history out of the patriarchal malaise by focusing nonjudgmental attention on the tale of Rankwana. At the most fundamental level, and unlike other tragic heroines, Rankwana refuses to take the entire blame for the traditionally unpermissible relationship she has with her lover. She refuses to be a "tragic" victim. And indeed, why should she be the only one who recognizes Makobi as her child when he belongs to Sembembele as well? She demands the same courage from Sembembele as she manifests herself, namely, publicly recognizing the love that leads to the conception of her child.

Even though Rankwana's demand of equal courage from Sembembele results in their expulsion from their homeland, she never once gives in, never once thinks of effacing herself into the "inevitable." She is not only bold but brazen and demands the same from her lover. Head's anthology of short stories commences appropriately with Rankwana throwing the gauntlet of challenge to all African women who have consistently taken a backseat to history. Even though her own actions lead to geographical exile, Rankwana challenges African women to "belong" to their societies and cultures in meaningful ways and not to take the exiled place demarcated for them. Her challenge consists of getting women to know their own desires in the relationships they have with men. Rankwana implies that women should seize the power that their own experiences illustrate to them but which "their" societies want to deny them. Head's choice of beginning her anthology with this story as the starting point of "women talk" is not surprising. The ancestress claimed legitimacy for herself, her relationship to the new chief, and her son. She refuses to suffer. What remains is the question about what or whether her descendants have contributed to this discourse and tradition of strong independent womanhood.

When the subject of polygamy emerges in the anthology, one finds that despite their apparent discomfort with the institution, women have not forced the dialogue to thicken by seizing Rankwana's gauntlet. Rankwana has challenged the notion that women of traditional Africa are perfectly content with their lot, which very few of them take up. There are several stories in *The Collector of Treasures* that depict the hardship and suffering of women because the ideology of polygamy was distorted through the imbalance that colonialism creates and also through the changing awareness that women impose on traditional societies. Often, the suffering caused through polygamous alliances is not economical but emotional and neither suffering is recognized as a problem facing the family structure of Southern Africa. Colonialism seemed to have started the trend of separation and erosion of the Black family structure, economically and emotionally, a little differently from the way slavery did, through transporting a male labor force to mines and other work areas while the women were more or less left to tend to the needs of the old people and the children. The men who did not see their families except for brief visits were saints if they stayed loyal to one family, regardless of all the deprivation that women had to face while they were gone.

Head does not become an apologist for male sexuality or polygamy as her male counterparts often do. She tends to distinguish sharply between postcolonial and Third World feminist discourse, without jeopardizing either. She overemphasizes questions of polygamy as it was manifested in the family structures in postcolonial times. In "The Special One," the problem of polygamy is not entirely economic but rather it is emotional.[14] The emotional bonding in this story is between women friends who pray for each other's happiness, Mrs. Maleboge and Gaenametse. Even though the elder woman has been denied economic stability as soon as her husband dies, by his brothers, and is forced to support herself by becoming a schoolteacher, the focus is on the younger Gaenametse who seems to be utterly distracted and over-wrought by the incessant sexual wanderings of her young husband.

The inherent otherness of female sexuality is portrayed very starkly in "The Special One," and it is Gaenametse's husband who tends to be seen, even by the women in the village, as the innocent one. After the protagonist is seen talking to Gaenametse, one of her neighbors tells her with utter contempt: "No one will talk to *her*. She's a wash-out! Everyone knows about her private life. She had a terrible divorce case. She was driving the husband mad. She pestered him day and night for the blankets, and even wanted him to do it during the time she was having her monthly bleeding."[15] Simultaneous with this patriarchal discourse is the one the women articulate. Even though this particular woman seems to have absorbed patriarchal notions of the sexual dialectic between men and women and has no regard for the idea that Gaenametse might have overcome her traditional taboo at great cost in order to make a desperate attempt to prevent her husband from going to his lover, while tradition dictated that she remain sexually unavailable to him during menstruation, there is a subtext. The neighbor adds: "Many women have killed men by sleeping with them during that time. It's a dangerous thing and against our custom. The woman will remain alive and the man will die. She was trying to kill the husband, so the court ruled that he'd better be parted from such a terrible woman." [16] Head's comments are illuminating. The protagonist and the teller of the tale sharply disagree with the village interpretation of this woman's sexuality.

The protagonist sees through the village gossip after the husband's renunciation and through Gaenametse's assumed piety. Head writes, "He must have anticipated this social reaction to his wife and deliberately invoked the old tribal taboo to boost his image. How she must have cringed and squirmed, and after the divorce tried to build up an image of respect by dressing up like old Mrs Maleboge." [17] The reaction of the village and the court is easily manipulated by the husband and consists of a deliberate misunderstanding of what a woman wants or needs, emotionally and sexually. This notion of making public certain aspects, even if untrue, about a woman's private life gives inordinate power to the husband who can always count on the eternal predictability of society—a society that invariably censures women's demands for exclusivity and monogamy without even mentioning the man's sexual wanderings.

In "The Special One," an older woman's recourse to sexuality is denied in the light of day by her "boy" partner because any manifestation of sexuality in women, especially older women, is immediately translated into perverse "promiscuity," frowned on by society, while the "virility" of even the older man is rewarded in terms of numerous sexual partners, marriage, and easily obtained divorce. Gaenametse tells the protagonist that the only recourse to sexual or emotional life that old women have, even though they don't have to worry about being pregnant anymore, is thickly veiled from society. Here, Gaenametse touches upon female *jouissance,* a subject especially taboo for old women who are past child-bearing age. "When you are old," she said, "that's the time you make love, more than when you are young. You make love because you are no longer afraid of making babies. You make love with young boys. They all do it but it is done very secretly. No one suspects, that is why they look so respectable in the day time." [18] However, Gaenametse cannot tolerate the patriarchal emotional/sexual, public/private split that is forced upon her sense of self. She confronts her boy lover while he is strolling, in broad daylight, with a young woman, whereas he only comes to her in the secrecy of night. This confrontation has all the tones of finality even though not one word is exchanged between them.

When the protagonist catches up with Gaenametse again, she seems happy and "complacent" because she has found someone for whom she is "mosadi-rra, the special one." There seems to be, at last, peace in Gaenametse's emotional yard and the subtext takes over: "The old days of polygamy are gone and done with, but the men haven't yet accepted that the women want them to be monogamists."[19] The Botswana woman's sexuality is also "characterized by desire." Head focuses on the moment she "names" her own experience, ignoring social censure and moving it out of the realm of illusive desire and longing, in which a slave mother's motherhood or a South African "nanny's" motherhood is frozen. She wants to be able to expect love, respect, and constancy from the man she marries and contentment from the children she bears.

Another ugly face of polygamous relationships is seen in the story of Mma-Mabele in "Witchcraft."[20] As in "The Deep River," a woman's strength and perseverance is pitted against tradition. Mma-Mabele's fiancé disappears soon after she begins to show signs of pregnancy, thereby ignoring a fundamental African custom of looking after one's progeny. She is left to fend for her child and herself along with a younger sister who is in a similar situation as herself. In this story the "naming" of a woman's discourse is crucial to the survival of a new family unit, tolerated yet unrecognized by society. Even though the reason why the *baloi,* supernatural evil spirits, are sent after Mma-Mabele remains obscure, it is often implied that her refusal to suffer in the ways that society designates makes her a subject of male sexual scorn and jealousy.

After her fiancé betrays her, she makes certain decisions about her sexuality which cause her to be ridiculed and minimized by men who simply cannot stand being rejected by her. "She was called 'he-man' and it was meant to imply that something was not quite right with her genitals, they were mixed up, a combination of male and female. The rumour had been spread by a number of men who had made approaches to her and whom she had turned down with quiet finality: 'I don't want to show myself anymore,' she'd said."[21] Again like Gaenametse, Mma-Mabele feels that she has been emotionally violated by the man to whom she entrusted a valuable part of a vision of her future self. She does not deny herself sexual recourse but seeks it elsewhere. However, because of the economic hardship and the possibility of taking care of another child singlehandedly, Mma-Mabele refuses to "show" herself.

Even though she has refused to have sex, her sexuality is controlled by the public domain of mythologizing villagers. She is considered half male and half female because she decided to take charge of her own sexuality given the limited options open to her. After all, she chose celebacy because relationships with men did not open up any but the old sexist venues. Head comments: "The men never looked up as far as a quiet, sensitive face that might have suffered insult or injury. The only value women were given in the society was their ability to have sex; there was nothing beyond that."[22] This sort of colonial and patriarchal, polygamous betrayal of female sexual and emotional consciousness is the one that the protagonist combats by shutting herself entirely out of the sexual domain of village life. This scorn of male sexuality is a dangerous space to inhabit for it results in the attack of the *baloi*, through which she nearly loses her life.

The "naming" of women's experience that occurs in this story evokes pathos and humor. When Mma-Mabele has gone through a visibly harrowing experience and emerges having defeated tradition— a tradition that did not protect her sexuality, her health, or her well-being, she can afford to utterly disregard it. She reacts in anger to the village people who expected the *baloi* invasion to kill her: "'You all make me sick! There is no one to help the people, not even God. I could not sit down because I am too poor and there is no one else to feed my children.'"[23] In recognizing the struggle before her, she is naming women's work experience, poverty, and the help they can expect from any patriarchal tradition, be it God, Lekena, the medicine man, or the income of a partner and husband who takes responsibility for feeding their children especially when she is unable to do so. The finality with which she eats those oranges, recommended to her by the European doctor while rejecting the costly offer of Lekena, who wishes to charge her an exhorbitant fee for discovering who wishes to kill her, has little to do with her belief in the superiority of Western medicine and more to do with how much money she can spare on the brutal threat of the *baloi*. She knows that she has to continue to struggle, no matter what happens to her health, because no one else will take care of her child if she dies.

Two aspects of Mma-Mabele's dialogue with tradition and society are important. One is her rejection of male sexuality which assumes polygamy and the other is her resistance against traditional beliefs and punishments. Her "secret," if any, is her iron will and her subversive negotiation of her systems of economic and emotional energy.

The most poignant story in this collection, "The Collector of Treasures," also relates to women's economic hardships because of a neocolonial misunderstanding of traditional polygamy.[24] I am not trying to uphold the tradition of polygamy here, but rather to examine Head's critique of this ancient institution, especially in regard to its modern, postcolonial manifestations. Whether this misuse of the idea of polygamy comes from the erosion of the family structure during colonialism or whether it is yet another way that dominant patriarchal structures oppress women while letting the men go scot-free is as hard to determine here as it is elsewhere.

A very important aspect of this longer short story, which, like "Looking for a Rain God," got its inspiration from a newspaper report that Head read in Botswana, is the analysis of women's sexuality within the context of "women talk" and male dominance.[25] This talk between women incorporates a complaint about polygamy especially, as it is practiced today, and about male sexuality and its manifestation within societal sanctions for men, that is, an acceptance of numerous sexual partners for men, a disregard for female *jouissance* during sexual contact, and male irresponsibility regarding economic support for any children that they have created within or outside wedlock.

Head's narrative strategy is different here because she begins with an extreme situation. We are at first aware not of the events that lead to the killing but just of the fact of the killing itself. In the jail cell, Dikeledi Mokopi meets four other women who have also killed their husbands in a terribly brutal, sexual way. The women's dialogue about men's sexuality as it defines theirs begins after the legal consequences of these extremes have situated themselves spatially and discussion about sexual identities has become limited by time and place. They are all in jail and do not expect to be released for the rest of their lives. This last, very sobering factor of their lives while they experience incarceration is not really touched on by the author. Rather, the emotional and social solidarity that these women feel in their critique of male sexuality, their own lives, and thus the society that sanctions male brutality toward women, constitutes the narrative thrust of "The Collector of Treasures."

In this story, death becomes the subject of dialogue for women. Women's role as giver of life is complicated enough but this story ponders their position as takers of life. Executing death which is the exact opposite of the life-giving capacity of women's physical capacities is the starting point of the dialogue between Kebonye and Dikeledi. The first aspect of the subject of killing, albeit provoked, comes up when Kebonye asks the newcomer Dikeledi whether she feels sorry or guilty about this crime, for their actions are classified as such. Dikeledi decides, "'Not really.'" Why is this question on Kebonye's mind? Even though we are not told anything about the religious persuasion of either woman, the subject of being "sorry" is introduced into their dialogue with each other not as an experienced emotional reality but rather as an act of "naming," which is a mental activity, not an emotional one. We only know that Dikeledi is a "good person" and, in spite of her situation in life, she has made some of the most valuable friendships anyone could make. She is also a capable woman and not afraid to fend for herself and her children, as well as to provide help for her friends. For instance, she helps Kenalepe when she is recovering from a miscarriage by taking care of her own and her friend's children.

Head establishes what became a feminist issue in the United States only in the 1970s, that perfectly sane and good women are driven to near insanity through mental and physical abuse. Abused women often take recourse in the most extreme way. Both Kebonye and Dikeledi want to seize power over their own lives in a straightforward way, but what compels this desire is an anger that can no longer be contained. And it is out of this brutal anger that a brutal punishment for these men first takes shape in their minds and then in actuality. The mode of killing is specifically sexual. Both women say that they have cut off the "special parts" of their husbands. Kebonye's contribution to "women talk" is a tale of her life that makes her jail sentence seem orderly and peaceful. She tells Dikeledi: ""Our men do not think that we need tenderness and care. You know, my husband used to kick me between the legs when he wanted that. I once aborted with a child, due to this treatment. I could see that there was no way to appeal to

him if I felt ill, so once I said to him that if he liked he could keep
some other woman as well because I couldn't manage to satisfy all his
needs."[26] Kebonye's marriage seems to be particularly horrific but it is
strange that she speaks of sexuality between herself and her husband
as a means to keep him "satisfied." The husband certainly does not feel
any reciprocal obligation and is not called upon to return the marital
"task," which is felt only by the woman. In a curious way her husband
must have regarded his own sexuality as something to be "satisfied,"
almost separate from himself and not complicated by any other desire.
Because of this treatment and a lack of any pleasure on Kebonye's part,
it is no wonder that she pleads with him to employ other lovers to
"satisfy" his needs. His behavior is further complicated by the fact that
he is an educated man, who should, supposedly, know better.

However, it is still awfully peculiar that both these "killers" would
kill their oppressors in such a horribly sexual way. There is something
strangely personal yet detached about the sort of punishment meted
out to these men by their wives. There is a hint of revenge at being
humiliated in an intimate sexual way by their own men, much as
women reporting rape situations feel rage at male sexuality in general
and at the man's "special parts" in particular. The rage is the starting
point of the punishment in the case of both Dikeledi and Kebonye and
manifests itself in their taking away the offending organ, the accompa-
nying death being almost incidental to the primary focus. So powerful
is Dikeledi's message to the men, regarding their own and the men's
sexuality, that "it made all the men shudder with horror. It was some
weeks before they could find the courage to go to bed with women;
they preferred to do something else."[27]

This blow becomes a collective message from the women to the men
of the community. Dikeledi takes up Rankwana's gauntlet and throws
it back as a challenge to the patriarchal society. Even though she is in
jail for life, Head's narrative denies that that is a justified incarceration.
Both Kebonye and Dikeledi first reaffirm to one another that what
their husbands did was wrong, and, second, they imply that society is
to blame for taking them away from their children and for not protecting them from the patriarchal sexual prerogative.

After Kebonye learns of her husband's actions at the school he is
teaching in, she kills him. Her act is motivated by undisguised fury, but
also a desire to protect other young girls in her husband's care. Dikel-

edi's act of fury was motivated by the sexual assumption that Garesego made in coming "home" without any concern for the three children he had helped to produce. A woman's sexuality, as I have argued elsewhere, is tied to her children and Garesego's denial is a curious annihilation of her and of his own sexuality. When he is killed, it is simply a grotesque symbol or spectacle rather than a human being, father, or husband who is savagely eliminated. However, neither woman comments on her own sexuality at all. They both seem to imply that the husband's behavior is reprehensible but expected and the only recourse was to remove his "special parts"; as if both the expectation and the murder constitute larger aspects of women's fate that remains unquestioned.

This revelation in jail is shortly followed by the exchange between Dikeledi and her friend Kenalepe, who has a totally different idea of marriage and sex. Kenalepe is deeply shocked when she learns that all sex means to her friend is something unpleasant to be gotten over or even as a means for having children. She insists that women are here in the world "to make love and enjoy it." This is a new addition to the discourse on Dikeledi's sexuality. It is no coincidence that her name means "mother's tears." Kenalepe is even more shocked because Garesego seems to have the reputation as a Don Juan in the village and, thus, the whole aspect of economics is added to the sexual gender discourse. It does not matter whether a man like Garesego has earned a reputation as a splendid lover or is simply somebody who "just jumps on and jumps off" a woman, because he has a big pay packet and no financial responsibilities, at least not ones he is willing to recognize. Women who are connected to postcolonial manifestations of polygamy have to fight with each other in addition to being very quiet about their own sexual desires for fear of losing the major income provider. In the creation of Kenalepe and Paul, Head is introducing a new feminist dialectic in the discourse on women's sexuality. Women want a relationship of sexual pleasure and social equality with the men in their lives. Kenalepe and Paul lend an optimistic balance of possibility to relations between men and women, as opposed to the devastating silent fury of the impasse that exists between Dikeledi and Garesego.

There is a striking parallel between the women who are forced to fight for a man's pay packet and the man whose sexuality Head compares to that of a dog. She describes in graphic detail the sexuality of such a man: "If one watched the village dogs chasing a bitch in heat, they usually moved around in a pack of four or five. As the mating progressed one dog would attempt to gain dominance . . . and oust all the others from the bitch's vulva. . . . No doubt during that Herculean feat, the dog imagined he was the only penis in the world and that there had to be a scramble for it . . . [such a man] accepted no responsibility for the young he procreated and like the dogs and bulls, he also made females abort." [28]

Head's tone becomes a little more compassionate toward a man like Garesego who has not taken the opportunity to form a "family life of a new order" when the chance was provided after the overthrow of colonialism. In describing such a man, she writes that he was "a broken wreck with no inner resources at all. It was as though he was hideous to himself and in an effort to flee his own inner emptiness, he spun away from himself in a dizzy kind of death dance of wild destruction and dissipation." [29]

There is a level of pathos in the man with "no inner resources," even though his family suffers from his behavior, which culminates in the fight for the patriarchal jackpot by economically disadvantaged women in the village who attach themselves to him. Garesego is immediately contrasted with the other kind of man, Paul Thebolo, who had the "power to create himself anew," after the White man was finished trying to make him into a "boy." This man was a "poem of tenderness" and turned "his resources, both emotional and material, towards his family life and he went on and on with his own quiet rhythm, like a river." [30]

Paul's sexuality is contrasted to Garesego's in one of the sessions that Dikeledi and Kenalepe have together, after which the latter, wanting her friend to experience the same *jouissance* she herself experiences, offers her husband to Dikeledi. Kenalepe breaks a taboo by exclaiming "'Oh, it isn't enough,'" when her friend implies that her reward after the bad sex and marriage with Garesego are her children. It is unusual for a rural African woman to verbalize that she wants more from a sexual relationship than just children. Yet in the context within which Kenalepe confides the following to Dikeledi, it is perfectly understandable. They are both able to continue a dialogue about their experience as women and thus the subject of sexuality as a vehicle, for recognizing their identity is one of great interest to them. Later Kenalepe talks even more explicitly about sexuality: "Oh, if you knew what it was really like, you would long for it, I can tell you! I sometimes think I enjoy that side of life far too much. Paul knows a lot about all that. And he always has some kind of new trick with which to surprise me. He has a certain way of smiling when he has thought up something new and I shiver a little and say to myself: 'Ha, what is Paul going to do tonight!'"[31]

Even though she admonishes herself for enjoying "that side of life far too much" and is perhaps a bit embarrassed, she anticipates having sex with pleasure and desire which she does not hide from her friend. Her husband seems to have a great deal invested in not letting his marriage become stale.

The "women talk" which first began between women friends in this story, and then later struck "horror" and fear in the men, constitutes part of the sexual dialogue between men and women in the postcolonies. Paul, an unusual person, encourages this friendship and takes it as a matter of course rather than being threatened by it. It is, however, fairly clear that women, in spite of inhibitions about aggressive sexual behavior—after all, it is Paul who thinks of new things to do, not Kenalepe—have progressed in terms of what they desire in their relationships with men. However, most of the men in the story, with the exception of Paul, are still continuing to hold the dominant yet regressive sexual-economic clout over women's heads. It is with a combination of powerlessness and anger that the subject of death is introduced to women's discourse about their intimate experience.

It is clear, even from the kind of fairly explicit "women talk" on sexuality, that it is neither easy nor very commonplace for women to talk openly about their relationships with men even to their best friends. Kenalepe begins hesitatingly and so does Dikeledi, and they keep halting, afraid to demand more from friendship or from their men, always grateful to a society that denied them so much, or as with Kenalepe a husband and parents who gave too much. Both seem to make the same assumptions about the role of women even though one is happy in her marriage and the other miserable. For women, happiness comes only accidentally. The predominant lot of the woman is burden, sexual or economic, and only the lucky ones, the ones with good husbands or families, can expect happiness. This ideology, shared by both friends, implies that even though it is the defined task of a

woman to make the man "happy," he is not under a similar obligation
toward her. Head keeps reverting to the whole question of feminine
jouissance. Why is it that sexuality is a man's pleasure and a woman's
burden? For Head, the question itself lends a dimension to "women
talk" which begs to be explored. Kenalepe and Dikeledi, who represent
polar opposites in their experience with sexuality, talk about it, but it
is Dikeledi who achieves a sense of personal empowerment and control
at the end of the story, through the murder of Garesego.

THE COLLECTOR OF TREASURES is a collection of tales not just about the
problematics of women's sexuality but also a discourse on women and
power as it is manifested in the desire to control oneself and others,
within particular social institutions such as marriage. Women are often
just as interested in seeking power as their male counterparts, but Head
tells us that the strategies are very different and the chance of punishment far greater if one is caught in one's "facade" than if one were a
man. It is a fairly common societal assumption that a man wants
power. The same argument cannot be made about women. They are
supposed to be loved but not because they control; rather they "de-
serve" to be loved and respected, and that love and respect is always a
favor bestowed on them by society and can be taken away with equal
whimsicality. The woman is always forced to live a duplicitous life if
she wants power. The systems of judgment are very different for a man
and a woman. Head is making a feminist critique of a society and of
the limitations of the kinds of power it allows a woman to have. A
woman must never forget that social censure will destroy her—she
must never try to attain the kinds of power that a man has and wants.
She must forever be underhanded. In this regard there must be certain
gymnastics of identity politics occurring in each woman who aspires to
power, like Mma-Mompati. Perhaps she has even convinced herself of
the facade she offers to her village for inspection, but it works only
while it remains unchallenged. The moment Mary Pule challenges her
facade—it crumbles. Part of Head's subtext is to engage with the questions of who are the powerful women in the village and what kind of
power they are allowed to have and at what price. It seems that a
pretense of piety will help a woman in hiding secrets that she knows
will bring her social censure. Like Mrs. Maleboge, in "The Special
One," who hides her sexuality behind religious piety, like other old

women, Mma-Mompati, in "The Village Saint," uses her piety to wield a different kind of power. So clever is her disguise that all the villagers, who are never easily fooled by facades, are devastated when their "patron saint" loses her position and "fool-proof facade" of piety and good works.

The narrative not only implies the dubiousness of the limited and precariously held power that women are allowed to enjoy but also delves into the straightforward realism of the tale at hand without too much commentary. The history of the Bamangwato tribe is intermingled with this realism, in that this tribe is famous for "unexpected explosions." There are clues like the one just mentioned about what will transpire, yet this is such a splendid tale of how families set up various games with each other and outsiders in order to maintain those very facades that they later come to believe as inherent to their identities. These sorts of secrets, which are at first guarded by Mompati as a little boy or as he is called, "policeman," erupt the moment a stranger to those secrets is taken into the fold. In this case Rra-Mompati first loses all credibility in the village when he takes another wife, and, later, when his son marries allowing yet another stranger to become privy to the family secrets, Mma-Mompati is revealed as the pathetic old tyrant she really is. It is curious that the entire family believes in the facade of Mma-Mompati. Rra-Mompati looks "shame-faced at his appalling deed," of leaving the saint for somebody else. The village, her son, and husband all collaborate in maintaining the facade she has created; it seems that this is the only way for a woman to enjoy some control over her life and power over others.

It is with a fascination and intensity similar to his mother's dedication to her facade of piety that her son, Mompati, focuses on his "poor blood" and becomes an invalid at seventeen. Along with this external manifestation of an internal obsession, he develops the same sort of relationship with Mary Pule, a village girl whose facade is one of a "wilting, willowy dreamy girl with a tremulous voice," which hides her "tenacious will." Mma-Mompati does not realize the strength of the girl her son married and is secretly contemptuous of the seemingly "weak" Mary. Of course, as is to be expected, the mother-in-law goes too far and ends up losing her reputation, her power, and her son. Her place of power in Mompati's life is replaced by his wife's. Head raises very interesting questions about the traditional relationships between women. Where does the communication break down and where is there an intense struggle for power? What does this power consist of?

Neither woman is a victim *par excellence* nor are they the opposite. Mma-Mompati is a woman who by her very nature would be somebody seeking power. She is right to realize, in a rather Machiavellian fashion, that she simply would not be allowed, by her gender-conscious society, to enjoy the same power that her husband can potentially have. She makes the only decision that allows her the good opinion of the people and through that she has some power in the community. She knows that if she did not have the facade of piety she would be disenfranchised by the society as was Mrs. Maleboge, whose property was taken away from her as soon as her husband died. Not so Mma-Mompati. She is so well thought of that it is her husband and his new woman who cannot show their faces in the village and are forced to leave. Rra-Mompati would not have dared take everything away from his wife as Mrs. Maleboge's brothers-in-law did.

Mary Pule becomes the new Mma-Mompati because she exhibits the same tenacity, but with a different facade. She, too, cannot have recourse to legitimate power—a power she can claim and adopt unabashedly, but has to hide behind her facade in order to wield it. Neither character is sympathetic, but Head's subtext makes us aware of the unfortunate fight between women for the limited amount of power that is allotted to a few of them in any traditional society. Thus the manifestation of their power itself can reside only in a very traditionally feminine domain, that is, control over the earning abilities of a man—husband, son, or lover—and enjoying a "good" reputation only by working tirelessly, doing good deeds all the time. Power as represented by violent aggression in a woman would never be tolerated, let alone praised as it is in a man. Thus, when women negotiate strategies to gain power, it is always gender-specific and socially limited. This limitation often traps women into an identity space that is usually controlled and defined by their society.

Head's awareness of the minute level of competition between women is remarkable, especially since her critique is encompassed in the narrative of women who desire power but are caught in "narrow, airless" rooms. The claustrophobia necessarily felt by Mma-Mompati and Mrs. Maleboge must be unbearable. Head makes a case, here, that as a woman one cannot burst out of an unpleasant situation but must slyly coax power out of the system in order to invest it in oneself. The pathos, of course, lies in that neither Mary Pule nor Mma-Mompati have any real power, for all they do is control the opinion of the villagers over small matters.

Upon contrasting what is expected of women in the whole sphere of piety to that expected of men one finds a great difference. There is really no social benefit to be gained by men like Jacob in "Jacob: The Story of a Faith-Healing Priest," for all his devotion to his "Lord."[32] In fact, quite the reverse happens to men who "give up worldly" materiality. Jacob is thought slightly stupid for not living as luxuriously as Prophet Lebojang, especially since, unlike a woman, economic success is expected from a man's involvement with any profession. Even though Jacob is somewhat respected, it is odd that he goes about without shoes when he does not have to. Jacob is seen, in spite of his religious vocation, as somebody without any power because he does not want to acquire the external manifestations of power, which are always social and public.

The desire for power in women, on the other hand, is represented by another sort of claim on freedom. Women who do not want to be owned by men sexually also desire to claim a certain kind of power from their societies. But, in their case, in doing so they are stepping outside the bounds carefully allotted by "decent" society and consequently these women are punished, unlike the women who maintained social standards of piety or decency. Society will not stand up for them even though the crime against them is sometimes fatal. The woman Life, in the short story by the same name, was claiming a nontraditional power with the "bold, free joy of a woman who had broken all the social taboos."[33] It was the same society that sanctioned her murder, committed by her husband who was outraged by her promiscuity—the same "crime" for which they had socially and economically endorsed her, earlier. On the other hand, the husband's crime is not punished with equal severity.

In the brief months that she is the wife of the only man who really fascinated her in the village, Lesego, her economic and sexual freedom is taken away from her. For Head, female sexuality is complex because in this story it is unclear whether desire is sociologically determined. Why do women seek bondage and why do men want to control them? Oppression becomes the price they have to pay in order to have relationships. After all, several women, like Mma-Mabele, refused to "show" themselves to men any longer. Life is fairly clear about her attraction to Lesego at first, but very soon after they marry, she feels hemmed in. While they are together he even tries to control her mind by not letting her listen to the radio all day, claiming that "'women who keep that thing going the whole day have nothing in their heads.'"[34] This story is riveting because it involves us in the dramatic occurrences of the death of Life and the trial of Lesego, or "Death." He gets off very lightly while Life, ironically enough, loses her life in refusing to "become a woman." In the last analysis, only females who are ready to "become women" are given any consideration by a discriminating society. They are the only ones allowed to live. Even their lives are the property of their fathers, husbands, sons, or tribes. The only power they can have is the one that does not challenge any of these power structures and the social taboos created in order to maintain them as subordinates. Life is known as the village "fuck-about." At the same time, and as her husband points out, that there is hardly anyone in the village who doesn't fit the same description. But, unlike Life, they are discreet about their "fucking about" and do not earn money or live ostentatiously from the proceedings as she insists on doing. Thus if a woman claims sexual power and freedom, she is eliminated, for she is challenging the very root of social structures. Her subversive discourse has to stay underground and hidden for her survival. The moment her desires surface, she is destroyed. Women's real piety is punished less severely, though punished it is. Both Life and Galethebege demand control over certain spheres of their lives which is denied them.

The tale of women's piety, in this case a deeply religious belief, is linked to the coming of colonialism and the erosions it caused in family life and society. If it had not been for imperialism, Life would never have left Johannesburg from where she was exiled after Botswana received independence in 1966. She would simply have stayed in a place where she felt more at home. Life was twice exiled geographically while Galethebege was twice exiled spiritually and emotionally. The anxiety that this exile caused in the lives of these two women cannot be underestimated because they both paid dearly for it, even though Galethebege was able to muster more resistance against the dilemma that plagued her throughout her life.

Galethebege would have wanted the Christian as well as the Setswana tradition to allow her to live in peace, but the narrow-minded
priest excommunicates her and she becomes the symbol of somebody
who is divided in her soul, in her loyalty, and in her life. Even though
she never consciously thinks about the initial trickery of the missionaries, as her husband Ralokae does, she makes her peace with both sets
of customs and even in death manages to display her double loyalties
by having a non-Christian pose in death. Modise, who has known her
all her life, is amused and quickly puts her in the correct posture for a
Christian death.

The way she dies symbolizes the way she has lived, balanced precariously between Setswana custom, which is a little more understanding,
and the Christian faith which insists on petty formalities and details.
She has become, because of colonial missionaries, a perfect symbol for
exile by not being entirely at home in the religion she was raised in
nor the custom of her people, which she was born into, but forever
caught in the middle. However, the village is more tolerant toward her
exile from Christianity to Setswana custom because she is, after all, one
of them. The villagers are not so kind to someone who is an outsider to
their customs and beliefs. The woman Rose, in the story "Kgotla," is
an outsider and even though everybody acknowledges she is in the
right and much admired for it, she continues to be treated like an outsider—an exile.[35]

Rose is treated like a foreigner in some subtle and some not so subtle
ways. One of her first complaints when she is asked to relate her side
of the events is this: "It's the first time I have seen jealousy and spite
such as exists in this village and people here have no love or respect
for a foreign person. My name is Rose but I hear myself referred to as
"'that Sindebele woman.'"[36] The reason Rose is offended by being
treated like a foreigner is that one does not have to be careful about
how one treats outsiders, for they can, by definition, never belong to
you and yours. And interestingly enough, the Kgotla (the village council of wise men) defends their position about that matter first since
they know there is grave truth in what Rose has accused them of. They
make light of the matter by insisting that "the good lady had misunderstood our customs." They further elaborate, while refusing to take any
of the blame for a fairly standard response to foreigners in most cultures. They explain: "It is well known from times past that a woman

from a far off place has more attraction than the woman who is known at hand every day. . . . The men found virtue in the foreigner and they were ever commenting about it. This drove the women wild. . . . So they decided to poison this happy marriage because they were wild with jealousy."[37] It is curious, yet expected, how even though the men in the Kgotla think that Gobosamang is a "senseless man," they try to save his face by blaming the women's jealousy which does not seem to have featured at all in this case. In fact, even his mother seems to think that the entire blame rests with her son because she kept telling him that his wife did not have any other lovers, which he stubbornly refused to believe.

The ultimate irony of the story occurs when it is that "Sindebele woman," a title she is to have in spite of her complaint, who, understanding perfectly well that the fault lies with the childlike blind husband, offers in the spirit of womanly discourse all the money back to Tsietso. In spite of the fact that village women have been blamed for the stupidity of the men, it is the women who save that "impossible case." The praise that Rose earns at the end does not take away from the stigma of her foreignness, but rather adds to it. One of the old men says at the end of the case, "'The Sindebele woman fills me with wonder. . . . The forefathers were right when they said the finest things often come from far-off places.'"[38] This last, in the very least, is an extremely dubious compromise because it insists on exiling Rose to the position of someone who does not and never can "belong," in spite of all the praise heaped on her. Rose, foreigner though she is, insists on the right to "belong" as a human being and as somebody who adopted their community through marriage.

Several times the women's discourse breaks down and they are pitted competitively against one another in order to win the man or societal acceptance of one form or another. In these stories, Head implies that there are fewer men ready to marry than women, thus the fierce battle for emotional and financial resources. "Snapshots of a Wedding" is a fascinating little story and like nearly all the others in this volume begins with the way things are in a traditional Botswana village.[39] In this case the Batswana are making preparations for a wedding, and it seems the whole village is participating in a designated way that is slightly different from the traditional ceremony.

This story is a combination of new-age relationships for men that are still polygamous but have an interesting component of educational and financial advantage thrown in as a ruse for social discussion. There is no criticism at all from the village toward Kegoletile for having polygamous relationships or for succumbing to the greater ability of one of his partners to earn money because of the education she has. There is no criticism for Mathata for being uneducated or getting pregnant out of wedlock. Implicit is a societal recognition that men will have sex with women and the women will conceive children but that will not ensure the beginning of a monogamous family unit or even a traditionally polygamous one. It becomes clear that even though Kegoletile loves Mathata, and she is a charming woman, though uneducated, who bears him children that he will support, he is going to marry only one woman and that is the educated one, Neo. He is fairly ruthless about the whole procedure and does not come off lightly in the story, even though he does in the minds of the village people and largely because they disapprove of the manners of the educated marriage prospect. Head writes, "He knew what he was marrying—something quite the opposite, a new kind of girl, with false postures and acquired, grand-madame ways. And yet, it didn't pay a man to look too closely into his heart. They all wanted as wives, women who were big money-earners and they were so ruthless about it!"[40]

Because of her lack of good manners, Neo has to be able to provide everything that Mathata provides, which is why she plans to become pregnant. The mode for "women talk" breaks down between these two women, for instead of finding out what their man can offer them or why both of them are being treated like pawns for the comfort of the man, they compete with each other for the takings. The competition is always between the two women, as if the man does not have anything to do with it, a curious emotional dialogue between women who have probably never met. Neo's society does not feel sorry for her, because she is "bad-mannered rubbish." It is strange that in spite of her education and her earning abilities she is marrying a man who she knows does not love her; the reason is clear, she needs to marry to attain the status of a married woman.

However, women's discourse continues, in this story, as a model of patriarchal demands on a woman even though they come from the mouthpiece of a matriarchal symbol, Neo's aunt. There is a definition of what is acceptable for a person in that community in regard to her behavior toward elders, and that is the sphere where any amount of education would not help Neo. Education and manners become the focus of this critique of Neo. Everybody, even Neo's relatives, want Kegoletile to marry Mathata because she knows how to treat people with respect, and the matriarchal warning does tend to sober even Neo. Her aunt tells her she is "hated by everyone around." None of this disapproval casts any aspersions on her future husband at all. It is assumed that a man would want to marry somebody who earns well even if everyone hates the person of his choice and she is not very lovable.

The sirenlike message from the outspoken aunt, "Be a good wife! Be a good wife!"[41] as she pounds the earth on either side of the bride's legs, is the ultimate double message to Neo: no matter how educated you are, your primary task is to be polite to everybody in the community and to be a good wife to your husband. Implicit in this ideology is that education will help you in the race for a husband but it will not help you after that. Even the traditional wedding ceremony prepares Neo for that role. His aunts tell her in ritualized greeting, "Daughter, you must carry water for your husband. Beware, that at all times, he is the owner of the house and must be obeyed. Do not mind if he stops now and then and talks to other ladies. Let him feel free to come and go as he likes."[42] However, in this story Head never allows us to slip behind Neo's and Mathata's masks in order to discover what they desire. Do they regard Rankwana's gauntlet with complacent distaste and indifference, or do they have desires that are totally submerged by the race for Kegoletile? This short story, like many others, ends with a question, but this is quite deliberate on Head's part for she wants to allow women's discourse to emerge from the questions posed by the text.

In "Hunting," Thato's experience bears out this male response toward education and consequently a greater income.[43] "Hunting" is told from the perspective of a woman who, like Mathata, is uneducated because of circumstances and angry about being treated as an appropriate sexual partner and parent but not a marriage partner. Unlike Mathata, Thato is very bitter about this treatment. When her first lover leaves her, after finding out that she is pregnant, she is very upset. "'Uneducated women,' she had said, in an exact precise way. 'They are just there to be misused by men. The men all want to marry educated women, and still they treat them badly. Those women work for them and support them and get no happiness out of marriage.'"[44] It seems that Thato is predicting what is going to happen to the marriage of convenience between Neo and Kegoletile, and the subtext implies who it is really convenient for. Why then, one may well ask, does a woman work so hard and often duplicitously to get married? Perhaps happiness is not what Neo is looking for at all, but rather an acceptable social status which only marriage can provide, that is, another "facade." Happiness for women, in nearly all the stories in this collection, is almost accidental if it happens and does not fit into the norm of expectability. Marriage seems to be a value in and of itself in most cultures today and tremendous covert pressure is placed on a girl-child to prepare her for the "inevitable." Unmarried people are often viewed with great suspicion in any society. Thus, even though Neo is doing her best to get married, she is not, according to Thato, going to get any "happiness" out of it.

In "Hunting" a new kind of man and family unit is introduced, thereby suggesting a hope for the emotional space that neocolonialism creates in Botswana. Like Paul in "The Collector of Treasures," Tholo tends to look for the deep residues of beauty in women and is faithful to the idea of a family even as it is being eroded by other men in the aftermath of colonialism. Like Paul, he is caught up in the daily round of work, while practicing, like his wife Thato, great generosity toward people who are not as fortunate as he is. The communication between men and women is being reestablished here. Before she met Tholo, Thato had decided not to become emotionally involved with any men because she was convinced that they were only interested in sex. This is very similar to the decision that Dikeledi, Mma-Mabele, Gaena-metse, and many others in Head's fiction make. For some women, communication with men is halted entirely and it is partly because of that that they turn to the solace of other women and recommence that dialogue.

"The Wind and a Boy," is really the only story in this collection that directly deals with women's relationship to mothering.[45] Sejosenye, even though she is biologically a grandmother, raises her grandson, Friedman, who she names after the attending obstetrician because he is kind to her daughter. It is the story of devotion between a child and his grandmother who raises him to admire heroism, and even though he is just as naughty as the other village boys, his charm helps him avoid getting into trouble, while other children often get punished. However, because of the beauty of their relationship, and the narrative strategies of Head, one can sense doom for this perfect pair, from the onset of the story. The child is killed in adolescence by a careless speeding car and the grandmother goes insane with grief and has to be put in an asylum.

Charlotte Bruner reconstructs this short story ambitiously, seeing Friedman as "Africa today . . . thwarted, abused, betrayed." It is very possible that Head became aware of the analogy after writing it, but this story seems to me to be woven out of the fabric of village life. Bruner herself is quick to add that Friedman is "also a child."[46] He is simply a child who lives in a village with his grandmother and is unaware of the dangers of motorized vehicles.

The poignancy of the tale comes from its "universality." Women as mothers have always worried about the safety of their children in graphic and agonizing ways which may seem utterly irrational to anyone but another mother. "The Wind and a Boy" brings that nightmare home. The scene where Friedman is flirting dangerously, while on his bike, with the oncoming speeding truck is described with accuracy and precision. This scene subjectifies the victim and his vulnerability by presenting him as a favorite, daring, and beloved child of the village, minutes before the fatal accident occurs. This scene is reminiscent of another in its grandeur and its ability to evoke pathos. King Lear's admission to a dying daughter of being a "foolish fond old man" seems identical to Friedman's grandmother's response when she is told about the accident.

The pain of a parent who loses the right to die before his or her children is far greater in "traditional" cultures. This loss is a recognition that one will not see one's child come to adulthood because of a totally unexpected freak accident. Friedman's grandmother cannot bear the loss of her motherhood and goes insane, dying very shortly after her grandson is buried by the village.

What I have suggested here is that "women talk" is not only a device used by Head to create an authentic Third World feminist discourse but this same mode is used to suggest that inherent to that discourse is the experience of women resisting phallocratic societies, seizing power, and insisting on "belonging" to their cultures. In Head's collage, *The*

Collector of Treasures, I have shown how even when the dialogue between women breaks down what emerges is a pattern of analysis that records women's history and resistance in the context of sociopolitical colonial struggle. Another aspect of the same debate is the whole notion of historiography as a collective story or an extension of a collector of stories. Sungari and Vaid have contributed to feminist historiography "involved in questioning all that we think we know, in a sustained examination of [our] analytical and epistemological apparatus."[47] In chapter 6, I will examine some of that epistemological apparatus at greater length and forge a model for Third World feminist historiography.

6

TALKING BACK:
Visioned and Envisioned History

It will take a long time for living cannot be told, not merely told: living is not
livable. Understanding, however, is creating, and living, such an immense gift
that thousands of people benefit from each past or present life being lived.

—Trinh T. Minh-ha, *Woman Native Other*

HEAD DID not see any contradiction between what Trinh T. Minh-ha
has called "gossip" and fact or history. For her the transition from the
collector and writer of village tales to the research historian did not
present any conflict. Especially toward her later career, Head thought
that inventing a history became one of the most important aspects of
the postcolonial intellectual and sociopolitical challenge facing a colonized peoples as they began to take account of the history that had
been made of and for them by others. Head wrote two histories about
Botswana and complementary shorter pieces in order to "overturn a
dominant colonial myth," as Cherry Clayton suggests. The theoretical
and creative links between the shorter pieces and the two longer histories have already been established in chapter 1. She did not write
about South Africa, except in a back-handed way in *A Bewitched Crossroad*. For the most part, Head was evasive about the complex and problematic history of South Africa, but the South African shadow looms
large in the background. Instead, she chose to deal with a history that
she was entirely unfamiliar with and had to approach as a research
scholar. Relying heavily on Head's histories *Serowe: Village of the Rain
Wind* and *A Bewitched Crossroad* as texts, I am going to explore how

Head implements the idea of rewriting history or as Toni Morrison would say, "rememorying the past."[1]

Where does this need, this longing for rewriting, for envisioning, come from? After all, there are in existence "documented records" of history told by the White invader as well as oral records handed down for generations. However, the larger question remains: Why does Head need to rewrite or, what I call "envision," history? What function does this rewriting have in the process that postcolonial discourse has taken? Why does this longing to envision the past manifest itself primarily in oppressed colonized groups of people and nations?

I find the word *envision* to bear more resemblance to this act of rewriting and recoding because, along with the historian's sociocultural know-how, Head is using her imagination to fill in the details of life lived in particular contexts. Minh-ha validates imagination thus: "The story has become *just* a story when I have become adept at consuming truth as fact. Imagination is thus equated with falsification. . . . Literature and history once were/still are stories: this does not necessarily mean that the space they form is undifferentiated, but that this space can articulate on a different set of principles, one which may be said to stand outside the hierarchical realm of facts. On the one hand, each society has its own politics of truth; on the other hand, being truthful is being in the inbetween of all regimes of truth."[2] Head creates history, which directly contributes to Minh-ha's analysis. For Head, an informed imagination becomes the fundamental tool used by the postcolonial historian who is interested in systematically excavating the "inbetween[s]" of the "politics of truth."

Head's two histories, *Serowe: Village of the Rain Wind* (1981) and *A Bewitched Crossroad* (1984), reenvision and thus reclaim Botswana history from racist missionary accounts. As Clayton has suggested, "*A Bewitched Crossroad* is the fullest statement of her critique of South African history and society, because its reach into the Southern African past illuminates the complex causes of two contrasted colonial fates, and this comparative base enables her to project an ideal platform for a Southern African future. . . . Head's historical work on Botswana subtends at every point the shadow of the South African nightmare."[3] In reclaiming a part of Southern African history, Head makes a strong case for reappropriating individual subjectivities as well as postcolonial history in its conceptual totality. Even though several Third World writers have attempted with great success the collective histories of their people, what is unique about Head's histories is that this is precisely where her autobiographical and historical interests coincide with her overtly political ones. In these histories she deliberately undercuts the actual sequence of events in order to excavate where each individual destiny determined and was determined by colonialism as well as resistance. She deliberately debunks the established parameters of past, present, and future: for Head, these categories were merely artificial impositions of an unimaginative mind. She thought that the most profound political engagement relied heavily upon historians perceiving the point where the individual and collective destinies coincided and not on a linear calendar. By bringing time, events, and destinies out of exile, Head globalized, or to use her word "universalized," the exploration and experience of exile. Femi-Ojo Ade comes fairly close to outlining important aspects of the unity between individual and collective history. He writes, "Now the autobiographical element does not preclude an interest in what one might call 'other people's business.' . . . The writer engaged in telling a story may explore the trauma of her life, she may trace her particular journey, but, by so doing, she is also engaged in the vicissitudes of her people, in their destiny, in 'other people's business.'"[4] *The Collector of Treasures,* which I discussed in chapter 5, and the two histories reveal Head's interest in "other people's business" in a different way. In Minh-ha's words, "The story as a cure and a protection is at once musical, historical, poetical, educational, magical, and religious. In many parts of the world, the healers are known as the living memories of the people. Not only do they hold esoteric and technical knowledge, but they are also kept closely informed of the problems of their communities and are entrusted with all family affairs. In other words, they know everyone's story."[5]

Head becomes the storyteller-healer *par exellance* in the postcolonial context. Rankwana creates the ultimate feminist challenge for women in an "Ancient Migration," just as Head begins a dual process of healing and retelling as an example to historians and scholars of all decolonized nations. Leslie Marmon Silko adds, "I feel the power that stories still have to bring us together, especially when there is loss and grief."[6] For Head, retelling not only becomes a process of expressing solidarity in togetherness but also a way of reconfiguring energy systems depleted through imperialism and colonialism.

This chapter begins by taking issue with the fictive character of recorded history and Head's challenge to what, in missionary accounts, has falsely been passed off as truth or fact. An analysis of truth as it is perceived to be distinct from fiction has been done splendidly by Trinh T. Minh-ha in the last chapter of her book *Woman Native Other.* Some of Minh-ha's critique is useful for an analysis of Head's histories because Head is working with a similar dialectic between truth/fact and imagination/fiction. But in Head's case this act of reenvisioning becomes a simultaneous act of redefining and reclaiming one's identity within spaces determined by the imperialist intervention and then equally successfully by other patriarchal discourses which replaced them. I posit that in challenging existing records, Head is not only anticipating postapartheid discourse but she is actively informing and recoding the dynamic flow of neocolonial history and thus critiquing a rather male-dominant postcolonial discourse. For instance, she systematically includes testimonies from old women who lived in the reign of the Khamas as well as the men.

Further, it is through Head's process of reenvisioning and reclaiming Botswana history that she is able to resolve several discursive problems. The "rememorying" of history, thus, becomes in part a quest for individual and collective identity. One acute but surmountable problem is the task of taking back from Western hegemonic discourse that part of our historical and collective identity which comes under the cloud of colonialism. Minh-ha has talked about the "re-naming" of concepts, ideologies, identities, and histories in order to "un-name" the same. "No repetition can ever be identical," she says. It is only through the renaming that these histories can be brought home from their place in exile, to take their place as a history of a people by the same people. "The story of a people," Minh-ha argues, is "of us, peoples. Story, history, literature (or religion, philosophy, natural science, ethics)—all in one."

> When history separated itself from story, it started indulging in accumulation and facts. Or it thought it could. It thought it could build up to History because Past, unrelated to the Present and Future, is lying there in its entirety waiting to be revealed and related. The act of revealing

bears in itself a magical (not factual) quality—inherited undoubtedly from "primitive" storytelling—for the Past perceived as such is a well organized past whose organization is already given. Managing to identify with History, history . . . thus manages to oppose the factual to the fictional (turning a blind eye to the "magicality" of its claims); the story writer—the historian—to the story-teller.[7]

Head's "revealing" Botswana history institutes credibility to the telling of a "true story," creating assent and dissent in the idea of what is history and what are just stories. When Silko takes on the part of individual history as a thinly veiled device to talk about the whole of a people's history in her book, *Ceremony*, she is reclaiming, rewriting, reforming, and "coming into being." Silko writes, "It will take a long time, but the story must be told. There must not be any lies."[8] Head balances the said and not said precariously, both in her novels and histories. It is through her two histories that she is able to bring colonial experience "home," out of linearity and exile. She succeeds collectively where she had failed individually. In her last novel, in spite of the "gesture of belonging," Elizabeth's peace with exile is very superficial. The peace is not so much with the place of exile as it is with her place in exile. Even though her earlier novels ended somewhat idyllically, the mood at the end of *A Question of Power* is tumultuous—a small shelter in the middle of a storm. The histories, on the other hand, document the loss of land and power in some instances, and, in the case of Khama the Great, it shows how a conscientious ruler saved his people from becoming another extension of South Africa. These histories substantiate and recapture the experience and culture of migration and exile as it existed among the Bamangwato tribes.

Exile and migration, as presented in the novels, is an individual and communal necessity, often taking place because of dissension among the members of the same family or tribe or nation as it became increasingly problematized in the neocolonies. Even though in Head's writing migration is not explicit, the connection between certain sorts of historical migration and exile is clear. Both the South African exile and the Bamangwato tribespeople put themselves in exile, never to return home, in order to avoid internal and external strife. This theory is individualized in Head's first novel. Makhaya, in *When Rain Clouds Gather*, leaves South Africa because he can no longer personally bear to live in a state of complete embattlement with the apartheid state. Tshekedi

Khama goes into exile for much the same reason: he does not wish to battle with his kinsmen. These are very different ways to define identities within tribal-national spheres.

Head is not the only writer of fiction who has envisioned history in this way, even though she was to call her second history a "novel" or an "African saga." Toni Morrison, Maryse Condé, Chinua Achebe, and many others have expressed a necessity to write about the customs and history of their peoples, and it has not been, especially in the colonial context, because it was not written before. It is certainly there to be read, or, to put it more succinctly, some accounts of specific histories determined by specific biases are available. However, there is a distinction to be made. Minh-ha tries to do just that: "Something must be said. Must be said that has not been and has been said before."[9] This particular dilemma becomes the task of the Third World writer, historian, or literary figure. The systematic resituating of events, customs, and individual lives in a historical context is a task carried out with meticulous energy by Third World writers. Minh-ha relates the retelling of history to the telling of a story. A story as narrative can only exist between the reader/listener and writer/teller much as history/gossip would. This particular relationship is more acutely problematic given the continuation of the very subtle and inherent viewer/viewed dialectic that can be easily perceived in the whole colonial world. On the other hand the same dialectic of gossip/history takes on curious ramifications when the act and motivation for gathering that history are evaluated. Head spends large parts of her first history documenting the various oral data she collected from the Batswana.

Thus, Minh-ha's distinction between gossip/story/history and science is very pertinent to what Bessie Head does in *Serowe: Village of the Rain Wind.* Head's variant accounts for another, equally inherent problem in the "real" history, or what I will call "visioned" history, silenced histories of peoples that these authors are envisioning or "re-memorying" from a peoples' vast pool of historic consciousness. Upon studying patterns of migration among various tribes living in Botswana, Head comes across blatant contradictions inherent in historical emphasis. She comments, "All that was written of this period by white historians trod rough-shod over their history dismissing it as 'petty, tribal wars,' denying for a long time that black men were a dignified part of the human race. Almost overnight they invented a new name for a black man, that of 'boy.' It had seemed more important that a black man should be known as a 'good boy' or a 'bad boy' and hurry up and down with the suitcases of his master, who was creating 'real' history."[10]

Here, she is drawing connections between racist ideology and the study or recording of historical events or facts, and indeed the purpose of her histories is not just to "show" that Africans have a legitimate historical identity but rather to save it from the way it has thus far been viewed and recorded by Western historical discourses. In addition, this exercise challenges these discourses, which successfully disenfranchised the sometimes orally transmitted histories. Envisioning thus becomes a process of reclaiming the identities of African historical figures from exile and placing them in specific sociohistoric contexts.

Minh-ha's distinction between gossip and scientific data follows closely Head's basic concern. Minh-ha says:

A conversation of "us" with "us" about "them" is a conversation in which "them" is silenced. "Them" always stands on the other side of the hill, naked and speechless, barely present in its absence. Subject of discussion, "them" is only admitted among "us," the discussing subjects, when accompanied or introduced by an "us" member, hence the dependency of "them" and its need to acquire good manners for the membership standing. The privilege to sit at table with "us," however, proves both uplifting and demeaning. It impels "them" to partake in the reduction of itself and the appropriation of its otherness by a detached "us" discourse. The presence of a (grateful) witness serves to legalize such discourse, allowing it to mimic, whenever necessary, the voice of truth.[11]

The passage from Head substantiates the problematic relationship that must exist for the writer between the discourse of "us" and "them." Trinh's passage implies the "(grateful) witness," which in Fanon's critique is the African psyche internalizing the colonialist agenda. Chinweizu implies similar problems for the process of what he calls "decolonizing African history." He writes: "The history we write has to meet the needs of our times. Franz Fanon has taught us that 'each generation must, out of relative obscurity, discover its mission, fulfil it, or betray it.' As I see it, our mission is not to transfer Western technology and transplant Western culture onto African soil; it is rather, to prepare the grounds for a new flowering of African civilization."[12] The recommended way for the "flowering of African civilization" for Chinweizu and many others is the rewriting through "rememorying" and bringing the past out of exile—not just the colonial past but also the precolonial patterns that determined life and history in Africa.

On the other hand, Trinh's "(grateful) witness" by his or her very nature is not interested in envisioning history but is rather caught up in situating him or herself in the discourse set up by "us." In this regard, the "witness," usually the colonized historian, grateful or not, jeopardizes real analysis by confusing it with inauthentic discourse and seeks and often succeeds only in perpetuating Western discursive historical hegemony, which proves inapplicable for the Third World writer, historian, and critic. Such a person, Fanon tells us, has the proverbial "white mask, black face." But this study is really not concerned with the pathology of the "wretched of the earth," except where it is concerned with the envisioning of history. The main concern here is the recounting of historical events or the telling of "the story," as an historical and intellectual exercise devoted to reclamation. As Silko, whose concern is with envisioning Native American history, noted, "The story must be told. There must not be any lies." There have been too many lies in the past.

The foregoing discussion of history by writers manifesting different sociological, intellectual, and literary interests outlines a real need and investment in discovering the "lies" that have continued to be told and written especially about colonized cultures. Silko's warning about the length of time it would take to tell the story is a warning well taken, simply because there are two processes going on simultaneously in the rewriting and envisioning of history, or in Head's work, "rememorying" historical identities. Head is bringing her exiles "home." Through the process of envisioning this history, she is dissipating the exilic consciousness by returning the identities back to the individuals crystallized by a different historical presupposition, namely, that of the Western ideologue. Her exploration of exile is precisely where personal and collective historical data coincide. Chinweizu tells us how those two processes will help us break out of the two "mental attitudes derived from our colonial experience."

> Because the West has played a dominant part in shaping our recent past, we all too often allow ourselves to see the key to our affairs as lying in Europe or North America where the dynamo of history is supposedly lodged. To cure us of this tendency, it is necessary, in decolonizing Afri-

can history, to reconnect us fruitfully with our entire precolonial past and so reduce the European intervention to its proper minitude. . . .

This means that the new African historiography must seek out and highlight the adventurous and highly creative periods in African history so we can draw inspiration from them.[13]

Thus, the colonial part of African history is put into a spatially determined trope out of which the Third World historian makes it possible to emerge only through rewriting and envisioning the past. The emergence is linked to the other activity of "telling the story" in its entirety and not in its fragmentary reality. Chinweizu rightly tends to include all of Third World history in this analysis of possibility and emergence, for when one starts to apply envisioning to one set of colonized peoples and their histories, the trope can easily be extended to another colonized peoples and to a completely different set of oppressive actions.

Chinweizu's analysis informs Trinh's discourse. She writes, "The story depends upon every one of us to come into being. It needs us all, needs our remembering, understanding, and creating what we have heard together to keep on coming into being."[14] For Head the coming into "being" is through historical "rememory"; but the being is the collective and individual identity dynamically emerging out of exile into "a sense of belonging." The important factor of this "coming into being" is that the rewriting and envisioning becomes part of a larger process that determines new ways of understanding the past, way that are never spatially or historically static. Trinh's analysis of the process of coming into being that includes "all of us" is useful and inevitable for the Third World historian. Further elaborating on the distinctions between "fiction" and "history," and here Bessie Head's two histories are informed by this dialectic, Minh-ha points to another problem: "As long as the transformation, manipulation, or redistributions inherent in the collecting of events are overlooked, the division continues its course, as sure of its itinerary as it certainly dreams to be. Story-writing becomes history-writing, and history quickly sets itself apart, consigning story to the realm of tale, legend, myth, fiction, literature. Then, since fictional and factual have come to a point where they mutually exclude each other, fiction not infrequently means lies, and fact, truth. . . . Which truth? The question unavoidably arises."[15]

The dialectic of "lies" and "fact" or fiction as opposed to history is of immediate concern for the evaluation of Head's *Serowe: Village of the*

Rain Wind and *A Bewitched Crossroad*. But perhaps the conclusions are not foregone as one might suspect, given the rigors of Western hegemonic absorption that any Third World critic, writer, and historian faces.

In the historical dialogic, Abdul R. JanMohamed's analysis of "racial romances" are crucial to the understanding of this particular part of the colonial experience. What the colonizer "visioned" historically fits the definition of JanMohamed's "racial romance" in several ways. Visioned history was the history of "them" constructed and written by "us," for an audience of "us," therefore it could be romanticized to an extreme degree and manipulated for the audience. In addition to the gleaning of these racially romantic histories from envisioned ones that Third World historians and scholars are working on, there has to be a simultaneous dispelling of these racial fictions which are ideologically determined by the colonizers.[16]

If indeed, as has been the case, one were to delegate Head's "history-writing" to the realm of "lies" or "story-writing," then too much of the speculative element is injected and her histories discredited historians, which were, as we see in her acknowledgments, researched as rigorously as written data allowed. If, however, as I shall be arguing in this chapter, one were to break down this artificially created binary opposition between fiction and fact, as Minh-ha urges, this could compel oral discourse, as in the case of Head's first history, into gaining a respectability even in this realm of print media. Orality, after all, functions in limited contexts and spheres but can still be frozen into categories that nonorality seems to transcend. Even in regard to the process of oral telling, the retelling becomes as important as the rewriting or envisioning, gaining authenticity through repetition, something that written records seem to share. But more important even than the desire for respectability is the exploration and reenvisioning of African history by otherly invested interest groups as opposed to the silencing Western one. Thus, envisioning takes on another task, to actively liberate Western accounts by imagining the position of a subject peoples and situating events in a "believable" context. Envisioning must relieve the African from the status of "boy," which the focusing eye of colonization froze into the "romantically" inspired consciousness of history but presented as a recorded, written, and read experience. To envision is to revision a history that was visioned only by the colonizer. Perhaps one can go so far as to say that the vision of the colonizer was a hallucinatory one, with half truths strung together in order to maintain sociopolitical control over the colonies. This vision, as Marie Louise Pratt and others point out, was developed, in addition, for the public back home.[17] I would add that this vision became very useful to the incoming younger colonials as well. The usage of this vision has been documented by fiction writers from the West as well as the Third World, for instance Achebe and E. M. Forster, to name just two who tended to use White characters who came into the colonies with appropriately vicious ideologies, which could be used to perpetuate certain sorts of moral, social, and political control over the "native" ideologies.

The dangers of looking at colonial history as only part of African, or by extension Third World, history are amply discussed by Chinweizu. The four points he outlines as a program for the decolonization of African historiography are well worth discussing. The four parts are

> 1. the expansion of the horizon of African history to include its full temporal span . . .
> 2. the recovery and correct interpreting of long available materials which were suppressed, misrepresented or sidelined by the objectives of colonial historiography;
> 3. vigorous research efforts to expand our knowledge and fill gaps in our inventory of events in African history;
> 4. a jettisoning of the colonialist habit of imposing on African history schemes of periodisation derived from those of European history.[18]

He sees African historians collaborating with European historical time frames such as the medieval age, to talk about African kingdoms. Chinweizu thinks that there is little or no correspondence of these periods, for they are two very different systems of history; so even as a simplifying gesture, this periodization is inappropriate for the African historian.

His second and third points are most pertinent to the analysis under discussion in this chapter. In her acknowledgments, Head formally thanks the curators of the Khama papers that were made available to her for this project. Head also relied on the oral testimonies of old people in the tribe to piece together what really happened in regard to colonial and imperial attempts to control Botswana. She is able to show how the subjugation of a people was kept at an absolute minimum by the integrity of Chief Khama. But the testimony in the form of the old people she interviewed is disappearing very rapidly. Perhaps that explains, in part, why African historians have concentrated on colonial history, rather than delving into precolonial history. It is easier to reinterpret and rewrite cases of misrepresentation but almost impossible to reinstate history, for even historians usually follow only the larger trends of periods instead of minute details.

Precolonial history does not have the advantage that Head was to experience in terms of oral records while doing her first history. In the second she was able to take even more liberties than her first, just because she was unable to rely on the oral testimonies of a people long dead. The task that Chinweizu sets historians of an oral culture are far more difficult than one imagines. Some of the Arab conquest of northern Africa and the influence of Islam is documented by the conqueror, and oral testimonies of the conquered are lost. Upon recording the history of Botswana, Head found that the historiography of Serowe was what she called "precariously oral." Condé tries to recreate the life of the Bambara before during and after Arab colonization, gleaning it from larger patterns, but again these accounts can be called "fictional" or "unscientific," not truthful.[19] And the challenge to Western historical hegemony has to be, at certain levels, as scientific as it is possible for them to be. Therefore the task of the Third World historian, though not impossible, is a very difficult one.

This is not to say that the realm of the speculative is alien to any recorded history or that speculation itself is to be discredited but, rather, that the kind of concerted effort made by, for instance, Condé in *Segu* or the sequel, *The Children of Segu*, is an incredible *historical* feat that relies heavily on speculative historical facts. Condé's two histories do what Head's *A Bewitched Crossroad* does, that is, take the skeleton of the historical pattern and fill in the details. One might well ask whether any historian of any time period can hope to do, or indeed, does do more.

Histories like Margaret Walker's *Jubilee* and Toni Morrison's *Beloved* are different from each other and from what Condé and Head were trying to do in their histories. Walker takes her own family history and gives fictional character status to her great grandmother Vyry, most probably filling in detail from family hearsay, but it is clear that Vyry's internal life remains a mystery to Walker and her reader. On the other hand, Morrison's Sethe has a complex internal life and her story is based on an actual slave mother's extreme act regarding her children and her own motherhood. Morrison's history is very distinct from other sorts of histories in the kind of attempt it makes to dip into the pool of consciousness that all slaves and former slaves must have recourse to. Here, I mean, that everybody in that community understands that all houses inhabited by them are full of some "dead nigger's grief."[20] Most African Americans hear stories about common ancestors who struggled against slavery in one way or the other. It is quite literally this "grief" that is being gathered and accounted for as collective testimony, tales, or history.

But Head's purpose in *Serowe: Village of the Rain Wind* is distinct from her thrust in *A Bewitched Crossroad*. In her first history, she is more interested in collecting data and often fuses the oral with the written records. As an exile, her enduring interest lies in a country that, because of a combination of strategies that the rulers of Botswana employed, was able to avoid the extreme brutality of colonial apartheid, which Head had experienced in South Africa. There is a mood of nostalgia in the beginning of this history that closely resembles the mood in *When Rain Clouds Gather*. Bessie Head writes, "Something about that day was lovely—it was like stepping back into an ancient world where everything had been balanced and sane; a daily repetitive rhythm of work and kindly humourous chatter. I thought: Serowe may be the only village in southern Africa where a black man can say with immense dignity: 'I like some of the things the white man brought, like iron bolts . . .' The white man hasn't trampled here on human dignity possibly because the Bamangwato produced a king like Khama who fought battles of principle on all sides against both white and black."[21]

This sense of desire or longing, which is determined by nostalgia for precolonial Africa, allows Head to use devices that situate historical Botswana in the archaeology of postcolonial understanding. It is interesting to note that Head considered this activity of rewriting or envisioning as her primary writerly task for the last decade of her Botswana sojourn.

In reference to this desire or longing, which is clearly seen in Morrison's *Beloved* as fusion of mother and daughter, child and lover, the historian needs to bring the defamed aspect of her history into the lived experience of reality. The journey is always out of exile into belonging. Head's nostalgia for a precolonial Africa, which is fictively negotiated in her first novel, *When Rain Clouds Gather,* functions in a way similar to the personal biographical longing in *Beloved.* Head's historical discourse longs to record and relive the comparatively uncomplicated simplicity she finds in Botswana, and simultaneously she seeks to escape the potentially conflictual relationship between Whites and Blacks that she leaves back in Southern Africa. There is tremendous yearning in the tone when she mentions that "a black man can say with immense dignity: 'I like some of the things that the white man brought.'" This is exactly the kind of tone that a South African would find it impossible to use, especially under apartheid where human interchange is totally reduced to its barest level.

The desire for "stepping back into an ancient world" in Head's case is replaced by a concerted effort to understand various aspects of Botswana history, which allows an African living fairly close to South Africa to do that. She manages to do this rather systematically. Even though *Serowe: Village of the Rain Wind* is not shaped with a historical format in mind, her focus is on three important men who out of altruistic feelings shaped the destiny of Botswana, as it was separate from the rest of Southern Africa. But the testimonies of these three men, Khama the Great, Tshekedi Khama, and Patrick van Rensburg, are given in a fairly democratic form. The village people who were most affected by their schemes are interviewed and their testimonies included. Since Head was not writing for either the government or some other interest group, it might be safe to assume that she takes down the testimony as it was told her and further reports it as accurately as possible.

The most revelatory parts of the history are the testimonies of these people who were directly affected by the social, political, and sometimes religious schemes of their rulers. It is also important to remember that part of the dialectic Head sets up in her histories is a poetic one. She begins *Serowe: Village of the Rain Wind* with an invocatory air, quoting a line from Harold M. Telmaque's poem: "Where is the hour of the beautiful dancing of birds in the sun-wind?" She remembers this line out of the literature, which "hoarsely and violently asserted blackness."[22] This longing for a place for the Black people of South Africa to be able to have time and space to enjoy extremely beautiful and simple things along with the rest of humanity was an enduring refrain in her work, and, as I mentioned earlier, it comprised part of her notion about "universalism." As I have already shown, to Head, universalism includes the unalienable right of every human being, and this is especially true of those living under apartheid, to enjoy life at its simplest.

When Head discovers, as she tells us, that Telmaque's words are more prosaically echoed by people in Botswana, who say, "The birds are playing," she does not regard this lightly especially since she comes out of the South African context. She immediately theorizes it into a human right, a human right that history, colonialism, and apartheid have systematically taken away from Black South Africans. She marvels at it and then constitutes it in her historical discourse.

Head's historicity sets out to "tell a story," a story that was carefully left out of the half truths that were documented by White missionary historians. In a telling reversal of fiction versus fact, Head uses "fiction" to elaborate "truths" about the collaboration of Africans in their history which the "facts" had left out. She does this at two levels. At one level she includes the tales of the leaders of the African people quite prominently left out of earlier accounts. At the other level, she includes the testimonies of people who were not in powerful leadership positions, which is unusual in historical accounts in general. Head writes, "Serowe has several arms and my book shuttles to and fro all the time, linking up the other dwelling places of the Bamangwato tribe."[23]

Head's status as both an insider and an outsider in Botswana helped her record various aspects of nonpolitical migration. In the late 1800s Khama moved his tribe three times in order to find water. Head complements this information as an outsider by recording her own impressions of rainfall in Serowe, which was the final stopping place of the Bamangwato. She notes,

> We have more drought years than rain years. During my ten-year stay here, the two or three seasons when it rained for a whole month in one long, leaden downpour were so exceptional and stunning that I cannot even describe them. I am more familiar with the rain pattern of drought years. It rains sparsely, unpredictably, fiercely and violently in November, December and January. Before the first rains fall, it gets so hot that you cannot breathe. Then one day the sky just empties itself in a terrible downpour. After this, the earth and sky heave alive and there is magic everywhere. The sky becomes a huge backdrop for the play of the rain—not ordinary rain but very peculiar, teasing rain.[24]

This description crystallizes the movement of the Bamangwato far more than a fact about the scarcity of rain would have done. In this way, Head's outsider/insider's status helps historical envisioning. The description further situates the Bamangwato relationship to land and water while representing Head's own longing to belong in a specific geographical way. The Bamangwato have unbreachable ties to both land and migration; they leave their lands over and over again to continue to till the soil under more hospitable conditions.

Head's historiography particularizes Serowe because this village seems to have closer ties to the people who have lived there for at least a hundred years. The people of Serowe have a history of building their own town as opposed to other more recently instituted government towns like Gaborone. The history of the new towns was not inextricably linked to migration or to the people for they were built by construction companies. Head's historical biases are very clear. She is not only trying to envision a history that did not give too much credence to the Africans, but is also interested in envisioning the history of the Bamangwato people's movement. Even though she does not loose sight of the leaders, she substantiates their existence through direct inclusion of whole villages that were tied to the decision of these leaders. Head remarks, "This book is built around the lives of three men— Khama the Great, Tshekedi Khama and Patrick van Rensburg—and the story of Serowe is told through their contributions to the community and the response of that community to their ideals and ideas."[25]

Head, very carefully, sets up a traditional pattern of relationships between leaders and their peoples. A good relationship is one of dialogue between the leaders and those they lead. Inherent in this pattern of historiography is the counterbalance of tradition and migration that continues to affect the Bamangwato. Migration in the later half of the twentieth century tends to be brought about because of political changes. For instance when Seretse Khama, the heir of the Bamangwato, disregards tradition and marries an English woman, the balance is disturbed for the tribe and for Tshekedi Khama who was regent for the tribe, at that time. And even though these two Khamas went into exile renouncing their own and their children's claim to the kingship, the older people pressed for tradition and leadership and made conciliatory gestures toward Seretse Khama's son, who was later installed as chief.

These interwoven relationships between tradition, people, migration, and power are intricately envisioned by Head's recounting of history. Throughout this book, Head calls her history a "story." A story suggests that it has not been completely told before and can certainly stand to be retold. In this regard the testimony of the responses of the Bamangwato people to their leaders is particularly important.

The introduction makes the life of Seroweans whole. Head explains how names of children are linked to the actual difficulties of life in Botswana. Children are named for seasons, specific political time periods, or even in defiance at a culture that might look down on poverty. The eternal historical dialogue between people, which makes up stories and histories, seems to be captured in its essence in the introduction to Head's *Serowe;* village dogs, names of months and what they signify, are inclusive of the overall makeup of the history of Serowe and the identity of a people in a place-specific way. This history focuses only on the happenings connected in and around Serowe.

Head follows the demands set by Chinweizu in his book *Decolonizing the African Mind* almost completely. She becomes a researcher of what is academically called folklore, anthropology, sociology, as well as history. The meanings of the names of the months she provides are indications of the people's love for ironic specificity. This specificity contributed to a total knowledge of a people rather than simply through events; this is exactly where history, sociology, and folklore coincide. The names of the months are indicative of the people's intimate tie to the land they cultivated, and the seasons that determined the crops determined the social activities of the people. For instance Mopitlwe (March) is further named "'Ngwaga wa pitle' . . . 'The year is narrowing.' The sun rises later; the first sign of winter."[26]

Not only do the names given to children have individual significance but they show collective struggle as well. She writes: "*Rebatho* means "Now we are people." The grandparents had seen no grandchildren in the family for a long time. Then a young grand-daughter married and gave birth to a son. This caused joy and relief to the grandparents. They exclaimed: "*Rebatho,* now we are people again."[27] There are numerous subtleties in a culture which a mere history of events can never hope to record, but at the same time these elaborations tend to create a whole picture rather than an incomplete one. Head's role as a novelist informs her task as a historian. She covers ground that neither a novelist nor a historian would cover, bringing to African historiography in particular a wholeness that did not exist before.

She is in the process of gazing inward and then out from that vantage position. Indeed, a gaze with which the whole postcolonial world is beginning to regard itself is valuable not just in terms of beginning to take its legacy seriously but in using the realities of its people's lives as they intersect with those histories in order to glean ancient wisdom for the modern world. At the end of the introduction to custom and way of life, Head poses another teasing question. In a traditional society to raise this issue is very problematic but nonetheless she does talk about how hard a death can be for the immediate family members who sometimes end up giving away things, which is part of custom, to all the relatives and often have nothing left to live on themselves, even though they might have lost the only wage earner.

For Head, these problems, and these customs, are the backdrop of what happened in terms of the larger patterns of history, colonialism, and the coming of Christianity. The conflict becomes very apparent when the people represent customs and religious practices that vary from the chief's. Traditionally the Bamangwato believe that the people should always respect and follow the chief who in turn safeguards traditional practice and people's interest within that context. But in Khama the Great's case, it is the chief who gets baptized as a Lutheran in his youth and thereby begins to stand outside and inside his traditional role as a ruler. Head, as historian, feels an affinity for the three leaders under discussion in their role as insiders/outsiders to their culture, a role which, as an exile, she shares with them.

This insider/outsider dialectic is different from the one set by colonialist discourse, because there is no recourse to an insider's position which often makes that historiography invalid. But Head, who, like Patrick van Rensburg, is certainly not a Bamangwato, is still a South African with affinities for the Batswana. On the other hand, Khama, who is a Bamangwato, does not share the same traditions and religion with his people. The historian and the historical characters, as well as the historiography, bring to a historical accounting a validity that neither a complete outsider nor a complete insider could negotiate.

Head begins Khama's discourse by elaborating exactly how he was an insider/outsider. For Head, the Victorian era's Eurocentric approach to history, as found in John Mackenzie's exceptional treatment of Khama, is a historical mistake. She writes, "Unfortunately too, according to the language and values of the Victorian era, he is treated as an exception to the rule and hailed from all sides as the one 'kaffir' or 'native' who somehow made it straight to God amidst the general 'savagery,' 'abominations' and 'heathendom' of his land. Overlooked is the fact that all men are products of their environment and that only a basically human society could have produced Khama."[28] Head's tone of extreme mockery is instrumental in implementing a system of doubt about the accuracy of the White Victorian missionary's historical record. She formulates different patterns of focusing through her use of sarcasm.[29]

Head debunks colonialist discourse by showing how it functioned in the minds of the readers in the colonies as well as "back home," in this case, England. About Chief Sekgoma's treatment in "history," Head writes, "The drum of 'heathen' and 'savage' was to be beaten loudly each time the name of Sekgoma I appeared in the history books."[30] Through this device of envisioning, Head renders the ideology behind Mackenzie's words ludicrous. Mackenzie's treatment of the son, Khama, not only valorizes but also reasserts the notions of the benevolent purposes of the missionary in the colonies. It further sets up as a worthy task Eurocentric "Manichean" ideas about the "civilizing of savages." And it perpetuates, on both sides of the colonial divide, a value system integrally tied to the stronghold of imperialist and racist ideology, especially in its Southern African manifestation. One of its most brutal manifestations is the ideology expounded by the Dutch Reform Church.

What John Mackenzie saw in Khama the Great, the "good" native amid the savagery, was that this former savage was also the leader of his people. Mackenzie's vision was simple and clear, to sanction and perpetuate certain ideologies and impose them on the people through the control of a puppet and tool of Christianity. Even though Khama was a convert and a devout Christian, he was also a good leader and used his influence and "civilized" status to the advantage of his own people. This last Mackenzie did not include; instead Head had to envision it out of the information available to her from Mackenzie's records of the impressions young Khama made on him, as well as from the older people who remembered events of that time.

It is no doubt true that Khama's disapproval of some Bamangwato customs had to do with the influence of Christianity, but it is also plausible that the austere, hard-working Khama wanted to rid his people of customs that represented cruelty of some sort or another. He could have abolished polygamy because of the influence of his adopted religion, but he did not, although he refused to take a second wife. He made exceptions when the problem of polygamy caused economic hardship for the woman's family. Head also makes it clear that in spite of his own Christianity, Khama did not see the colonials as benevolent figures in the region; he knew he had to use his influence with them so that his country would not become another Rhodesia or South Africa. In this last, he was supported by his people. Head writes that "his life did not only benefit the Bamangwato. It reached out and benefited Botswana as a whole, for he was a founder of the British Bechuanaland Protectorate which, so people firmly maintain, prevented Botswana from becoming another South Africa or Rhodesia and resulted in independence for the country in 1966."[31] The battle between Sekgoma and Khama is not the simplistic one that Mackenzie or his successor J. D. Hepburn might want to see, that is, Christianity triumphing over "abominations, savagery or heathenism." The battle between the father and son seems even in the little that Head is able to glean from the Mackenzie record a complicated generational one between a ruler and his successor who no longer wishes to understand leadership as a tool for safeguarding the traditions handed down to him.

Upon getting back to Mackenzie's record, Head is very careful to point out that "it was not his aim to mock and despise black people."[32] However, she does not make the same concession for Hepburn. Here, she records the shock that a new colonialist recruit from Europe experiences upon finding a people so unlike the ones he is used to; this would certainly influence his "objective historical" testimony. For instance, Head talks about Hepburn's account beginning with "a storm of hysteria." One can only imagine an extremely ignorant young man from England, arriving in a country torn politically as well as socially, being given the task of historian either by his own arrogance or by other colonialists. Head writes: "The first two chapters of Hepburn's book are very misleading. The whole society is damned as consisting of 'heathens, abominations and savages.'"[33]

When Head's own account enters the testimonies of the old people whose lives came into contact with Khama's, the historiography adopts anecdotal value. Incidents that contribute to the making of a historical figure as she makes daily decisions, stealthily slips out of accounts when this sort of anecdotal information is not included. Upon consulting Mokgojwa Mathware, described as a ninety-six-year-old "traditional historian," Head finds that there are certain aspects of Khama's reign that are traditionally taboo for Mathware to talk about, such as openly criticizing the chief. Yet she makes it her task to relay information that he gives her thereby evoking the context of opinions and values tied to the political emergence of Khama. The transcription of Mokgojwa Mathware's account describes a commonly held opinion of Khama. He says: "There is only one thing I would like to say about Khama. He thought about the man who was nothing. At the head of each ward was a headman. This headman was really a chief but when he lived under a chief like Khama, he was called a headman. When a headman died, his wife sometimes chose a commoner as the second husband or man friend. The people of that ward would then deny her children because they were not of royal blood. Khama changed that custom." [34] One cannot imagine a Hepburn or even a more benevolent Mackenzie consulting a "traditional historian" to aid in their recounting of that history. Both were too busy constructing a lopsided vision, which had vested colonialist-imperialist interests from the beginning, to really pay minute attention to the patterns of opinions that supported the chief they were supposedly writing about.

More valuable than Mathware's account of Khama is his recounting of the creation of the Bamangwato Nation by Ngwato and the ties that the Batswana have to migratory patterns of exile. Head's record of this aspect of the history of Botswana is integral to the way colonialism and the Batswana fears about their own leaders coincided. And later, as Head elaborates in *A Bewitched Crossroad*, this phenomenon of migration became intertwined with the mandatory migration that the colonials imposed, especially as the process of disenfranchisement of land intensified in Southern Africa. Head begins to envision this phenomenon through Mathware's precolonial account.

Even though Mathware's account does not relate the exact lineage of Ngwato and his relationship with his direct descendant, Khama, it is important to recognize that there is a link between the way Ngwato avoids "trouble" with his brother Kwena through migration and Khama does the same when Sekgoma feels threatened by his son and heir, many years later. In addition, Mathware relates and Head reports, how the Phuti became the totem for the Bamangwato. Here, I do not wish to valorize the connection that colonial discourse reaffirms about the link between the "natural" man with nature, but rather a connection between all beings that complex societies with higher degrees of consciousness were able to perceive. It is interesting to note that the higher religious being that Sebina and his people, whose story is "lightly fictionalised,"[35] worshipped, represented the manifest life in all creatures. Sebina becomes "a core of tribal memory amidst change and upheaval."[36] The concept of Ngwale is very similar to the one upheld by Buddhism, another very ancient religion. This discovery must have been particularly delightful for Head who herself was attracted by Buddhism. Ngwale, representing an extremely complex religious ideology, leaves Hepburn sputtering incoherently about idolatry when quite obviously Christianity manifests far more overt idolatry than did Sebina's religion. Hepburn can silence his own doubts by simply refusing to engage in a theological dialogue, which shows that his religious interests are immature and unscholarly while his imperialist interests remain untouched.[37]

The most valuable inclusions by Head are several testimonies of people who were directly affected by Khama's interest in their personal welfare. He sent several young men to school, at personal cost, in order to meet the demands of his people and to prepare the way for launching education in Botswana, which was severely lacking, especially higher education. His successor Tshekedi Khama stepped up this personal patronage in order to inculcate education as a value in the younger generation of Batswana. Khama was to pioneer the building of schools and later colleges in his own country so that the young people would not have to go to South Africa to study.

The testimonies of people are not always full of praise for Khama. He believed that the teachers "were working for their country to improve it, not working for money," which created a lot of personal hardships for teachers who could no longer count on their cattle as income. His ideology of service for the nation is important for he never shirked it himself. Teachers' salaries did not start till 1929, which must at some level have changed the concept of the relationship of education and the nation-state. Head's concentration on the educational development of Botswana is again particularly valuable for its historiography, because educational systems, in most history books, are skimmed over and the long personal sacrifices that the Batswana made to have schools for their children would be unheard. This sort of negligence can occur to any record of events under colonial rule.

The existence of meticulous hierarchies to perpetuate social harmony in societies that were perceived as "savage" is another aspect of Head's description of how individual and collective destinies coincide. Rannau Ramojababo, head of Seetso village ward and retired schoolteacher relates, "The headman is expected to keep peace in his area. The quarrel that most often happens is trouble in early marriage between young people. A young man usually has other girls; when his wife is beaten severely or not kept in food and clothing, she will come and report to me. So I keep in touch with everything in my ward."[38] The levels of social and legal hierarchies are extremely complex in their legal ramifications. But additionally, the headman is supposed to know what is going on in his ward and not let the Western notion of "privacy" interfere with his care of the people. Even in traditional societies, if there is wife battering the inclination of the neighbors is to leave the contentious pair to work it out. However, if the injured party decides to make a legal complaint to a headman, then the state is ready to intervene and, depending on the case, can propose different solutions.

In the testimony of Tsogang Sebina, a very important aspect of Khama's reforms, continued by Tshekedi Khama, is introduced. The whole cooperative venture that Patrick van Rensburg perpetuated through collaborative effort constitutes part of Head's novels, most seriously described in *A Question of Power*. Head explains in *Serowe* how the foundations for collective farming, cattle and agriculture, building, thatching, and many other tasks that villagers in Serowe are engaged in, have their roots in traditional culture. It was not considered unwholesome or untraditional for Khama to call the different age group regiments to go out into the bush to build schools for the community. Even though several people died during this long venture, for lack of food supplies; they built schools in spite of shortages of building materials.

In Tshekedi Khama's time, and later with Rensburg, the system of regiments and brigades became far more sophisticated but the economic struggles of the cooperatives remained a constant source of problems for the participants who had precious little to fall back on. The cooperative venture was not initiated out of any desire for socialist communal sharing, though various testimonies indicate that community does mean a watchfulness toward other members of one's village ward, but rather these ventures were appropriate especially in times of trouble. Tsogang Sebina reports that "Tshekedi had organized something like co-operative marketing. It was planning for drought years when the crops fail. Each village ward was given a piece of land to plough corn. When harvested, this corn was taken to two big grain silos Tshekedi had built near the kgotla, for times of need."[39] These cooperative ventures, especially in a drought-stricken country, made immediate sense. Even though farmers had, before the advent of cooperative grain reserves, put their lot in with the weather, getting greater or smaller yields, after Tshekedi's plan starvation was not as big a threat as it had been in earlier times.

For a Third World historian, one of the most problematic parts of Khama's personal life must have been his total devotion to Christianity, the colonial religion. Head devotes a whole chapter to the examination of his interest in not only his adopted religion but also the remembered historiography of his people's reaction to his faith. Head reports that he was not blind to the aims and prejudices of the London Missionary Society (LMS), for which he had a preference. This balancing act becomes even more obvious in her second history. Head reports that "at a certain stage one begins to keep a joyful tally of all the missionaries Khama expelled from his country after reading such books as *Native Life on the Transvaal Border* by W. C. Willoughby and *Three Great African Chiefs* by Edwin Lloyd."[40]

Head does not tell us in so many words, but it seems that there was a ban placed on any other religion but Khama's brand of Anglicanism, propagated by the London Missionary Society, until after Tshekedi Khama's death. This ban does indicate that Khama's belief in Christianity led him to disenfranchise his people from their own religion. This particular aspect of Khama's benevolent tyranny is problematic at several levels. Even though he believed in modernization at fundamental levels, such as secondary and college education in Botswana, personally he still must have thought the religion of the Bamangwato less appealing than the Christian religion, which seduced him as an individual if not as a ruler. This interest manifested itself politically as well for he wanted to impose the Christianity he had adopted on all his peoples by banning African religion.

However, when Khama abolished *bogwera* (the practice of polygamy) and other traditions that were either cruel or disenfranchised commoners, he was not propagating Christianity per se but trying to bring a new world into his kingdom, a world that functioned more compassionately than the old traditions did. But the old religion could not be separated from the traditions of his people.[41] Thus the destruction of the traditions led to the annihilation of the religion of the Bamangwato. Khama's religious practices were an incredible deterrent to the continued practices of the Bamangwato specially since the relationship between the leader and his people was one of constant dialogue.

Some people continued to fight in order to maintain the traditions of their peoples, in spite of the divisions that Khama's religion was creating between people. One of Head's informers tells of her own family history and the problematic rifts that Christianity caused at an individual and communal level. Segametse Mpulambusi relates,

> Like everyone else, my whole family attended the L.M.S. church up till the time my grandmother wanted to get married. When grandfather proposed to my grandmother he told her that he had married his first wife under Setswana custom and he was going to marry his second wife under Setswana custom too. . . . L.M.S. people said that was one thing they could not allow.
> . . . My grandmother chose to marry grandfather under Setswana custom. The next thing was that the L.M.S. people forbade grandmother to attend church. She was chased away. The whole family came together to talk this matter over. They could find no fault with grandmother, who was a good woman and they could find no fault with Setswana custom, which was also good. So they said: "We shall all no longer attend L.M.S."[42]

This sort of rift must have occurred much more frequently than is reported, simply because Setswana religious practices are inherent to the Batswana custom and had been functioning without being challenged for hundreds of years. It must have taken a lot for a traditional society to gradually give up their customs, and it probably did not happen right away but took several decades. Khama the Great not only imposed his religion on his own people but made it a condition for other migratory tribes who sought his territorial protection. Since he did not feel any ambivalence toward the Anglicanism preached by the LMS, he assumed that the same attitude toward his chosen religion was held by other people. However, what is important about Head's history is that it shows the rifts between the Bamangwato from within rather than from the perspective of somebody who did not share their culture or religion.

This tyranny is recorded over and over again by the testimonies that Head collected over several years, and the historiography implies that Khama had to pay this price; even though he seems fairly convinced by the LMS, he had to work hard to keep the colonials at arm's length. Perhaps the LMS gave him certain sorts of immunity in order to have exclusive colonial, religious, and economic privileges, which he might not have been able to enjoy without the sanction of the chief of the British Bechuanaland Protectorate.

However, upon turning to the Khama papers themselves, parts of which Head includes in this history, his actions seem full of contradictions; Khama was addressing himself to the problems of his people and not so much to his adopted brand of Christianity. Even when he talks about the evils of polygamy, it is not Christianity that he evokes as a higher guiding light but the circumstances that numerous divorces cause in the economic makeup of an agricultural community. He says, "Young men were perpetually in the habit of divorcing their wives, and that a remedy against this habit was to prohibit them from marrying many wives. Polygamy, I said was unavailable to young men of the present day, because after their divorce their fathers-in-law have to meet great inconveniences in providing the divorcees and their children with all the necessities for living."[43] Khama's papers affirm that the cause for changing a centuries-old tradition was not upstart Christianity but rather the economic burden on older men caused by the divorces tolerated by Christianity. These divorces also absolved the economic responsibility of the father, while precolonial polygamy did not cause a breakdown in family structures. Thus Khama is really addressing and counterbalancing the bastardization of polygamy through colonization by abolishing the material reality of polygamy, rather than critiquing it for some abstract Christian ideal.

The refusal of the Batswana to follow Khama's suggested reform on polygamy is causing controversy and debate to this day. Obviously colonialism was responsible in part for the "breakdown in family life," yet old patterns of polygamy thrown into the modern context devastated the family structure. Head writes that "this breakdown affects men and women of the age groups from forty to fifty and all the young people who follow on after them, so much so that most mothers are unmarried mothers with children who will never know who their real father is. Out of every one hundred children born in Serowe, three on the average are legitimate; the rest are illegitimate."[44]

This status of legitimacy as opposed to illegitimacy causes great economic and social hardship for the children, their mothers, and often the mothers' families who try to help raise them. When Head inquired whether this strain in family life was caused by the abolition of bride price, the answer for several possible reason was unanimous: "No one would attribute it to Khama's reforms."[45] In Khama's time, Christianity had solved the problem of uncared-for single mothers, but in present-day Botswana no compunction of that sort takes care of the rapidly changing family unit—a unit that has broken down since colonialism.

Khama also makes it clear in his papers that the reason he could not tolerate beer-drinking parties was because it was the "source of fights, disturbances and quarrels common among my people."[46] In Head's second history, *A Bewitched Crossroad,* the other more important reason for banning liquor among all his inhabitants, the few white settlers included, surfaces. The colonials used brandy or as the locals called it "brandewyn," illicitly, to get land from reigning chiefs. In *A Bewitched Crossroad,* when Khama's party offers protection to the Sebina clan, they inform him of the sinister aspects of the Boers land-grabbing techniques. One of those present in the Khama party relates, "A further trouble arose from the Transvaal Boers. It was claimed by the Boers that Chief Botlhasitse had placed his mark on a document offering all the country of his people to the Boers. There is no love between us and the Boers so it is not known how the Boers came upon it, though the faults of Chief Botlhasitse were well known. He was fond of the white man's brandewyn and while drunk might have given his land to the Boers."[47] Khama was very aware of the Boers' use of alcohol to take land away from various Tswana chiefs and probably banned it in both the settler community and among his own people to prevent illegal land sales. The example of land loss through alcohol was extremely common and well known everywhere, and Khama, as a clever leader, used "his" religion which was conveniently also the colonials' religion, to make the drinking of alcoholic beverages illegal. Later, Khama is very critical of his people because they disobey the law over which he sat in council with them, implementing it only after they agreed to it.

This criticism was over the sale of cattle. This law makes it very clear that if the Batswana sell, especially their cows, to foreigners they will lose all their income. The foreigners were offering them quick money, which they needed, but they were also pressuring them to sell their precious livestock, which helped the Batswana survive through long drought years. Khama made it illegal to sell cattle for short-term economic gains that would destroy long-term valuable assets, which were not easy to replace.

In all three of these cases, Khama did not display even a hint of divided loyalty between Christianity and the good of his people. He seemed very clearly to be combating at several levels the onslaught of colonialist imperialism. The record of this is not as important when it is in some obscure "nativist" library, but Head pries it out of its limited context to one that is recognized and read. It is interesting to note that Head was doing, in her histories in the 1970s, what critics like Mary Louise Pratt have done in the late 1980s, documenting subtle individual resistance to overt colonialism that affected the whole community; in other words, bringing truth and knowledge out of exile and into experienced reality.

Khama also seemed, as a serious leader of his people, to have a great deal of foresight, especially in regard to sale of the breeding cattle. He was, in addition, especially wary of cattle sales at the railroad stations, partly because stolen or straying cattle could be sold easily without detection, and partly because if one drives cattle to a station then it is more advantageous to sell it for a lower price rather than drive it back home. No doubt, this aspect of the sale was ever-present in the mind of the buyer, who could get the best price, and a bane for the seller. Thus, the cooperative movement, a direct offspring of old traditions in Botswana, seems to be a deliberate plan to combat colonial interests and not an accident. It is important to record this kind of governmental finesse because it actively dispels the idea of clever White colonials taking over from a nonresistant bunch of savages with no clue about ruling their peoples.

Another way in which Khama deliberately combated the coming of South Africa–style colonialism was by reinforcing that the sale of land was illegal because "we cannot depart or forget the ways of our forefathers." In traditional Botswana, land was apportioned to whomever wanted it and not passed on from father to son like the cattle were. As a leader, he was only too aware of what was happening in the neighboring country and how the people of South Africa were being systematically disenfranchised, through land sales and heavy land taxation, by the colonials. When he went to England in 1895, the land issue was one of the first things he addressed. He told a gathering in Leicester, a gathering, no doubt taken with the Christian ways of this "savage" as advertised by their own countryman, John Mackenzie, "We think that the Chartered Company will take our lands, that they might enslave us to work on their mines. We black people live on the land; we live on the farms. We get our food from the land, and we are afraid that if the British South Africa Company begin in our country we will not get these things and that it will be a great loss to us."[48] He was never blinded by his adopted faith or by the "Christian" mission in his land because he had already seen it functioning in horrendous ways across the border and among the Southern Tswana tribes. The maxims that he set for the Bamangwato seem to have repercussions even a hundred years later, because they are very unwilling to sell land to this day. Head reports that Khama was the only one "who preserved this ancient way of life intact."[49] Obviously, he was not scared of changing or discarding certain very ancient traditions, but he never refrained from using his Christian faith to safeguard his people from the most pernicious aspects of British colonialism. Much as the Christian faith was used to resist slavery in the Americas, so Khama used it to resist the active colonization of his nation.

However, he was not afraid of disputes with the British in Serowe either. Over a dispute that came up in Kgotla, where a White man had attacked a Motswana over a woman, much to the indignation of the Batswana people and the British colonials, Khama stayed firm. The British tried to use this incident (as recorded history proves they did over the most trivial issues) to show Khama how to rule his country. Khama went on record as having said something to them that no other Southern African chief had ever said. "'Well, I am black, but if I am black, I am chief in my own country at present. When you white men rule in the country, then you can rule as you like; at present I rule.'" Head further records that the reason colonials listened to him was that he "had also made the white man's tenure in Bamangwato country very insecure; if they riled him they had to leave, in spite of their brick houses and shops."[50] In her second history, she records the time that he banned liquor and the Europeans could drink it only secretly and only among themselves. When they defied him, which they did deliberately and without regard to their status as guests, they had to leave.[51] Through this precarious balance of power, Khama carefully steered his country out of the direct control of greedy imperialist interests, over-eager to swallow bigger or little chiefdoms. Head's record of imperialism in Southern Africa changes the way history is viewed.

The tradition of migration among the Bamangwato tribes seems to have been a time-honored one, integral to the history of Botswana; this tradition was used by colonials for their own ends. The old people whose testimonies Head collected, and who are referred to fondly in the community as "traditional historians," tell her: "'Whenever trouble broke out,' they said, 'people would rather move away than fight. Once far away, they could discuss the trouble and so could the enemy.'"[52] The desire to avoid trouble with fellow members of the same tribe helped, as far as possible, to settle peacefully the turmoil of the colonial era. A show of force would most certainly have devastated the Bamangwato because like all Southern Africans, they did not have guns like the enemy did.

Recording individual episodes of what Head called "irrelevant" details became her primary task, especially since old people like the man of 104, Ramosamo Kebonang, who are the repositories of this information, were not going to be alive for very much longer. Her task of envisioning oral history becomes more urgent, because it was literally disappearing before her very eyes. *Serowe* then proceeds in its historiography to take account of the educational advancement projects that Tshekedi Khama undertook during his regency for Seretse Khama. As I have mentioned earlier, these are really testimonies of the struggles of various age groups to give Botswana and its people primary and secondary schools and a college.

Head envisions history in another very useful way. She records the conflicts between traditional and Western medicine as a Third World historian would record it and not through a glorification of the "ignorance" or "wisdom" of the "savage" customs of the Botswana. She documents illnesses familiar to the Batswana, which seem like warnings against breaking taboos that are there for specific social benefits. But Head is not afraid to show how this traditional society tends to base even medicine on rather sexist principles. She interviews a Western doctor familiar with traditional medicine on Malwetse sickness, which a husband gets after sleeping with an unfaithful pregnant wife: "I do not think Malwetse sickness describes a particular set of symptoms, but it is probably the name for the offence."[53] Thus, it becomes clear that the traditional Batswana were much more interested in keeping social order in the village than in naming certain diseases. Later on in the account, the same doctor tells Head, the historian, about "Tshenyegelo sickness: The prescribed abstinence is a useful custom to protect the woman who needs to recover after an abortion. European medicine prescribes six weeks' abstinence and six months without getting pregnant after an abortion. Our customs aim at protecting the woman. It is interesting to note how these Tswana concepts of sickness always assume that the male victim is completely innocent. The woman was blamed for breaking the custom and causing the sickness. One wonders whether this was due to male chauvinism or to a high incidence of infectious diseases."[54] Head's historiography is valuable because it takes the traditions into account from a feminist perspective, which is rare even in the few histories that have been envisioned by Third World scholars and writers. She takes patriarchal traditions to task throughout her histories and in recording the histories of herbalists and other local crafts and remedies which traditionally belong in the domain of women's work. This focus helps put women's historiography in sharp relief to the traditions that undermined them sociosexually.

The Swaneng Project, started by Patrick van Rensburg, is amply fictionalized in Head's *A Question of Power*. It seems that this Afrikaans man from South Africa is very well regarded by the Batswana because he, without discarding the long-standing traditions of cooperative ventures introduced and implemented by Khama, consolidated them into nontraditional areas of activity. These three leaders that Head chose to bring out of exile through her historicization are not only important to the envisioned history of Botswana but also to the continuation of the envisioning process for histories of other oppressed peoples.

In *A Bewitched Crossroad*, her last book, Bessie Head is able to cope with the history of South Africa and incorporate it into her envisioning of Botswana history. The Southern Tswana tribes were threatened by the same land disenfranchisement that occurred in the Cape and the Transvaal. This was the first time that she handled Southern African material with a degree of detachment, examining patterns in a colonialism that were single-minded though not systematic. Through her envisioning, it becomes clear what a painful task it is for a Third World historian and writer to embark on. The only protection that the Southern African tribes seemed to have arose from the animosity between the Boers and the English. However, the basis for this animosity was the race for imperial power between these two European tribes, with one only a fraction less brutal than the other. In *A Bewitched Crossroad*, the patterns of migration take on added meaning. Traditional migratory patterns and the imperialist onslaught become integrated from the beginning of the colonial period just as apartheid and exile did later. No doubt to a European colonizer the existence of migratory patterns among the African tribes of Southern Africa must have seemed like a window of opportunity. It would be easier to assume detachment from a particular piece of land belonging to specific tribes if they migrated often for specific reasons.

In the Americas, the Native Americans' concept of land and ownership was used against them by the European colonizers' desire and avarice for owning property, and land sales occurred in equally brutal and sinister ways. Neither the Native Americans nor the Southern African tribes bargained for the complete loss of their land. One of the most clear examples of how migration served colonial ends is the case of Sebina and his followers. The Sebina clan was at first terrorized by the Matebele people who took human and agricultural resources away from them. Later the Boers threatened to do the same, forcing them to accept the hospitality of the Bamangwato. They moved twenty days' journey away from their homeland, leaving their lands to the Boers who were already "siding with one party against the other, under cover of which, once war broke out, they would seize the land."[55]

Another little-known fact that the Third World historian and writer has to envision, especially in regard to South African history, something that most visioned accounts leave out, is the extent of slavery that the Boers introduced with their brand of imperialism. As late as 1852, when Schele was attacked by the Boers, some two hundred women and children were taken as "apprentices," a thinly disguised term for slavery. Perhaps the necessity for calling them apprentices arose because Britain had outlawed slavery in all its colonies in 1808.[56]

In regard to the protection that many Southern African tribes sought from the English, it is important to remember that slavery was instituted in Southern Africa seven years after the British came there in 1652. These "apprentices" were used in order to provide the work force that the Boers lacked and needed especially after amassing and looting thousands of cattle and land. This sort of slavery is a direct precursor of other Boer phenomena such as apartheid and the Bantu education programs. An envisioned history must make apparent connections between settler colonialism and its manifestations and developments in more recent "colonies" like South Africa. Head makes these connections much more obviously in *Serowe: Village of the Rain Wind,* where she is more interested in recent colonial history, than she does in *A Bewitched Crossroad,* where her interest is in the actual land wars that South African tribes had with the Boers and the British.

Another aspect of history envisioned by the Third World historian and writer is the attention Head pays to the religion of the Tswana tribes as they were converting to Christianity for different sociopolitical reasons. If one could hypothesize that colonialism itself was a deeply impoverishing experience especially at a spiritual level, then it is no wonder that one finds all over the colonized world people following a religion that does not belong to their forefathers. These conversions in themselves signify experiences of exile—exile from one's own traditions and ancestry. Christianity, especially in Southern Africa, as Head has documented in *Serowe,* takes on interesting and socially destructive manifestations.

One of Head's informers tells her that the charismatic religions seem more popular today. And as we see, when Hepburn is proselytizing Sebina, the Christianity that was implanted there by missionaries seemed to flourish. First, when Hepburn comes to Sebina, Sebina assumes that this missionary has come to talk, not to impose his narrow-mindedness on the old chief. After Sebina talks about Ngwale's complicated spirituality and world view, Hepburn is embarrassed because the alien religion seems "appealing" to him. Fearing his own attraction, Hepburn quickly seeks recourse in a narrow view of Christianity which sought to undermine the "other" spirituality. He dismisses his own doubts and fears very quickly: "There is only one God and his name is Jehovah and his Son is Lord Jesus Christ, our Savior, the source of eternal life. All else is idolatry"—as if any spiritual or moral concept can be only "one thing."[57]

So, then, what is it about the charismatic churches that attracts the spiritually impoverished colonized subject? It is not uncommon in the postcolonies to see the younger generation reject Christianity with as much fervor as their fathers and grandfathers took it on. This sort of pattern occurred commonly among Afroamerican people as well. It seems as if Christianity tended to represent a simplifying mechanism, though one of the major tasks of the postcolonies is to reflect on spiritually complex aspects of African religions, as Sebina did. His worship of Ngwale seems to encompass a whole scheme of highly sophisticated ideologies. He tells the somewhat dense Hepburn: "Ngwale . . . is a spirit who dwells in all things. . . . He is worshipped in song and dance. His praises are sung and he is requested to bestow favors on life."[58]

Since the Third World historian has to be wary of making the same distinctions between "heathen" and "Christian" ritual that the colonizer did, she must understand the significance of ritual in any sociospiritual context; the worship of Ngwale in "song and dance" sounds no more inappropriate than an Easter service does. And further, since Hepburn was only "obsessed with the salvation of heathen souls" he is thereby "impervious to dialogue and an exchange of thought," much to Sebina's regret. Thus colonial imperialism becomes a silencing experience at the historical level as well. It is no wonder that this spiritual silence leads to Diele's condition, which Sebina notices after his exchange with Hepburn: "He had the lonely look of a man who had forsaken the gods of his forefathers."[59] In Diele, there is an echo of inconsolable loss.

In *A Bewitched Crossroad*, Head is careful not to glorify "Old Africa" nostalgically. She concentrates on "rememorying" history which is slipping away even as she writes. Her task is important, yet complex. Head's recording and recoding the delicate balance that Southern African chiefs had to maintain in order to keep their land from the ruthless Boers and less ruthless British is well worth commenting on. When one looks at T. Dunbar Moodie's *The Rise of Afrikanerdom*, where the ideology of the Dutch Reform Church stands in direct contradistinction to Southern African chiefs keeping their own land, then the form of imperialist expansion that occurred in South Africa becomes clearer.

In Moodie's book one discovers the concept of history held by the Boers. Moodie quotes D. F. Malan:

> Our history is the greatest masterpiece of the centuries. We hold this
> nationhood as our due for it was given to us by the architect of the
> universe. [His] aim was the formation of a new nation among the na-
> tions of the world . . .
>
> The last hundred years have witnessed a miracle behind which must
> lie a divine plan. Indeed, the history of the Afrikaner reveals a will and
> a determination which makes one feel the Afrikanerdom is not the work
> of men but the creation of God.[60]

If the Boer believed his actions and his history were directly sanctioned
by his Calvinist God, then it stands to good reason that he also thought
he could do anything to tip the balance of colonialism on his side. He
could loot cattle, he could loot land from their rightful owners by not
recognizing them as owners, and he could enslave African peoples
with the historical and political blessings of his God.

This extremely compelling ideology enabled the Boer to be utterly
ruthless in his amassing of power. And even though chiefs like Khama
and others were confused about the desire for power among the British
colonials, they were never unsure of what the Boers wanted and how
they would go about getting it if they did not scramble for British protection, which was usually forthcoming only when it suited British colonial interests. The Boer ideology, which was a simple recognition of
themselves as the chosen people often martyred, seemed to function
hand in hand with their expansionist policies in South Africa.

The Boers visioned their own history as one of a martyred yet chosen people of God whose destiny it was to be served hand and foot by
the "unchosen" Africans. They had no qualms about first asking to use
African land for watering and grazing their cattle, and later taking over
that land entirely, as they amassed some of the cattle that did not belong to them.[61] When the African tribes whose land had been taken
away confiscated the Boer cattle, armies of Boers swooped down killing children and women and making the rest slaves and permanently
taking the land away from the vanquished tribe. Their complex ideology later became the system of apartheid that was imposed on South
African Blacks and that held legal sway till Mandela's presidency, and
its legacy will continue in subtler ways for some time to come. Until
Mandela's release, any reforms, though the term *reform* has to be used
advisedly, were voted down by the predominantly Boer-controlled
Pretoria government.

Head's envisioned history forces us to give up the view of Africans as either villains or victims; instead we see them as peoples who tried to save their land and resources from cut-throat imperial interests as best they could. It is important also to see that their failure to protect their land did not come from stupidity or greed, as the colonizer would have us believe, but rather from the military arsenal of the imperial interests. One of the tricks that the Boers and the British used was to offer guns to the chiefs, and, if they accepted them as gifts, the hidden colonial agenda surfaced very quickly. When Cecil Rhodes's emissaries offered guns and ammunition to the Ndebele chief, Lobengula said, disdainfully, "I don't want your guns. If I take your guns you will take my land."[62] The chiefs were becoming vigilant about the complexity of market economy exchanges, which were used as tools of deception against them and their people both by the British and the Boers.

When two Ndebele headmen tried to go to England to get the British queen's protection, they were sabotaged by Rhodes. First their lives were in danger before they boarded the ship and then the colonial secretary planned that they should not be allowed into the presence of the queen but instead be "humiliated and insulted."[63] Thus, even the British colonial interests in South Africa were kept carefully guarded and hidden from the government at home, especially when it suited them. In this case the British went so far as to pretend that Maund, Rhodes's servant, was independently acting in the interests of the Ndebele delegation. And even though the Ndebele delegation was able to get an audience with the queen—she simply absolved herself of any responsibility in the actions taken by her countrymen. This history of systematic sabotage takes Third World historiography out of a simplistic nondiscursive valorizing of victimhood and instead shows patterns of resistance and comprehension about the design of the colonizer—a design not always obvious to the colonized.

Head's record of South African history replaces the contempt that Third World historical identities, especially as they are subjects of nations, have fallen into because they were on the losing side. Envisioned history has to recognize the struggle and resistance, rescuing these exiled figures, for truth must determine the collective identity of any postcolonial nation.

Nonetheless, Rhodes's philosophy—"If you want the black man's labor, take it"—became all-pervasive by 1893.[64] Head writes that "any white settler was allowed to collect hut tax of ten shillings per hut from all black people in his area. The hut tax was imposed on a moneyless economy so that the people were forced to pay tax in cattle, goats, sheep and grain.[65] Even though Khama saved Botswana from overt colonialism, the Cape, the Transvaal, Nataal, and many other areas of Southern Africa fell under a ruthless colonialism that continued to flourish for hundreds of years.

The connections that Head is able to make for us in her two histories are manifold. She envisions the long-term historical reality of a people, her people—for she is Southern African—in order to understand colonialism in the context of a people and their leaders and not a people in the context of colonialism. This focus, as I have tried to argue in this chapter, changes the viewer/viewed dialectic considerably. The otherized colonial subject begins to view herself, her historical identity, and that of her leaders as separate from the continued presence of the colonizer. This presence takes socioeconomic and actual political forms. The process of envisioning, thus, becomes a disidentifying one. It is through this wedge, systematically created by the Third World writer and historian, between the historical destinies and identities of colonizer and colonized, that a "rememorying" of "our" past, through which a future with potential can be compelled—can begin.

Colonial histories, written with colonialist interests, systematically blur the distinction between the interests of the colonizer and the colonized simply because the masters' ideology sees its interests as synonymous with the interests of the colonized. Missionary ideology does much to engage the identity of the colonized with that of the colonizer through phenomena such as Christianity in order to maintain control over other "spiritualized" beings. This onslaught breaks down the defenses one employs to protect one's identity from this objectification, resulting in the confusion of the oppressed. This confusion of revolutionary purpose and method functions much as gender oppression does in most cultures. Thus the recognition of a separate identity and purpose from the oppressor becomes a prerequisite to any revolutionary activity. Retelling history is just such a revolutionary activity for Head.

Her historical data and analysis, no matter how "fictionalized" in their narratology, intend to and do break the stronghold of colonialist historicity and presence in Southern Africa. In a curious way, her recording and recoding anticipated the postapartheid era, even though both of Head's histories were written before the release of Nelson Mandela. She is able, through her histories, to contraindicate the continuance of apartheid. Implicit in the "rememorying" and envisioning of the histories of resistance and loss, migration and exile, is a cyclical pattern in which colonialism constitutes a part, visibly on the decline. The awareness of leaders like Khama, among others, pervades the consciousness of any aspect of the freedom fight found in Southern Africa today—and that is precisely the connection that Head's historiography illuminates.

CONCLUSION:
Toward a Third World Feminist Aesthetic

MY ANALYSIS of Head's texts argues that she is doing serious damage to preconceived ideas about postcolonial women's literature, by developing a feminist aesthetic. I have tried through the course of this book to suggest that Head's narratives are important precisely because they use Third World women's experience to create a feminist aesthetic. Bessie Head's interest in exploring the complexities of women's inherently subversive identities within the context of the various ways that women are exiled by patriarchal structures is clear from the beginning of her writing career.

However, an enduring picture that emerges from *Maru*, after the rejection of nostalgia begun in *When Rain Clouds Gather*, is the artist's identity. Margaret Cadmore's role as an artist is the one that emerges as the strongest icon in Head's second novel. Her resistance lies at the level of her artistry. Even though Dikeledi takes away her paintings soon after she has painted them, Margaret is no longer tied to them. Her woman artist's identity is the one that engages Head most and that identity is subversive in that it refuses dialogue but rather turns inward to examine and create. Even though her marriage to a paramount chief coerces her status as a woman, it is finally her pictures that communicate and not her. The part that draws the pictures, unlike any other part, belongs to herself alone not to the Masarwa and certainly not to Maru.

It is the artist's identity in *Maru* that renders any other struggle, either with gender or with race, secondary to that exploration. Perhaps this is the reason why Head wants to escape after just teasing into existence the subjects of race, gender, and oppression. Her primary concern remains with the role of an outcast, exiled artist. As an artist, Margaret does survive even as she is unable to survive as a woman and Masarwa. She survives, in that she enters the domain of the "soul" to create, which perhaps is the only value of her marriage to Maru. It removes her from Dilepe where her "enormous vitality" would be wasted on another sort of struggle, and not the one she would choose. Therein lies the only choice she is interested in making. For the rest, she does remain a passive woman and a Masarwa. However, in that she resists as an artist, Head is making a very strong statement about her own priorities and the importance of a woman's artistry. Margaret gives up everything, society, power, economic viability, and independence, but never the inalienable artist in her, which Maru recognizes but cannot curb for she continues to "totally love Moleka," in the "other" room.

What is most crucial to the development of a Third World feminist aesthetic is Head's creation of uncompromising women characters. They marry, they bear children, they struggle to survive as single mothers, but they never give in to their victimhood—indeed they celebrate life through their work. For Margaret Cadmore, it is her paintings. For Dikeledi in "The Collector of Treasures" the joy comes from her children and her working hands, which like Margaret's are artist's hands and can craft whatever is placed in them. In jail, she is able to knit and create beautiful things as she was able to sew and earn her living before she killed her husband. Her *jouissance* comes from her relationship with her close woman friend, which becomes the treasure she finds, like an artist, amid the ashes.

In *The Collector of Treasures*, one of the most enduring images that Head negotiates is a space for what I have called "women talk." This sphere allows Head to create a theory of women's dialogue by expressing the desire and experience of women in her short stories. Postcolonial feminist discourse is rooted in the experience and desire of women as they struggle and resist enormous odds. Since their identities are tied to that resistance, it takes as many forms as one perceives in Head's narratives.

In *A Question of Power* "the gesture of belonging," after the artist, woman, and exile's horrendous "workout," constitutes the postcolonial woman's aesthetic domain. In her narratives, Head creates that domain, functions in that domain, and presents it to a postcolonial feminist audience. The whole question of power as it relates to individual/societal good and evil is not just appropriated by Head, but, rather, it is "feminized" by her. The "journeys into the soul," an aesthetic that had primarily belonged to the patriarchal persuasion, is unhinged from its old foundation and placed in the center of a woman artist's dialogue with herself and other women.

I have shown that, in the histories *Serowe: Village of the Rain Wind* and *A Bewitched Crossroad,* Head's purpose is a little more general, even though she pays special attention to comparing Mackenzie and Hepburn's missionary accounts with those of local Black historians who were still alive when she was doing research for these books. However, she brings to these histories not only a Southern African's outrage at the recorded accounts of her history but through "rememory" and envisioning she is able to create a model for other postcolonial historians. She sees the coincidence between the individual and collective identity creating a model for dialogue in postcolonial nations. In her shorter historical pieces, she is much more specific about challenging local traditional authority over the roles women played in the migratory patterns of several branches of the Bamangwato tribe. In "The Deep River: A Story of Ancient Tribal Migration," Rankwana refuses to take the blame for stepping outside tradition because as the youngest wife of a very old chief she fell in love with his son and had a child with him. I believe that these stories and other historical data are informed by Head's feminist commitments even though she always hesitated in adopting that title.

What emerges from Head's narratives is a dialogue on several aspects of women's identities. In *A Question of Power,* the text challenges into focus women's sexuality, and even though Head ultimately halts Elizabeth's understanding of her own sexuality by making her reject it altogether, she has carved out a space for women's dialogue with their sexual-political identities.

In the last analysis, Bessie Head, woman writer exiled from South Africa and never allowed to really "belong" in Botswana, through her narratives did far more in terms of contributing to postcolonial feminist discourse than anyone has recognized thus far. She is and will remain a pioneer of feminist dialogue and historiography. She began what became a way of talking about postcolonial feminist aesthetic concerns.

NOTES

Introduction

1. Gayatri Chakravorty Spivak, *Outside in the Teaching Machine* (New York: Routledge, 1993), 217–41.

2. I am indebted to Judith Butler for the idea of "subversive identities."

3. See bell hooks, *Talking Back* (Boston: South End Press, 1989).

4. The term *postcoloniality* has to be used advisedly since many situations, both political and emotional, exist without the luxury of a postcolony but rather as the new or neocolonies such as South Africa. For a fuller understanding of the term see *Callaloo* 16 (Fall 1993) and *Social Text* 31/32 (1994), special issues devoted to the study of this term. On "identity politics," see Biddy Martin, "Lesbian Identity and Autobiographical Difference[s]," in *Life/Lines: Theorizing Women's Autobiography,* ed. Bella Brodzki and Celeste Schenck (Ithaca: Cornell Univ. Press, 1989), 77–103.

5. Zoe Wicomb, "To Hear the Variety of Discourses," *Current Writing* 2, no. 1 (1988): 35–44.

6. Teresa de Lauretis, *Technologies of Gender* (Bloomington: Indiana Univ. Press, 1987), 9–10.

7. Martin, "Lesbian Identity," 82.

8. Bessie Head, *A Question of Power* (London: Heinemann, 1974).

9. Teresa de Lauretis, "Issues, Terms and Contexts," in *Feminist Studies/Critical Studies,* ed. Teresa de Lauretis (Bloomington: Indiana Univ. Press 1986), 9.

10. Simon Gikandi's paper at the African Studies Association Meeting in Boston, December 5, 1993, "On Reason and Tradition: Professional Identities and Conceptual Constraints," describes the terms *modernity* and *tradition* as a false dichotomy no longer a valid expression of the postcolonial situation.

11. I am indebted to Lemuel Johnson for pointing out the connection between Shakespeare's *Othello* and Bessie Head's Elizabeth.

12. See Gillian Stead Ellersen, *Bessie Head: Thunder Behind Her Ears* (Portsmouth, N.H.: Heinemann, 1996).

13. Franz Fanon talked at length about this idea in regard to the Algerian Revolution in *The Wretched of the Earth* (New York: Grove Press, 1981),

but he did not include it in conjunction with its relationship to exile, which coincides with my interest in Head's work.

14. Trinh T. Minh-ha, *When the Moon Waxes Red* (New York: Routledge, 1991), 14.

15. To examine concepts of Third World feminisms, see bell hooks, Chandra Mohanty, Gayatri Spivak, among others.

16. Cornel West, "The New Cultural Politics of Difference," in *Out There*, ed. Ferguson, Gever, Trinh T. Minh-ha, and Cornel West (New York: New Museum of Contemporary Art, 1990), 29.

17. Trinh T. Minh-ha, "Not You/ Like You: Post-Colonial Women and the Interlocking Questions of Identity and Difference," *Inscriptions* 3, no. 4 (1988): 77.

18. Ibid.

19. "Linguistic mulatto" is meant to suggest the complex relationship and, indeed, the linguistic angst that writers of the "English language" have with the colonial's language as well as their own, for they are caught writing outside a tradition that excludes them in every way, yet they write and appropriate that language of inclusion/exclusion.

20. I am referring to how women's sexuality informs their political identity.

21. Edward Said, "Reflections on Exile," in *Out There*, 357–58.

22. Ibid.

23. Ibid., 364.

24. Bessie Head, *When Rain Clouds Gather* (London: Heinemann, 1968); *Maru* (London: Heinemann, 1971); *A Question of Power* (London: Heinemann, 1974); *The Collector of Treasures* (London: Heinemann, 1977); *Serowe:*

Village of the Rain Wind (London: Heinemann, 1981); *A Bewitched Crossroad* (Craighall, South Africa: A. D. Donker, 1984); *Tales of Tenderness and Power* (Oxford: Heinemann, 1989); *A Woman Alone: Autobiographical Writings* (Oxford: Heinemann, 1990); *A Gesture of Belonging*, ed. Randolph Vigne (London: Heinemann, 1991); *The Cardinals* (Cape Town: Africasouth New Writing, 1993).

25. Head herself is known to have said this about the South African apartheid state.

26. Head, *A Woman*, 24.

27. "Universalist" is a term used by Head to suggest human liberation from localities such as "race and nation." She develops this idea more fully in her novel *A Question of Power*.

28. Wicomb, "To Hear," 37.

29. Head, *A Question*, 96.

30. Said, "Reflections," 363.

1. Geography of Subversion

1. Linda Susan Beard, "Bessie Head's Syncretic Fictions: The Reconceptualisation of Power and the Recovery of the Ordinary," *Modern Fiction Studies* 37 (Autumn 1991): copyright by Purdue Research Foundation, 575.

2. Head, *Tales*, 16.

3. Ibid.

4. Ibid., 18.

5. Ibid.

6. Head, *A Woman*, 13.

7. Ibid.

8. Ibid., 16.

9. Ibid., 11.

10. Minh-ha, "Not You/Like You," 77.

11. Head, *A Question*, 132–33.

12. Head, *A Woman*, 12.

13. Ibid., 21.

14. Ibid., 22.
15. Ibid., 17.
16. Bessie Head, "Remote Lives," *The New African* 8 (1968): 29–30; "African Religions" (November 1969): 46–47; "Makeba Music" (Nov. 1969): 8.
17. Head, "African Religions," 46.
18. Head, *A Woman*, 58.
19. Head, "West-East-South," *The New African* (June 1966): 114.
20. Ibid.
21. Head, *Tales*, 32.
22. Head, "Things I Don't Like," *The New African* (July 1962): 10.
23. Head, *A Woman*, 95.
24. Head, *Tales*, 32–36.
25. Head, *A Woman*, 28.
26. Also collected in *A Woman*, 29–31.
27. Head, *A Woman*, 30.
28. Ibid., 31.
29. Ibid.
30. Head, *Tales*, 141–43.
31. Ibid., 143.
32. Ibid., 142.
33. Ibid., 141.
34. Head, *A Woman*, 43–50.
35. Ibid., 47.
36. Ibid., 50.
37. Ibid., 46.
38. Ibid., 95.
39. Ibid., 49.
40. Ibid., 31.
41. Ibid., 32.
42. Ibid., 31.
43. Ibid., 39–41.
44. Ibid., 40.
45. Head, *Tales*, 45–47.
46. Ibid., 46.
47. Ibid., 42–43.
48. Ibid., 48–55.
49. Ibid., 49.
50. *A Woman*, 73.
51. Head, *Tales*, 54.
52. Ibid., 37–40.
53. Ibid., 78–83.
54. Ibid., 125–30.
55. Ibid., 72–77, 84–101, 131–40.
56. Ibid., 65–71, 102–15, 116–24.
57. Ibid., 121.
58. Ibid., 102–15.
59. Head, *The Cardinals*, xiii.
60. Ibid.
61. Ibid., 116.
62. Ibid., 76.
63. Ibid., 116–17.

2. Euphoria and Subversion in Exile

1. Linda Susan Beard, "Bessie Head in Gaborone, Botswana: An Interview," *Sage* 3 (Fall 1986): 45.
2. The problematic issues related to binary opposites have been critiqued more completely by others such as Jacques Derrida, Gayatri Spivak, and Abdul R. JanMohamed.
3. Said, "Reflections," 360.
4. Ibid.
5. Gikandi, "On Reason and Tradition."
6. Stuart Hall, "Cultural Identity and Cinematic Representation," *Framework* 36 (1989): 69–70.
7. Christopher Miller, *Blank Darkness* (Chicago: Univ. Chicago Press, 1983), 241.
8. Head, *A Woman*, 187.
9. Carol Boyce Davies, "Private Selves and Public Spaces: Autobiography and the African Woman Writer," *College Language Association Journal* 24 (March 1991): 278.
10. Arthur Ravenscroft, "The Novels of Bessie Head," in *African Novels of Affirmation*, ed. Douglas Jefferson and Graham Martin (London: Open UP, 1982), 178.
11. Head, *Rain Clouds*, 187.
12. Ibid., 185.
13. Ibid., 22.

14. Ibid., 20.

15. Ezekiel Mphahlele's comment quoted in Lewis Nkosi, *Tasks and Masks* (Essex: Longman, 1981), 98.

16. Lee Nichols, *African Writers at the Microphone* (Washington, D.C.: Three Continents Press, 1984), 151–52.

17. Head, *Rain Clouds,* 10.

18. Ibid., 177.

19. Ibid., 103.

20. Ibid., 102.

21. Ibid., 154.

22. Ibid., 176.

23. Maria Mies documents many such cases in her *Lacemakers of Nasarapur* (London: Zed Press, 1984).

24. An Urdu word for a traveler, exiled from their home for some reason. There is a viable political party in Pakistan today that represents the interests of the Muhajareen, the exiles.

25. Michael Thorpe, "Treasures of the Heart," *World Literature Today* 57 (Summer 1983): 415.

26. Head, *Rain Clouds,* 182.

27. The character Gilbert uses the word "utopia" to describe Golema Mmidi, ibid., 31.

28. Ibid., 32.

29. Ibid., 16.

30. Ibid., 10.

31. Simon Simonse, "African Literature between Nostalgia and Utopia," *Research in African Literatures* 13 (Winter 1982): 468.

32. Nkosi, *Tasks,* 102.

33. Head, *Rain Clouds,* 82.

34. Ibid., 34.

35. Ibid., 186.

36. Randolph Vigne, *A Gesture of Belonging* (London: Heinemann, 1991), 58.

37. Nkosi, *Tasks,* 102.

38. Vigne, *A Gesture of Belonging,* 64.

39. Interview in *Between the Lines,* ed. Craig Mackenzie and Cherry Clayton (Grahamstown, S.A.: National English Literary Museum, 1989), 12–13.

40. Head, *Rain Clouds,* 16.

41. Ibid., 158.

42. Ibid., 110.

43. Ibid., 137–38.

44. Ibid., 71.

45. Ibid., 80.

46. Ibid., 133. Minh-ha, "Not You/Like You," 73–74.

47. Head, *Rain Clouds,* 134.

3. Race, Gender, and Exile within National Discourse

1. Head, *A Woman,* 68.

2. Ibid., 68–69.

3. Audre Lorde, *Sister Outsider* (Freedom, Calif.: Crossing Press, 1984), 115.

4. Vigne, *A Gesture,* 64.

5. Ibid., 104.

6. Ibid., 125.

7. Wicomb, "To Hear," 43.

8. Head, *A Woman,* 69.

9. Ibid., 69.

10. Ravenscroft, "The Novels," 180.

11. R. Nobantu's paper at the African Literature Association Annual Meeting, Madison, Wisc., April 1990, epitomize some of the contradictions in *Maru.*

12. Nichols, *African Writers,* 52.

13. Daniel Grover, "The Fairy Tale and the Nightmare," in *The Tragic Life,* ed. Cecil Abrahams (Trenton, N.J.: Africa World Press, 1990), 112.

14. Also look at Yakini Kemp, "Romantic Love and the Individual

in Novels by Mariama Ba, Buchi Emecheta and Bessie Head," *Obsidian II:
Black Literature in Review* 3 (Winter
1988): 1–6.
15. Wicomb, "To Hear," 43.
16. Said, "Reflections."
17. Head, *Maru*, 11.
18. Ibid., 6.
19. Ibid., 16.
20. Ibid., 17.
21. Ibid., 24.
22. Ibid., 126–27.
23. Lloyd Wesley Brown, *Women
Writers in Black Africa* (Westport,
Conn.: Greenwood Press, 1981),
158–79.
24. Wicomb, "To Hear," 43.
25. Head, *Maru*, 8.
26. Ibid., 16.
27. Minh-ha, "Not You/Like
You."
28. Head, *Maru*, 7.
29. Ibid., 64.
30. Ibid., 9.
31. Ibid., 8.
32. Ibid.
33. Wicomb, "To Hear," 43.
34. Head, *Maru*, 6.
35. Ibid., 7.
36. Ibid., 6–7.
37. Ibid., 127.
38. Ibid., 9.
39. Ibid., 10.
40. Ibid., 9.
41. Ibid., 34.
42. Ibid., 49.
43. Ibid., 50.
44. Ibid., 6.
45. Ibid., 7.
46. Ibid., 8.
47. Ibid., 67–68.
48. Ibid., 68–69.
49. Ibid., 72.
50. Ibid., 70.
51. Ibid., 71.

52. Vigne, *A Gesture of Belonging,*
124- 25.
53. Head, *Maru*, 108, 109.
54. Ibid., 109.

4. Women's Identity and a Question of Good and Evil

1. Michel Foucault, *Madness and
Civilization* (New York: Vintage,
1988).
2. Ravenscroft, "The Novels,"
183. "Head, Bessie," *Literary Exile in
the Twentieth Century: An Analysis and
Biographical Dictionary,* ed. Martin
Tucker (New York: Greenwood
Press), 306–08.
3. See Arlene Elder, also look at
Susan Gardner's piece "Don't Ask for
the True Story," in *Hecate* 12 (1986):
109–29, and the refutation of Gardner's "tribute" by Teresa Dovey, "A
Question of Power: Susan Gardner's
Biography versus Bessie Head's Autobiography," *English in Africa* 16 (May
1989): 29–38. See Françoise Lionnet's *Autobiographical Voices* (Ithaca:
Cornell Univ. Press, 1989) and Bella
Brodzki and Celeste Schenck's *Life/
Lines.*
4. Head, *A Woman*, 69.
5. Head, *A Question*, 20.
6. Ibid., 175.
7. Ravenscroft, "The Novels,"
184.
8. Head, *A Question*, 38.
9. Charles Larson, *The Novel in the
Third World* (Washington, D.C.: Three
Continents Press, 1976), 164–73.
10. Head, *A Question*, 44.
11. Julia Kristeva, "Stabat
Mater," in *The Kristeva Reader,* ed.
Toril Moi (New York: Columbia Univ.
Press, 1986).
12. Hélène Cixous, "The Laugh of

the Medusa," in *New French Feminisms,* ed. Elaine Marks and Isabelle Courtivron (New York: Schocken Books, 1981), 246.

13. Ibid., 256.

14. See Marianne Hirsch's *The Mother Daughter Plot* (Bloomington: Indiana Univ. Press, 1989), and Adrienne Rich's *Of Woman Born* (New York: Bantam Books, 1977).

15. Head, *A Question,* 13.

16. Ibid., 44.

17. Ibid., 44.

18. Rukmani Vanamali talks interestingly about Medusa as a mythical character in her article "Bessie Head's *A Question of Power*: The Mythic Dimension," *The Literary Criterion* 23 (1988): 154–71.

19. See Monique Wittig, "One is Not Born a Woman," *Feminist Issues* (Winter 1981), and Judith Butler, *Gender Trouble* (New York: Routledge, 1990).

20. Head, *A Question,* 181.

21. Ibid., 184.

22. Ibid., 105–6.

23. Margaret E. Tucker, "A "Nice-Time Girl" Strikes Back: An Essay on Bessie Head's *A Question of Power,*" *Research in African Literature* 19 (Summer 1988): 172 and 177.

24. Head, *A Question,* 117.

25. Ibid., 12.

26. Tucker, "A Nice-Time Girl," 178.

27. Minh-ha, "Not You/Like You," 71.

28. Head, *A Question,* 170.

29. Ibid., 192–93.

30. Ibid., 45.

31. Ibid., 47.

32. Ibid., 96. See Paulo Freire, *Pedagogy of the Oppressed* (New York: Seabury Press, 1968).

33. Ravenscroft, "The Novels,"

184. Beard, "Bessie Head's Syncretic Fictions," 578.

34. Jean Marquard, "Bessie Head: Exile and Community in Southern Africa," *London Magazine* 18 (Dec. 1978/Jan. 1979): 53.

35. Ibid.

36. Tucker, "A Nice-Time Girl," 179.

37. Head, *A Question,* 85.

38. Ibid., 129.

39. Ibid., 19.

40. Ravenscroft, "The Novels," 185.

41. Head, *A Question,* 52.

42. Said, "Reflections," 357.

43. Head, *A Question,* 133.

44. Ibid., 134.

45. Nkosi, *Tasks,* 99.

46. Head, *A Question,* 17.

47. Ibid., 11.

48. Ibid., 12, 206.

49. Ibid., 50.

50. Foucault, *Madness and Civilization.*

51. Wilson Harris, "Keynote Address," to the Association of Commonwealth Literatures and Languages, University of Kent, Canterbury, in August 1989.

52. Foucault, *Madness and Civilization,* 10.

53. Ibid., 11.

54. Ibid., 11–22.

55. Said, "Reflections," 360.

56. Head, *A Question,* 25.

57. Ibid., 206.

58. Ibid., 161.

59. Ibid., 19.

60. Ibid., 29.

61. Ibid., 35.

62. Ibid., 55.

63. Ibid., 70.

64. Ibid., 191.

65. Ibid., 191–92.

66. Ibid., 192.

67. Kolawole Ogungbesan, "The Cape Gooseberry Also Grows in Botswana: Alienation and Commitment in the Writings of Bessie Head," *Présence Africaine* 109 (1979/80): 98.

68. Head, *A Question,* 200.

69. Ibid., 200–201.

70. Ibid., 201.

71. Ibid., 203.

72. Ibid., 202.

73. Ibid.

5. "Women Talk": A Dialogue on Oppression

1. Beard, "Head in Gaborone," 45.

2. Ibid., 45.

3. Françoise Lionnet, "Geographies of Pain," in *Politics of (M)othering: Epistemology, Ontology, and the Problematic of Womanhood in African Literature* ed. Obiowa Nnaeweka (forthcoming from Routledge). Michael Thorpe, "Treasures of the Heart: The Short Stories of Bessie Head," *World Literature Literature Today* 57 (Summer 1983): 414.

4. This chapter is concerned with women's dialogue. For other analyses of Head's stories, see Craig Mackenzie, "Short Fiction in the Making: The Case of Bessie Head," *English in Africa* 16 (1989): 17–28; and Sara Chetin, "Myth, Exile, and the Female Condition: Bessie Head's *The Collector of Treasures," Journal of Commonwealth Literature* 24 (1989): 114–37.

5. Wicomb, "To Hear," 37.

6. Kumkum Sangari and Sudesh Vaid, *Recasting Women: Essays in Colonial History* (New Delhi: Kali for Women, 1989).

7. Chandra Mohanty and Satya Mohanty, "Contradictions of Colonialism," *Women's Review of Books* 7 (March 1990): 10.

8. Beard, "Head in Gaborone," 45.

9. Claudia Tate, "Allegories of Black Female Desire," in *Changing Our Own Words,* ed. Cheryl A. Wall (New Brunswick, N.J.: Rutgers Univ. Press, 1989), 98–126.

10. Especially Toni Morrison's *Beloved* (New York: Knopf, 1987) and August Wilson's *The Piano Lesson* (New York: Plume, 1990).

11. Head, *The Collector,* 1–6.

12. Ibid., 6.

13. Ibid.

14. Ibid., 81–86.

15. Ibid., 84.

16. Ibid., 84–85.

17. Ibid., 85.

18. Ibid., 84.

19. Ibid., 86.

20. Ibid., 47–56.

21. Ibid., 49.

22. Ibid.

23. Ibid., 56.

24. Ibid., 87–103.

25. Ibid., 57–60.

26. Ibid., 89.

27. Ibid., 101.

28. Ibid., 91.

29. Ibid., 92.

30. Ibid., 93.

31. Ibid., 96.

32. Ibid., 19–36.

33. Ibid., 40.

34. Ibid., 43.

35. Ibid., 61–68.

36. Ibid., 63.

37. Ibid., 66.

38. Ibid., 68.

39. Ibid., 76–80.

40. Ibid., 78.

41. Ibid., 80.

42. Ibid., 79.

43. Ibid., 104–9.

44. Ibid., 106.

45. Ibid., 69–75.

46. Charlotte Bruner, "Child Africa: As Depicted by Bessie Head and Ama Ata Aidoo," in *When the Drumbeat Changes*, ed. Carolyn A. Parker and Stephen H. Arnold (Washington, D.C.: Three Continents Press, 1981), 261–77.

47. Mohanty and Mohanty, 10.

6. Talking Back: Visioned and Envisioned History

1. Cherry Clayton, "A World Elsewhere: Bessie Head as Historian," *English in Africa* 15 (May 1988): 55–69. Morrison, *Beloved*, 216.

2. Minh-ha, *Woman Native Other* (Bloomington: Indiana University Press, 1989), 121.

3. Clayton, "A World," 55.

4. Femi-Ojo Ade, "Bessie Head's Alienated Heroine: Victim or Villain?" *Ba Shiru* 8 (1977): 15.

5. Minh-ha, *Woman*, 140.

6. Leslie Marmon Silko, *Ceremony* (New York: Viking Press, 1977), quoted on the dust jacket.

7. Minh-ha, *Woman*, 119–20.

8. Silko, quoted in Minh-ha's *Woman*, 119.

9. Ibid.

10. Head, *Serowe*, 67.

11. Minh-ha, *Woman*, 67.

12. Chinweizu, *Decolonizing the African Mind* (London: Pero Press, 1987), 87.

13. Ibid., 88.

14. Minh-ha, *Woman*, 119.

15. Ibid., 120.

16. Abdul R. JanMohamed, *Manichean Aesthetics* (Amherst: Univ. Mass. Press, 1983).

17. Mary Louise Pratt, *Imperial Eyes: Travel Writing and Transculturation* (New York: Routledge, 1992).

18. Chinweizu, *Decolonizing*, 90.

19. See Maryse Conde's *Segu* (New York: Viking, 1987) and *The Children of Segu* (New York: Viking, 1990).

20. Morrison, *Beloved*, 6. Margaret Walker, *Jubilee* (New York: Bantam Books, 1967).

21. Head, *Serowe*, 70.

22. Ibid., ix.

23. Ibid., xi.

24. Ibid., x.

25. Ibid., xiv.

26. Ibid., xx.

27. Ibid., xxi.

28. Ibid., 3.

29. More precise histories of this period have been written subsequent to Head's exposition. For further clarification, look at Jean and John Comaroff, *Revelation and Revolution*, v. 1 (Chicago: Univ. of Chicago Press, 1991). However, it is important to remember that Head was going something completely different in her histories though both challenge colonial records.

30. Ibid., 4.

31. Ibid., 9.

32. Ibid., 4.

33. Ibid., 6.

34. Ibid., 13.

35. Clayton, "A World Elsewhere," 59.

36. Ibid., 59–60.

37. Head, *Bewitched*, 132.

38. Head, *Serowe*, 22.

39. Ibid., 24.

40. Ibid., 27.

41. I am indebted to John S. Mbiti's *African Religions and Philosophy* (London: Heinemann, 1969). Head wrote a review of Mbiti's book.

42. Head, *Serowe,* 30–31.
43. Ibid., 38–39.
44. Ibid., 58.
45. Ibid.
46. Ibid., 38.
47. Head, *Bewitched,* 96.
48. Head, *Serowe,* 47.
49. Ibid.
50. Ibid., 77.
51. Head, *Bewitched,* 69–70, 142.
52. Head, *Serowe,* 67.
53. Ibid., 122.
54. Ibid., 122.

55. Head, *Bewitched,* 37.
56. Ibid., 47.
57. Ibid., 73.
58. Ibid., 72.
59. Ibid., 77.
60. T. Dunbar Moodie, *The Rise of Afrikanerdom* (Piennar, S.A.: 1964): 235–36.
61. Head, *Bewitched,* 92–94.
62. Ibid., 161.
63. Ibid., 158.
64. Ibid., 151.
65. Ibid., 184.

NAMES INDEX